P9-DWG-602

D0037729

ADVANCE PRAISE FOR
CONSCIOUS CAPITALISM

"Capitalism, done consciously, is the most powerful system for uplifting humankind to unimaginable levels of prosperity, peace, and happiness. This book identifies the forces of light and makes an impassioned plea for them. I can't imagine better advocates than John and Raj."

—Fred Kofman, author, *Conscious Business*

"In this wonderful antidote to the plethora of recent books on capitalism in crisis, Mackey and Sisodia set out a compelling and inspiring vision of a new form of values-based and purpose-driven capitalism. Essential reading for those who need persuading that the old ways of doing business will simply not suffice."

—Paul Polman, CEO, Unilever

"I have long believed that companies have a responsibility to balance profitability with a social conscience, yet few leaders have an inherent understanding of just how to do it. In *Conscious Capitalism*, John Mackey and Raj Sisodia provide a timely, realistic framework so companies can better serve a variety of stakeholders. I highly recommend listening to what they have to say."

—Howard Schultz, chairman, president, and CEO, Starbucks

"*Conscious Capitalism* is a welcome explication and endorsement of the virtues of free-enterprise capitalism—properly comprehended, there is no more beneficial economic system—and a simultaneously pragmatic and inspirational extolment of higher purpose and humanism in business. I hail and revere the tenets of Conscious Capitalism!"

—Herb Kelleher, former Chairman and CEO, Southwest Airlines

"This book provides the script for a much-needed different narrative for free-enterprise capitalism. Businesses need to be driven by a purpose higher than maximizing profit, and they must ensure optimal benefits to all stakeholders. Only if that happens can capitalism deliver to all humanity the full societal benefits it is capable of."

—Ratan N. Tata, Chairman, Tata Sons

"By so clearly and thoughtfully articulating the tenets of Conscious Capitalism, Raj and John have helped me understand the power behind the sustainable success in our business, raising my consciousness in guiding REI forward to serve a new generation of outdoor enthusiasts and environmental stewards."

—Sally Jewell, CEO, REI

"John Mackey's journey to awakening is an inspiration not just to entrepreneurs, but to anyone who believes in a new definition of success for capitalism—one that includes positive societal impact as well as traditional business metrics."

—Biz Stone, Cofounder and Creative Director, Twitter

CONSCIOUS CAPITALISM

LIBERATING THE
HEROIC SPIRIT OF BUSINESS

CONSCIOUS CAPITALISM

John Mackey
Raj Sisodia

Harvard Business Review Press

Boston, Massachusetts

Conscious Capitalism is a registered trademark of Conscious Capitalism, Inc., a nonprofit organization.

Library of Congress Cataloging-in-Publication Data

Mackey, John, 1954-
Conscious capitalism : liberating the heroic spirit of business / John Mackey & Raj Sisodia.
      p. cm.
  Includes bibliographical references.
  ISBN 978-1-4221-4420-6 (alk. paper)
  1. Social responsibility of business. 2. Business ethics. 3. Capitalism—Moral and ethical aspects.
4. Corporations—Moral and ethical aspects. 5. Social values. I. Sisodia, Rajendra. II. Title.
HD60.M28 2013
174'.4—dc23

                                                    2012025305

The paper used in this publication meets the requirements of the American National Standard for Permanence of Paper for Publications and Documents in Libraries and Archives Z39.48-1992.

To my father Bill Mackey and to my wife Deborah Morin—the two people who have taught me the most in life.

John Mackey

To my children Alok, Priya, and Maya, and my nephews Shiva and Krishna: don't fear the future, but welcome it with love, joy, courage, and optimism.

Raj Sisodia

CONTENTS

CONTENTS

Getting Capitalism Back on Track

This is the book I always wanted to write. As a committed capitalist, I worry a great deal to see how capitalism has gone off the rails the past quarter century and acquired such a bad name, much of it deserved.

In this book, John Mackey and Raj Sisodia return capitalism to its roots. They make a compelling case for capitalism as the greatest wealth creator the world has ever known. In these pages, they call their version *conscious capitalism*. I consider it just capitalism, as it is the only authentic form of capitalism. Other forms of doing business, including "crony capitalism," are simply inauthentic versions of the real thing. As we witnessed during the global economic meltdown of 2008 and the Great Recession that followed, these false versions of capitalism cannot be sustained and are doomed to fail over the long term.

I first discovered John Mackey's philosophies when I read his 2005 debate with Nobel Prize–winning economist Milton Friedman about the way capitalism works. Shortly before Friedman's death, Mackey challenged his view that the *only* responsibility of business is to its shareholders, which financial markets have translated into its short-term stock price. In his widely quoted 1970 treatise in the *New York Times*, "The Social Responsibility of Business Is to Increase Its Profits," Friedman excoriated business leaders who were concerned about their employees, communities, and the environment: "Businessmen that take seriously their responsibilities for providing employment, eliminating discrimination, avoiding pollution . . . are preaching pure and unadulterated socialism."

Mackey challenged that view, just as I have tried to do for many years. We share a much broader view of the role of the corporation in society. It was society that chartered the limited liability corporation and granted companies the right to operate. Violating those rights can result in loss of freedom, either by revoking a company's charter or restricting it with regulatory actions and laws that limit its freedom to operate.

In his leadership of Whole Foods Market, John Mackey has become a role model for conscious capitalism just as my Medtronic colleagues and I have tried to be. From our personal experiences of being in the trenches every day—Mackey in his stores and my time in hospitals with physicians and patients—both of us know that authentic capitalism is the *only* way you can build an organization that benefits its customers, employees, investors, communities, suppliers, and the environment.

Mackey and Sisodia demonstrate unequivocally that leadership matters. They show us how to become *conscious leaders*, a notion that is virtually synonymous with my concept of authentic leadership. They recognize how essential it is for leaders to integrate their hearts with their heads by developing self-awareness and emotional intelligence, while empowering other people to do the same. As the saying goes, "The longest journey that people must take is the eighteen inches between their heads and their hearts." With the enormous loss in confidence in our leaders in the past decade, developing conscious leaders is the best way to rebuild trust in our leaders and in capitalistic institutions and to ensure that they follow their True North.

Let me share my journey to my embracing these notions. By the time I graduated from Georgia Tech in 1964 in industrial and systems engineering, I had a passion to become a values-centered leader of a major company that contributed to the welfare of society. This passion started with listening to my father talk about how businesses should be operated at the age of eight. It continued into my teen years as I heard conversations with businesspeople while caddying and later at summer jobs for companies that included Procter & Gamble and IBM.

I chose business because I believe that well-run, values-centered businesses can contribute to humankind in more tangible ways than any other organization in society. My MBA studies at Harvard Business School exposed me to many great business leaders, opened my eyes to how global business operates, and strengthened my desire to make a difference through free enterprise. In my twenty-three years at the Department of Defense, Litton Industries, and Honeywell, I saw the good, the bad, and the ugly of business.

Joining Medtronic in 1989, I recognized the opportunity to create lasting value for all the company's stakeholders while sustaining its success. My thirteen years at Medtronic provided the platform, one well established by founder Earl Bakken, to turn this concept into reality. Some would cite Medtronic's increase in shareholder value from $1.1 billion to $60 billion as evidence of its success, but I believe a much more compelling case comes from the increase in new patients restored each year to fuller life and health from 300,000 people in 1989 to 10 million today. The healing stories of these patients are the real reward for Medtronic employees and the doctors, nurses, technicians, suppliers, investors, and communities that make up the Medtronic family.

Since retiring from Medtronic in 2002, I have taught at great academic institutions, most notably serving the past nine years on the Harvard Business School faculty. These years have enabled me to develop and solidify my ideas with gifted business scholars and great business leaders, discuss them in the classroom with remarkable students and executives, and write about them in five books and numerous articles.

Meanwhile, society has experienced an historic loss in trust in business leaders. Understanding what has happened to undermine conscious capitalism in the last decade requires going back to Friedman's theories, which have had monumental influence on generations of economists and CEOs who have followed his philosophy, unwittingly or not. The influence has grown as the stock market has become increasingly short-term and as average holding periods for stocks have fallen from eight years to six months.

Most regrettably, the drive for short-term gains has led to the destruction of many great companies like General Motors and Sears and the bankruptcies of Enron, WorldCom, Kmart, and Kodak, and more than one hundred large companies that were forced to restate past financial reports in 2003–2004 because of questionable accounting. These problems pale in comparison with the 2008 failure of major financial firms like Fannie Mae, Bear Stearns, Lehman Brothers, Countrywide, Citigroup, and scores of others, as overleveraged financial institutions collapsed while trying to maximize their shareholder value. In effect, Wall Street's pressure on corporations to increase short-term stock prices boomeranged, knocking out many of those same financial firms.

John Mackey, who calls Friedman "one of his heroes," challenged the economist's ideas in their 2005 debate, shortly before Friedman's death. To his credit, Friedman tried to incorporate many of Mackey's ideas into his theory of shareholder value creation, but Mackey pushed back: "While Friedman believes that taking care of customers, employees, and business philanthropy are means to the end of increasing investor profits, I take the exact opposite view: Making high profits is the means to the end of fulfilling Whole Foods' core business mission. We want to improve the health and well-being of everyone on the planet through higher-quality foods and better nutrition, and we can't fulfill this mission unless we are highly profitable. Just as people cannot live without eating, so a business cannot live without profits. But most people don't live to eat, and neither must businesses live just to make profits."[1]

I often made a similar argument about Medtronic's mission to "restore people to fuller life and health." In my first book, *Authentic Leadership*, I presented the case that business should start with its purpose and its values and use them to inspire employees to innovate and provide superior service, while creating sustainable increases in revenues and profits. This approach provides the basis for ongoing investment in the business while creating lasting value for shareholders and stakeholders—leading to a virtuous circle. This philosophy is not unique in any way to Whole Foods and Medtronic. It is widely practiced at such diverse firms as IBM, Starbucks, Apple, Novartis, Wells Fargo, and General Mills, all of which have sustained great success for decades.

In *Conscious Capitalism*, Mackey and Sisodia walk the reader through every constituency that corporations serve, including some like labor unions and activists, which are normally considered hostile to the company's best interests. The authors demonstrate why and how these organizations deserve attention and respect, even when there are ongoing disagreements.

To economists, Friedman's much simpler calculation of shareholder value is easier to compute and measure, but it fails to represent the more important long-term elements of the company's health, the validity of its strategy, the merits of its investments, the satisfaction of its customers, and the commitment and engagement of its employees. These factors have far greater impact on a company's long-term, sustainable value than does its short-term stock price movement. Other leading scholars, such as my Harvard Business School colleague Robert Kaplan, have provided a more resilient and nuanced way to measure long-term company performance with the balanced scorecard.

As a vivid illustration of how this works, consider Hewlett-Packard and IBM and the different approaches to leadership taken by CEOs Mark Hurd and Sam Palmisano in the last decade. Prior to being forced to resign for misconduct, HP's Hurd, who came from NCR Corporation, took over from the failed leadership of Carly Fiorina and seemingly got the company back on track, driving revenues and profits upward and more than doubling HP's stock. However, these gains were caused in part by sharp cuts in R&D spending from 6 to 3 percent (compared with historic levels of 10 percent) and a near-term focus that precluded investing in viable long-term strategies. Since his departure in 2010, HP stock has declined by $60 billion, or 55 percent.

Under Palmisano's steady leadership, IBM focused on serving its global customers through a values-centered "globally integrated enterprise." This long-term culture change took the bulk of Palmisano's ten years as CEO but resulted in an increase in IBM shareholder value of more than $100 billion, or 84 percent, in the past three years. Virginia Rometty, Palmisano's internal successor, is well positioned to sustain this success, whereas Hurd's externally chosen successors, Leo Apotheker and Meg Whitman, continue to search for a viable strategy.

I am deeply grateful to John Mackey and Raj Sisodia for giving business and society this invaluable treatise on how to integrate all the company's constituencies for the long-term benefit of creating sustainable organizations that serve society's interests simultaneously with their own. They refer to capitalism as a "heroic force" addressing society's greatest challenges. In that sense, their ideas dovetail perfectly with those of my Harvard Business School colleague Michael Porter, the pioneer of modern corporate strategy, who has issued a clarion call to corporate leaders to contribute to society by "creating shared value."

It is my fervent desire to see these ideas became a widely accepted and practiced mode of running corporations in the future, thereby enabling capitalism to flourish in the decades ahead as the dominant force contributing to a prosperous global society.

Bill George is professor of management practice at Harvard Business School and the former chair and chief executive of Medtronic, Inc. He is the author of four best-selling books, including *Authentic Leadership* and *True North*, along with his most recent book, *True North Groups*. He serves on the board of directors of ExxonMobil, Goldman Sachs, and the Mayo Clinic.

Awakenings

BY JOHN MACKEY

Before I cofounded Whole Foods Market, I attended two universities, where I accumulated about 120 hours of electives, primarily in philosophy, religion, history, world literature, and other humanities. I only took classes I was interested in, and if a class bored me, I quickly dropped it. Needless to say, with such a self-directed educational strategy, I learned many interesting and valuable things, but ended up with no degree. I never took a single business class. I actually think that has worked to my advantage in business over the years. As an entrepreneur, I had nothing to unlearn and new possibilities for innovation. I spent my late teens and early twenties trying to discover the meaning and purpose of my own life.

My search for meaning and purpose led me into the counterculture movement of the late 1960s and 1970s. I studied Eastern philosophy and religion at the time and still practice both yoga and meditation. I studied ecology. I became a vegetarian (I have been a vegan for ten years). I lived in an urban

1

co-op/commune in Austin, Texas, for two years, and I grew my hair and beard long. Politically, I drifted into progressivism (or liberalism or social democracy) and embraced the ideology that business and corporations were essentially evil because they selfishly sought only profits. In contrast to evil corporations, I believed that nonprofit organizations and government were "good," because they altruistically worked for the public interest, not for profit.

With that background, I was clearly "well prepared" to launch a business in 1978. Our original company, a natural foods market named Safer Way, was a small 3,000-square-foot store in an old house that I opened with my girlfriend, Renee Lawson. We had seed capital of $45,000 that we raised from friends and family. We were both very young (I was twenty-five and Renee was twenty-one) and idealistic, and we started the business because we wanted to sell healthy food to people, earn a decent living, and have fun doing both.

Despite working many eighty-plus-hour weeks, Renee and I initially took salaries of only about $200 a month and lived in the office above the store. There was no shower or bathtub there, so we took "showers" in the store's Hobart dishwasher when we needed to clean up (I'm pretty sure that violated several city health codes). After operating Safer Way for two years, we decided to relocate to a much larger building, merge with another small natural food store, and change the name to Whole Foods Market in 1980.

First Awakening: Creating a Business and Becoming a Capitalist

At the time we started Safer Way, the progressive political philosophy I believed in had taught me that both business and capitalism were fundamentally based on greed, selfishness, and exploitation: the exploitation of consumers, workers, society, and the environment for the goal of maximizing profits. I believed that profit was a necessary evil at best and certainly not a desirable goal for society as a whole. Before starting Safer Way, I had been involved in the cooperative movement in Austin. Besides living communally in a housing co-op for two years, I was also a member of three separate food

co-ops at different times. For several years, I believed that the co-op movement was the best way to reform capitalism because it was based on cooperation instead of competition. If a store was owned by its customers, rather
than by profit-hungry investors, it would be both less expensive and more
socially just. I agreed with the food co-op motto—"food for people, not for
profit." However, I ultimately became disillusioned with the co-op movement because there seemed to be little room for entrepreneurial creativity;
virtually every decision was politicized. The most politically active members controlled the co-op with their own personal agendas, and much more
energy was focused on deciding which companies to boycott than on how to
improve the quality of products and services for customers. I thought I could
create a better store than any of the co-ops I had belonged to, and decided to
become an entrepreneur to prove it.

Becoming an entrepreneur and starting a business completely changed my
life. Almost everything I had believed about business was proven to be wrong.
The most important thing I learned in my first year at Safer Way was that
business isn't based on exploitation or coercion at all. Instead, I discovered
that business is based on cooperation and voluntary exchange. People trade
voluntarily for mutual gain. No one is forced to trade with a business. Customers have competitive alternatives in the marketplace, team members have
competitive alternatives for their labor, investors have numerous alternatives
to invest their capital, and suppliers have plenty of alternative customers for
their products and services. Investors, labor, management, suppliers—they all
need to cooperate to create value for customers. If they do, the joint value
created is divided fairly among the creators of the value through competitive
market processes based approximately on the overall contribution each stakeholder makes. In other words, business is not a zero-sum game with a winner
and loser. It is a win, win, win, win game—and I really like that.

I also discovered that despite my best intentions and desire to create a good
business, there were many challenges. Our customers thought our prices
were too high; our team members thought they were paid too little; our suppliers would not give us good prices, because we were too small; the local
Austin nonprofit sector was continually asking us for donations; and various

governments were slapping us with many fees, licenses, fines, and various business taxes.

Not knowing much about how to operate a business didn't quite pay off for us in our first year, as we managed to lose more than 50 percent of the capital entrusted to us—$23,000. We discovered that creating a successful business isn't easy. Despite the losses, we were still accused by antibusiness people of exploiting our customers with high prices and our team members with low wages. Despite my good intentions, I had somehow become a selfish and greedy businessman. To my co-op friends, I was now one of the bad guys. Yet, I knew in my heart that I wasn't greedy or selfish or evil. I was still very much an idealist who wanted to make the world a better place, and I thought I could best do so by operating a store that sold healthy food to people and provided good jobs.

Once I realized this, I gradually started to abandon the social democratic philosophy of my youth, because it no longer adequately explained how the world really worked. I looked around for alternative narratives for making sense of the world.

As I steadily devoured dozens and dozens of business books trying to help Safer Way succeed, I stumbled into reading a number of free-enterprise economists and thinkers, including Friedrich Hayek, Ludwig von Mises, Milton Friedman, Jude Wanniski, Henry Hazlitt, Robert Heinlein, Murray Rothbard, Thomas Sowell, and many others. I thought to myself, "Wow, this all makes sense. This is how the world really works." My worldview underwent a massive shift.

I learned that voluntary exchange for mutual benefit has led to unprecedented prosperity for humanity. As we will show in chapter 1, the progress that human beings have collectively made during the past two hundred years is simply incredible. I learned that free enterprise, when combined with property rights, innovation, the rule of law, and constitutionally limited democratic government, results in societies that maximize societal prosperity and establish conditions that promote human happiness and well-being—not just for the rich, but for the larger society, including the poor.

I had become a businessperson and a capitalist, and I had discovered that business and capitalism, while not perfect, were both fundamentally good and ethical.

Second Awakening: Stakeholders Really Matter, and the Power of Love

One of the pivotal events in Whole Foods Market's history occurred over thirty years ago on Memorial Day in 1981, when we had only one store. We had been in business for only about eight months as Whole Foods, after we had relocated from Safer Way and changed our name. Our new store quickly became a big success. Customers loved shopping there, and our team members loved working there; they passionately believed in what we were doing, had a great deal of freedom to express their individuality, and enjoyed their fellow team members and serving our customers. But that day, Austin experienced its worst flood in seventy years. Thirteen people were killed, and the flooding caused over $35 million in damage to the city (equal to about $100 million today). Our store was eight feet underwater. All the equipment and inventory in the store were destroyed; our losses were approximately $400,000. The flood basically wiped us out. We had no savings, no insurance, and no warehoused inventory. There was no way for us to recover with our own resources; we were financially bankrupt.

When the founders and team members came to the store the day after the flood and saw the devastation, many of us had tears in our eyes. For our team members, it felt like the end of the best job they had ever had. For the founders, it seemed like the end of a beautiful but short-lived dream. As we despondently started trying to salvage what we could, a wonderful, completely unexpected thing happened: dozens of our customers and neighbors started showing up at the store. Since it was Memorial Day, many had the day off and had come in their working clothes, bringing buckets and mops and whatever else they thought might be useful. They said to us, in effect, "Come on, guys; let's get to work. Let's clean it up and get this place back on its feet. We're not going to let this store die. Stop moping and start mopping!"

You can imagine the galvanizing effect this had on us; suddenly, we found new energy and felt a flicker of hope that perhaps all was not yet lost. It didn't stop there. Over the next few weeks, dozens and dozens of our customers kept coming in to help us clean and fix the store. We asked them, "Why are you doing this?" In response, they said things like, "Whole Foods is really important to me. I'm not sure I would even want to live in Austin if Whole Foods wasn't here, if it ceased to exist. It has made a huge difference in my life." It's hard to overestimate the impact this had on us; we felt so loved by our customers that we were determined to open again. We thought, "These customers love us so much and they have given us so much that we owe it to them to do everything possible to reopen and to serve them as well as humanly possible."

It wasn't just our customers who helped us. There was an avalanche of support from our other stakeholders as well, all of whom pitched in to save us. We were bankrupt when that flood occurred and couldn't make payroll, so many of our team members worked for free. Of course, we paid them back when we reopened for business, but there was no assurance that we were really going to be able to reopen. Dozens of our suppliers offered to resupply us on credit because they cared about our business and trusted us to reopen and repay them. That created a commitment of loyalty in our company toward those suppliers, and we are still doing business with many of them more than thirty years later. Our investors believed in Whole Foods Market and reached into their pockets to make additional investments. Our bank loaned us additional money to help us restock. In fact, all the major stakeholders—customers, team members, suppliers, and investors—pitched in after the flood to make sure that Whole Foods Market didn't die and that we were able to reopen. And reopen we did, a mere twenty-eight days after the flood.

Our experience after the Memorial Day flood of 1981 drew our young company together. It demonstrated to us that all our stakeholders have the potential to form close relationships with us, to care and to commit intensely. Our team members grew closer, and our commitment to our customers was greatly deepened. We understood that we were actually making an important difference in people's lives.

It is humbling now to think about what would have happened if all of our stakeholders hadn't cared so much about our company then. Without a doubt, Whole Foods Market would have ceased to exist. A company that today has over $11 billion in sales annually would have died in its first year if our stakeholders hadn't loved and cared about us—and they wouldn't have loved and cared for us had we not been the kind of business we were. How many "normal" businesses would attract a volunteer army of customers and suppliers to help them in their hour of need? That is one of the reasons we understand so well the importance of stakeholders and the power of love in business, because they made us realize how important they were to our success. Not only would we not be successful without them, but we wouldn't have even survived. What more proof did we need that stakeholders matter, that they embody the heart, soul, and lifeblood of an enterprise?

More Awakenings

Business can be a wonderful vehicle for both personal and organizational learning and growth. I have experienced many more awakenings as Whole Foods has grown and evolved over the past three decades. We will share some of these throughout the book. Most importantly, I have learned that life is short and that we are simply passing through here. We cannot stay. It is therefore essential that we find guides whom we can trust and who can help us discover and realize our higher purposes in life before it is too late.

In my early twenties, I made what has proven to have been a wise decision: a lifelong commitment to follow my heart wherever it led me—which has been on a wonderful journey of adventure, purpose, creativity, growth, and love. I have come to understand that it is possible to live in this world with an open, loving heart. I have learned that we can channel our deepest creative impulses in loving ways toward fulfilling our higher purposes, and help evolve the world to a better place.

We have opened this book with a recounting of some of my awakenings because that is an apt metaphor for my journey of rising consciousness in my life and work. This journey has helped me to access some fundamental truths about business that were beyond my reach earlier. I have seen the power of this wisdom at work in my own company and at other companies and have come to realize that the world urgently needs a richer, more holistic, and more humanistic philosophy and narrative about business than the one we have encountered in economics textbooks, in business school teachings, and even from the mouths and pens of many prominent business leaders.

Why We Wrote This Book

My own awakenings to higher levels of consciousness have been paralleled by the evolution of Whole Foods Market to a deeper sense of its own purpose and potential for societal impact. Looking beyond our company, I see that so much about business and capitalism that for so long has been unconscious is now becoming conscious. The most exciting but unheralded change human society has experienced in a long time may be that we are beginning to collectively awaken to the incredible potential of business and capitalism being conducted much more consciously!

My coauthor, Raj Sisodia, has gone through his own journey of seeking deeper truths about business over his twenty-eight years as a professor, an author, and a consultant to numerous companies. He has come to discoveries similar to mine by studying a number of companies (including Whole Foods Market) that are loved by all their stakeholders and have consequently become extraordinarily successful at creating both wealth and well-being. He investigated and described what made these companies special in his influential and inspiring 2007 book *Firms of Endearment: How World-Class Companies Profit from Passion and Purpose.*

Over the last five years, together with a number of influential business and thought leaders, Raj and I have pursued our shared calling of changing the way business is thought about, taught, and practiced through our work in the Conscious Capitalism movement. In 2009, Raj cofounded the Conscious Capitalism Institute, which has now merged into Conscious Capitalism, Inc. (www.ConsciousCapitalism.org), a nonprofit of which we are both trustees. Our shared passion for the extraordinary potential of a more conscious form of capitalism makes it only fitting that we write this book together.

Our primary purpose in writing this book is to inspire the creation of more conscious businesses: businesses galvanized by higher purposes that serve and align the interests of all their major stakeholders; businesses with conscious leaders who exist in service to the company's purpose, the people it touches, and the planet; and businesses with resilient, caring cultures that make working there a source of great joy and fulfillment. We truly believe that this will lead to a better world for all of us. Together, business leaders can liberate the extraordinary power of business and capitalism to create a world in which all people live lives full of purpose, love, and creativity—a world of compassion, freedom, and prosperity. This is our vision for Conscious Capitalism.

How the Book Is Structured

In chapter 1, we provide some much-need historical perspective on free-enterprise capitalism: what it really is, how much it has helped transform our world for the better, and the challenges it faces today. Chapter 1 is also a call to adventure to you (the reader) to actively participate in changing the narrative of capitalism. In chapter 2, we expand on the idea of Conscious Capitalism, a more evolved form of capitalism and business enterprise that addresses the challenges we face today and offers the promise of a dramatically better future.

The next four parts of the book each deal with one of the four tenets of Conscious Capitalism. Part 1 (chapters 3 and 4) is about purpose: we explain why purpose is so critical, offer some generic kinds of purpose, and describe how every company can go about discovering its own authentic purpose. After that, we turn our attention to stakeholders. In part 2 (chapters 5 through 12), we discuss how conscious businesses think about each major and secondary stakeholder. We also discuss how they can leverage the interdependent relationships that exist among stakeholders, which lies at the heart of the Conscious Capitalism philosophy. In part 3 (chapters 13 and 14), we turn to the crucial issue of conscious leadership: what it means and how one can cultivate it. In part 4 (chapters 15 and 16), we discuss the fourth tenet: conscious culture and management. Chapters 15 and 16 describe the key elements of a conscious culture, especially love and care, as well as an approach to management that is consistent with a conscious culture and leverages its strengths. In chapter 17, we provide some suggestions on how to start a conscious business and offer guidance on how an existing business can move toward becoming more conscious. We conclude the book in chapter 18 by discussing how we can spread the Conscious Capitalism philosophy more broadly and more rapidly, and offer a credo for Conscious Capitalism.

The book also has three appendices. Appendix A describes how and why conscious businesses perform better than traditional businesses over the long run. Appendix B compares Conscious Capitalism with other recently proposed alternatives such as Natural Capitalism, Creative Capitalism, Shared-Value Capitalism, B Corporations, and Triple Bottom Line. Appendix C addresses some common questions and misconceptions about Conscious Capitalism.

A stylistic note: while this introduction is in my voice, the rest of the book is very much a joint effort and is in "our" voice, including instances in which we recount aspects of the Whole Foods story. In a few places, we revert to using my voice when describing episodes in my personal journey.

CHAPTER 1

Capitalism: Marvelous, Misunderstood, Maligned

In the long arc of history, no human creation has had a greater positive impact on more people more rapidly than free-enterprise capitalism. It is unquestionably the greatest system for innovation and social cooperation that has ever existed. This system has afforded billions of us the opportunity to join in the great enterprise of earning our sustenance and finding meaning by creating value for each other. In a mere two hundred years, business and capitalism have transformed the face of the planet and the complexion of daily life for the vast majority of people. The extraordinary innovations that have sprung from this system have freed so many of us from much of the mindless drudgery that has long accompanied ordinary existence and enabled us to lead more vibrant and fulfilling lives. Wondrous technologies have shrunk time and distance, weaving us together into a seamless fabric of humankind extending to the remotest corners of the planet.

So much has been accomplished, yet much remains to be done. The promise of this marvelous system for human cooperation is far from being completely fulfilled. Too much of the world still has not embraced the core principles of free-enterprise capitalism, and as a result, we are collectively far less prosperous and less fulfilled than we could be.

Much of the twentieth century can be seen as an extended intellectual war between two diametrically opposed social and economic philosophies— free-enterprise capitalism (free markets and free people) and communism (dictatorship and governmental economic control). By every objective measure, free-enterprise capitalism has won this battle. The United States was far more economically dynamic and socially evolved than the Soviet Union, its chief communist rival. The same held true for West Germany versus East Germany; South Korea versus North Korea; and Taiwan, Hong Kong, and Singapore versus China. With the fall of the Berlin Wall in 1989, country after country began to turn toward greater political and economic freedom in the 1990s and 2000s, as the dismal economic and societal results of the various socialistic experiments conducted in the twentieth century became better known. As this transition to greater freedom took root, many countries experienced rapid economic growth, and hundreds of millions of poor people were able to escape grinding poverty.

Of course, much of the Western world has benefited from the fruits of free-enterprise capitalism for about two centuries now. The success of free-enterprise capitalism in improving the quality of our lives in countless ways is the most extraordinary but poorly understood story of the past two hundred years. It has enabled humankind to progress at a rate unprecedented in all of history. Consider these facts:

- Just 200 years ago, 85 percent of the world's population lived in extreme poverty (defined as less than $1 a day); that number is now only about 16 percent.[1] Free-enterprise capitalism has created prosperity not just for a few, but for billions of people everywhere.

- As figure 1-1 shows, average income per capita globally has increased 1,000 percent since 1800.[2] It has increased 1,600 percent in developed countries. Japan's income per capita has increased by 3,500 percent since 1700. Adjusting for affordability and quality improvements, the standard

FIGURE 1-1

World population and gross domestic product (GDP) per capita

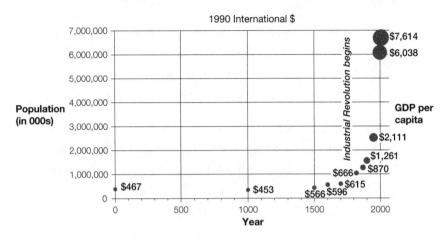

Source: Data from Angus Maddison, "Statistics on World Population, GDP and Per Capita GDP, 1–2008 AD," Groningen Growth & Development Centre Web page, March 2010, www.ggdc.net/MADDISON/oriindex.htm.

of living of ordinary Americans has increased 10,000 percent since 1800![3] Perhaps most startling, the gross domestic product (GDP) of South Korea has grown 260-fold since 1960, transforming it from one of the poorest countries in the world to one of the richest and most advanced.[4]

- Over tens of thousands of years, the human population grew very slowly and declined frequently as huge epidemics such as the plague and influenza claimed millions of lives. It finally crossed one billion around 1804 and has grown rapidly since to over seven billion, primarily because of progress in sanitation, medicine, and agricultural productivity.[5]

- In the past two hundred years, average life expectancy across the world has increased to sixty-eight years, from its long historical average of thirty years or less.[6]

- In just the past forty years, the percentage of undernourished people in the world has dropped from 26 percent to 13 percent.[7] If current trends continue, we should see hunger virtually eliminated in the twenty-first century.

- From a world of almost complete illiteracy, we have transformed, in only a couple of hundred years, into one in which 84 percent of adults can now read.[8]

- With the growth of economic freedom, 53 percent of people now live in countries with democratic governments elected by universal suffrage, compared with zero people just 120 years ago, as even democracies denied women or minorities, or both, the right to vote.[9]

- Contrary to popular belief, prosperous countries have a higher level of life satisfaction. The self-determination associated with free markets, along with greater prosperity, leads to greater happiness. The top quartile of economically free countries has a life satisfaction index of 7.5 out of 10, compared with 4.7 for the bottom quartile.[10]

Entrepreneurs: The Heroes of Free-Enterprise Capitalism

In her recent book *Bourgeoisie Dignity*, Deirdre McCloskey, an economist at the University of Illinois in Chicago, argues persuasively that the most important factors in free-enterprise capitalism's success have been entrepreneurship and innovation, combined with freedom and dignity for businesspeople.[11] The inventions that have changed the world—automobiles, telephones, gasoline, the Internet, antibiotics, computers, airplanes—didn't happen automatically or by government edict; they all required massive amounts of innovation. Human creativity, partly individual but mostly collaborative and cumulative, is at the root of all economic progress.

Entrepreneurs are the true heroes in a free-enterprise economy, driving progress in business, society, and the world. They solve problems by creatively envisioning different ways the world could and should be. With their imagination, creativity, passion, and energy, they are the greatest creators of widespread change in the world. They are able to see new possibilities and enrich the lives of others by creating things that never existed before.

Educator Candace Allen, wife of economics Nobel laureate Vernon Smith, writes movingly about the need for entrepreneurial heroes in society and the great impact they have on our lives: "Ultimately, the hero is the representative of the new—the founder of a new age, a new religion, a new city, the founder of a new way of life or a new way of protecting the village against harm; the founder of processes or products that make people in their communities and the world better off. What I will contend here is that in our modern world, the wealth creators—the entrepreneurs—actually travel the heroic path and are every bit as bold and daring as the heroes who fought dragons or overcame evil."[12]

Why Capitalism Is Under Attack

Despite enabling widespread prosperity, free-enterprise capitalism has earned little respect from intellectuals and almost no affection from the masses. Why is it so disliked by so many people? Does it need to change? Do we need to think about it differently?

Rather than being seen for what they really are—the heroes of the story—capitalism and business are all too frequently vilified as the bad guys and blamed for virtually everything our postmodern critics dislike about the world. Capitalism is portrayed as exploiting workers, cheating consumers, causing inequality by benefiting the rich but not the poor, homogenizing society, fragmenting communities, and destroying the environment. Entrepreneurs and other businesspeople are accused of being motivated primarily by selfishness and greed. Meanwhile, the defenders of capitalism frequently speak in a jargon that not only fails to inspire people, but often reinforces the ethical critique that capitalists only care about money and profits and that businesses can only redeem themselves through "good works." This is a fundamentally misguided view.

We believe that capitalism has long been under attack for several reasons:

1. Businesspeople have allowed the ethical basis of free-enterprise capitalism to be hijacked intellectually by economists and critics who have foisted on it a narrow, self-serving, and inaccurate identity devoid of its inherent ethical justification. Capitalism needs both a new narrative

15

and a new ethical foundation, one that accurately reflects its intrinsic goodness and virtue.

2. Too many businesses have operated with a low level of consciousness about their true purpose and overall impact on the world. Their tendency to think in terms of trade-offs has led to many unintended, harmful consequences for people, society, and the planet, resulting in an understandable backlash.

3. In recent years, the myth that business is and must be about maximization of profits has taken root in academia as well as among business leaders. This has robbed most businesses of the ability to engage and connect with people at their deepest levels.

4. Regulations and the size and scope of government have greatly expanded, creating the conditions for the spread of crony capitalism, restricting competition in favor of politically well-connected businesses. Crony capitalism is not capitalism at all, but is seen as such by many because it involves businesspeople.

These are significant challenges, but they must be overcome if we are to continue to spread freedom and bring dignity and the fruits of modernity to the billions on the planet who are still in dire need.

The Intellectual Hijacking of Capitalism

The early intellectual case for capitalism was built almost exclusively on the theory that people create businesses to pursue only their personal self-interest. Economists, social critics, and business leaders largely disregarded the second and often more powerful aspect of human nature: the desire and need to care for others and for ideals and causes that transcend one's self-interest. The founding father of modern capitalism, Adam Smith, recognized both of these powerful human motivations. His book *The Theory of Moral Sentiments* preceded his far better-known book, *The Wealth of Nations*, by seventeen years. In the earlier book, he outlined an ethics based on our ability to empathize with others and to care about their opinions. Through our ability to empathize, we are able to understand how other people are feeling and imagine what it would be like to be in their shoes.

Smith was far ahead of his time, both in his economic philosophy and in his ethical system. If the intellectuals of the nineteenth century had embraced and integrated his economic and ethical philosophies, we might have avoided the extraordinary strife and suffering that occurred in the nineteenth and twentieth centuries over competing political and economic ideologies.

Unfortunately, that did not happen. Smith's views on ethics were largely ignored, and capitalism developed in a stunted way, missing the more human half of its identity. This created fertile conditions for ethical challenges to capitalism, which were not long in coming. Karl Marx attacked capitalism as inherently exploitative of workers. Critics used the Darwinian idea of the survival of the fittest to describe markets as inherently ruthless and brutal. Just as nature was seen as "red in tooth and claw," business was seen as harsh, dehumanized, and uncaring. These descriptions ignored the higher-level human aspirations and capabilities that free-enterprise capitalism potentially taps into so well.

Another factor that fed distrust of capitalism was a failure to distinguish between the fixed-pie or zero-sum concept of mercantilism and the expanding-pie concept of free-enterprise capitalism. Much of today's animosity toward capitalism stems from a misconception that we need to share all resources fairly and equitably. But the reality is that by artfully combining resources, labor, and innovation, wealth can be greatly expanded. The poor can become wealthier without requiring the well-off to become poorer. The pie grows, and there is more for everyone. This idea is at the core of capitalism's extraordinary and unique ability to generate wealth.

The Unintended Consequences of Low-Consciousness Business

When businesspeople operate with a low level of consciousness about the purpose and impact of business, they engage in trade-off thinking that creates many harmful, unintended consequences. Such businesses view their purpose as profit maximization and treat all participants in the system as means to that end. This approach may succeed in creating material prosperity in the short term, but the resultant price tag of long-term systemic problems is increasingly unacceptable and unaffordable. Too many businesses fail to recognize the significant impacts they have on the environment, on other creatures that inhabit the planet (such as wildlife and livestock animals), and on the physical health and psyches of team members and customers. Many businesses have created stressful and unfulfilling working conditions and fostered and fed unhealthy appetites and addictions in their customers. Many companies tend to treat all these as externalities, outside the scope of their own concerns.

Symptoms of dysfunction and disaffection abound in the corporate world. The average level of engagement that American team members have with their work has remained at 30 percent or less for the past ten years, and almost as many people are hostile to their employers.[13] Top executives at the helm of many major corporations have rigged the game to enrich themselves at the expense of the company and its stakeholders. While employee wages in the United States have been virtually stagnant for decades, executive pay has skyrocketed, fracturing workplace solidarity. According to the Institute for Policy Studies, the ratio between CEO pay and average pay was 42:1 in 1980, 107:1 in 1990, and 525:1 in 2000. It has fluctuated in recent years, standing at 325:1 in 2010.[14]

Given all this, it is not surprising that the reputation of business has suffered. Corporations are widely seen as greedy, selfish, exploitative, and untrustworthy. Big business, in particular, has a terrible reputation today. Gallup has found that Americans' confidence in big business has declined steadily, from about 34 percent in 1975 to a historic low of 16 percent in 2009, rebounding to 19 percent in 2011.[15]

The Myth of Profit Maximization

The persistent myth claiming that the ultimate purpose of business is always to maximize profits for the investors probably originated with the industrial revolution's earliest economists. How did this myth originate? It appears to have come from two sources: a narrow view of human nature and an inadequate explanation of the causes of business success.

CAPITALISM: MARVELOUS, MISUNDERSTOOD, MALIGNED

Looking to create elegant mathematical models of economic systems, academic economists adopted the narrow view that we humans are maximizers of economic self-interest to the exclusion of all else. By logical extension, businesses, too, were deemed to be pure profit maximizers. These simplistic assumptions enabled economists to create models that seemed to explain some of the workings of the larger economy.

The classical economists also formulated their theories by observing and describing the behavior of various entrepreneurs and their businesses. They observed correctly that successful businesses were always profitable and that, indeed, the entrepreneurs who organized and operated these successful businesses always sought to make profits. Businesses that were not profitable did not survive for long in a competitive marketplace, because profits are essential to the long-term survival and flourishing of all businesses. Without profits, entrepreneurs cannot make the necessary investments to replace their depreciating buildings and equipment or to adapt to the always-evolving and competitive marketplace. The need for profit is universal for all businesses in a healthy market economy.

Unfortunately, early economists went far beyond merely describing how entrepreneurs always seek profits as an important goal, to concluding that maximizing profits is the only important goal of business. Taking it one step further, the economists soon asserted that maximizing profits is the only goal entrepreneurs should seek. The classical economists went from describing the behavior in which they observed successful entrepreneurs engage while operating their businesses, to prescribing the behavior as the correct one that all entrepreneurs should engage in all of the time. How did they come to this conclusion?

In the United States, we often take for granted the availability of large pools of capital to invest in new businesses because our economy has been producing these pools for more than 250 years. However, at the beginning of the industrial revolution, capital was quite scarce. Successful enterprises accumulated profits, and entrepreneurs and investors redirected accumulated capital into promising new opportunities, at unprecedented levels. Not surprisingly, then, classical economists became enamored with the importance of profits, because profits had historically been rare and were essential to the continued progress of society.

The principle of profit maximization even became codified into corporate law as the de facto definition of fiduciary responsibility. Economists and eventually business scholars integrated these ideas into their textbooks, shaping the thinking of virtually every student who pursued higher education thereafter. The enemies of capitalism used the ideas as powerful points of attack on the ethical basis of capitalism, to great effect.

But with few exceptions, entrepreneurs who start successful businesses don't do so to maximize profits. Of course, they want to make money, but that is not what drives most of them. They are inspired to do something that they believe needs doing. The heroic story of free-enterprise capitalism is one of entrepreneurs using their dreams and passion as fuel to create extraordinary value for customers, team members, suppliers, society, and investors.

This is a very different narrative than the one that sees history through the lens of profit maximization. Bill Gates did not start Microsoft with the goal of becoming the richest man in the world. He saw the potential of computers to transform our lives and was on fire to create software that would make them so useful that eventually all of us would own one. He followed his passion and, in the process, became the richest man in the world—but that was the outcome, not his goal or purpose.

The myth that profit maximization is the sole purpose of business has done enormous damage to the reputation of capitalism and the legitimacy of business in society. We need to recapture the narrative and restore it to its true essence: that the purpose of business is to improve our lives and to create value for stakeholders.

The Cancer of Crony Capitalism

True free-enterprise capitalism imposes strict accountability and strong internal discipline on businesses. For over a century, the U.S. economy demonstrated to the world that free-enterprise capitalism can deliver great benefits to all humankind. It created a large and prosperous middle class, belying the current inaccurate critique that free-enterprise capitalism necessarily concentrates wealth among a privileged few at the expense of everyone else.

But as the size of government grew, a mutant variation of capitalism has also grown, spurred on by those unable to compete in the marketplace by creating genuine value and earning the affection and loyalty of stakeholders. Instead, they have thrived by using the power of government for their own enrichment. Crony capitalists and governments have become locked in an unholy embrace, elevating the narrow, self-serving interests of the few over the well-being of the many. They use the coercive power of government to secure advantages not enjoyed by others: regulations that favor them but hinder competitors, laws that prevent market entry, and government-sanctioned cartels.[16]

While free-enterprise capitalism is inherently virtuous and vitally necessary for democracy and prosperity, crony capitalism is intrinsically unethical and poses a grave threat to our freedom and well-being. Unfortunately, our current system has the effect of corrupting many honorable business-people, pushing them into becoming reluctant crony capitalists as a matter of survival.

Moving to Higher Ground

This is what we know to be true: business is good because it creates value, it is ethical because it is based on voluntary exchange, it is noble because it can elevate our existence, and it is heroic because it lifts people out of poverty and creates prosperity. Free-enterprise capitalism is one of the most powerful ideas we humans have ever had. But we can aspire to even more. Let us not be afraid to climb higher.

Sandy Cutler, the chairman and CEO of Eaton Corporation (a global power management company with over $16 billion in revenue), says it well:

> In a period of time when so many questions and doubts have emerged about major institutions in society, business has not done a particularly good job of telling its own story—not in the form of puffery, but really trying to help people understand the role of capital formation, how important it is to providing livelihoods for families, what business does for communities and for institutions like our schools and universities, and

the role business has in helping solve so many societal problems. That is not the way so many people today think about business; they think of it as the source of societal problems. The great majority of companies are involved in doing pretty exciting work where people are having vital, exciting careers, earning a livelihood for their families and making a difference for their communities. That's a story that is worth telling.[17]

Far from being a necessary evil (as it is often portrayed), free-enterprise capitalism is an extraordinarily powerful system for eliciting, harnessing, and multiplying human ingenuity and industry to create value for others. It must be defended not just on the basis of the profits it generates but also on the basis of its fundamental morality. Free-enterprise capitalism must be grounded in an ethical system based on value creation for all stakeholders. Money is one measure of value, but it is certainly not the only measure.

Marc Gafni is the cofounder and director of the Center for World Spirituality. Honoring the tremendous impact of capitalism and business on human well-being, he says:

> Capitalism has lifted more people out of poverty than any other force in history, and it has done so through voluntary exchange. Communism tried to lift people out of poverty through coercion, but wound up killing countless millions. What does it mean to lift people out of poverty? It means babies not dying, it means mouths being fed, it means girls going to school and getting educated, it means a response to slavery that never existed in the world before. It means that all the values of the great (spiritual) traditions get enacted on two levels: by ending the physical oppression of poverty, and by opening a gateway for human beings to be able to grow emotionally, morally, spiritually, and socially.

> Lifting people out of poverty was never the conscious intention of business; it was the by-product of a business well-enacted. Now business is awakening to itself and becoming conscious. It is recognizing that it is a force with enormous power and responsibility. By becoming conscious, it can do what it does even better. It can create more community, more mutuality, and paradoxically, more profit, by engaging everyone in the system.[18]

Correcting the Narrative

In a way, the practitioners of capitalism created their own trap and fell into it. They accepted as fact a narrow conceptualization of business and then proceeded to practice it in that way, creating a self-fulfilling prophecy. Had they rejected the caricaturized version and embraced a richer, more complex definition of capitalism, this would not have happened. As pioneering stakeholder theorist Ed Freeman and his colleagues write: "Business is not about making as much money as possible. It is about creating value for stakeholders. It is important to say this and to enable businesspeople to enact the story. We need to hold up the numerous companies, large and small, that are out there trying to do the right thing for the stakeholders, as the real paradigm of business, rather than deeply flawed companies like Enron."[19]

We need to discover anew what makes free-enterprise capitalism what it has been: the most powerful creative system of social cooperation and human progress ever conceived. We next need to rethink *why* and *how* we engage in business to better reflect where we are in the human journey and the state of the world we live in today. We need a richer and more ethically compelling narrative to demonstrate to a skeptical world the truth, beauty, goodness, and heroism of free-enterprise capitalism, rather than continuing to harp on the tired maxims of self-interest and profit maximization. Otherwise, we risk the continued growth of increasingly coercive governments, the corruption of enterprises through crony capitalism, and the consequential loss of both our freedom and our prosperity.

Those who recognize and embrace the life-affirming power of free-enterprise capitalism must reclaim the intellectual and moral high ground. Gafni is eloquent on the need for a new narrative for capitalism:

> Narratives are the stories that infuse our life with meaning. The narrative of business matters greatly, not only to the business community, but to every human being alive. The majority of people on the planet work in some form of business. But the dominant narrative about business is that it is greedy, exploitative, manipulative and corrupt. The majority of human beings on the planet thus experience themselves as

furthering and supporting greed, exploitation, manipulation and corruption. When people experience themselves that way, they actually begin to become that way. But the true narrative is that by participating in business, they are creating prosperity and lifting people out of poverty. They are creating stable conditions for families to be raised, they are helping build communities that can create schools, they are creating places for people to exchange value, find meaning, build relationships and experience intimacy and trust. When people realize that they are part of the largest force for positive social transformation in history, their self-perception changes.[20]

In the next chapter, we introduce the core tenets of Conscious Capitalism, an approach to thinking about and practicing business that holds the rich promise of elevating the narrative of business in a way that accurately reflects its enormous power for good.

CHAPTER 2

Conscious Capitalism and the Heroic Spirit of Business

What does it mean to become more conscious as individuals and as businesses? Consider one of nature's many small miracles: a caterpillar transforming into a butterfly through the seemingly magical process of metamorphosis. For its brief existence, a caterpillar does little more than eat; that is seemingly its only purpose. Some caterpillars eat so much that they grow to one hundred times their original size. However, eventually the amazing process of metamorphosis begins. When the time is right, certain cells become activated in the caterpillar and it enters the cocoon phase, from which it emerges a few weeks later unrecognizably transformed into a creature of enchanting beauty, one that also serves an invaluable function in nature through its role in the pollination of plants and thus the production of food for others to live by.

This analogy can be applied to human beings as well as to the institutions that we have created in our own image—corporations. We humans can choose to exist at a caterpillar level, consuming all we can, taking as much as possible from the world and giving little back. We are also capable of evolving to a degree that is no less dramatic than what happens to a caterpillar, transforming ourselves into beings who create value for others and help make the world more beautiful. The same is true for corporations. They too can exist at a caterpillar level, where they strive only to maximize their own profits, extracting resources from nature and from human beings to do so. Or they can reinvent themselves as agents of creation and collaboration, magnificent entities capable of cross-pollinating human potentials in ways that nothing else can, creating multiple kinds of value for everyone they touch.

The difference is intent. Unlike caterpillars, we cannot wait for nature to trigger our evolution to higher consciousness. Instead, we must work to raise our own consciousness and make deliberate choices that further our personal and organizational growth and development.

A New Chapter in Human History

We human beings did not stop evolving when we became *Homo sapiens*; our evolution continued, but became more culturally and internally driven. The changes are most manifest in an increase in different types of intelligence and a rise in consciousness.

It may not seem obvious at first glance, but we are becoming smarter as a species. The Flynn effect shows that overall human analytical intelligence has been rising at an average rate of about 4 percent every decade for the past several decades.[1] In other words, a person testing at an average IQ of 100 today would have tested at close to 130 sixty years ago.

People are also far better educated worldwide. Literacy rates have risen rapidly, but the larger story is access to higher education. In the year 1910, only 9 percent of Americans had a high school diploma; today, about 85 percent do, and over 40 percent of Americans over the age of twenty-five have college degrees. Coupled with our overall higher collective intelligence, this means that many more of us are capable of comprehending and acting on greater complexity than ever before.

We will discuss the rise in consciousness momentarily, but first, let's take a look at a significant recent turning point in our history.

1989: The World Changes

An extraordinary historical coincidence occurred when Adam Smith's *Wealth of Nations* was published in 1776, the same year that the United States issued its Declaration of Independence. The world soon witnessed the incredible power of free people and free markets coming together, especially in the United States. This was unprecedented in human history; for the first time, ordinary people were masters of their own destiny as a matter of law, and could through diligence and enterprise rise from nothing to great heights of material prosperity and social esteem.

Another almost equally historic year occurred more recently in 1989, which marked several epochal changes in society and technology. Consider three momentous events that took place that year.

The Fall of the Wall

Preceded by the dramatic but failed Chinese uprising in Tiananmen Square in June, the fall of the Berlin Wall on November 9, 1989, triggered the collapse of communist regimes all over Europe, something that was unthinkable just a few years before. Without a shot being fired, the defining ideological debate of the twentieth century between competing systems for organizing human society was suddenly over. Capitalism and democracy decidedly won that epic battle, and the debates that remained were about the types of democracy and the degree of economic freedom that worked best.

The Birth of the Web

Working in Switzerland at CERN (the European Organization for Nuclear Research), British physicist Tim Berners-Lee invented the World Wide Web in 1989.[2] His creation has rapidly transformed the world in myriad ways. You could argue that Berners-Lee did more to transform the world than any single individual in the past hundred years, including Churchill, Roosevelt, Gandhi, and Einstein. His invention is at least as dramatically culture changing as Guttenberg's printing press was over five hundred years ago. In an extraordinarily short time, the Web has evolved into a shared nervous system that links much of humanity. We now enjoy

27

an unprecedented level of information egalitarianism; ordinary people today have access to virtually limitless information on any subject, anytime, anyplace, instantly at almost zero cost.[3] The richest billionaire in the world did not have such access twenty years ago. We have entered an era of extraordinary transparency, in which most corporate and governmental actions and policies can easily become public knowledge, particularly if they are controversial. We are far more connected, through the Web (especially through social media such as Facebook, which will soon have over one billion members worldwide) and through mobile technologies. There are now more phone connections in the world than there are people; we have zoomed from two billion phone connections in the world in 2001 to over seven billion now.[4]

The United States Enters Midlife

The median age of adults is rising rapidly in most countries as birth rates fall and life expectancies increase. For the United States, the year 1989 marked a major turning point: for the first time, there were more adults over the age of forty than below.[5] The "psychological center of gravity" for society as a whole shifted into midlife and beyond.[6] This silent passage marked a gradual but significant transformation of the zeitgeist toward midlife values such as caring and compassion, a greater desire for meaning and purpose, and concern for one's community and legacy. Even young people started to exhibit these characteristics; by many accounts, the millennials (the generational cohort born approximately between 1980 and 2000) are the most socially and environmentally conscious generation we have ever seen. The median age of adults continues to rise virtually everywhere in the world. It is now about forty-four in the United States, in the high forties throughout Europe, and in the fifties in Japan.[7] Midlife values are ascendant and will soon become dominant throughout much of the world.

These factors have dramatically changed society and created a transformed landscape for business. We care about many different things because our value systems are shifting, we have much more information, we are better equipped intellectually to process that information, and we can quickly connect with others who are similarly inclined and galvanize them into shared action.

Because people today care about different things and are better informed, better educated, and better connected than in the past, their expectations from businesses in their roles as customers, team members, suppliers, investors, and community members are rapidly changing. Unfortunately, most companies have not evolved to keep pace with all these changes and are still doing business using mind-sets and practices that were appropriate for a very different world. It is now time to change that.

Our Rising Consciousness

Perhaps the greatest change that we humans are experiencing is our rising consciousness. To be conscious means to be fully awake and mindful, to see reality more clearly, and to more fully understand all the consequences—short term and long term—of our actions. It means we have a greater awareness of our inner self, our external reality, and the impacts we have on the world. It also means having a greater commitment to the truth and to acting more responsibly according to what we know to be true.

One indication of our rising consciousness is that many practices that we found acceptable in the past are unthinkable today. Consider the following: Until 150 years ago, slavery was widely accepted by a large number of people around the world and was the law of the land in many countries; 100 years ago, most people (including many women) thought it acceptable to deny women the right to vote; 75 years ago, colonialism was still widespread and generally accepted; 50 years ago, most people accepted racial segregation as a way of life; 40 years ago, few people knew much or cared about environmental issues; 25 years ago, communism was still seen by many as a viable way to organize our economic and political lives.[8]

One key indicator of rising consciousness is declining violence. As Steven Pinker documents in his recent book, the present era is "less violent, less cruel and more peaceful" than any other in human history. There is less violence in families, in neighborhoods, and among countries. The probability of dying violently, through war, terrorism, attacks by animals, or murder, is lower than any time previously. People are also less likely than in the past to experience cruelty at the hands of others.[9] Values like caring, nurturing relationships, and compassion are ascendant throughout society. Billions of us have consciously expanded our circles of concern for whom we feel empathy.

Of course, we still have plenty of room for improvement. Decades from now, we will no doubt look back on many practices that are commonplace today (such as the treatment of livestock animals) in disbelief. On this journey of constantly rising and evolving consciousness, the scope of our concerns keeps growing wider but also somehow simpler. We are gradually becoming more caring, holistic, and long term in our thinking. Many of us now see and feel the essential interdependence of all people and of all other living things. We recognize more clearly that we are all in the same boat; we must act both individually and collectively to plug the many leaks that our shared boat has sprung. This is a never-ending journey; we will continue to evolve in this way because it represents the evolutionary imperative for us as the most sentient of beings on this planet. The future of life on our planet and the fate of generations yet unborn will be greatly affected by the choices we make today.

In a vastly different time and context, Abraham Lincoln said, "The dogmas of the quiet past are inadequate to the stormy present. The occasion is piled high with difficulty, and we must rise—with the occasion. As our case is new, so we must think anew, and act anew."[10] All of these changes and challenges offer great business opportunities, but they cannot be effectively addressed if we use the same mental models we have operated with in the past. "Business as usual" will not work anymore. We need a new paradigm for business, a new philosophy to lead and work by.

Imagine . . .

Imagine a business that is born out of a dream about how the world could be and should be. The founders are on fire to create something of relevance, resonance, and permanence—a business that will far outlive them, that delivers real value of multiple kinds to everyone it touches. They want to create a business that their parents and children will be proud of, that aspires to so much more than making money—a force for good that enhances the health and well-being of society. They dream of creating a business that enriches the world by its existence and brings joy, fulfillment, and a sense of meaning to all who are touched by it.

Picture a business built on love and care rather than stress and fear, whose team members are passionate and committed to their work. Their days race by in a blur of focused intensity, collaboration, and camaraderie. Far from becoming depleted and burned out, they find themselves at the end of each day newly inspired and freshly committed to what brought them to the business in the first place—the opportunity to be part of something larger than themselves, to make a difference, to craft a purposeful life while earning a living.

Think of a business that cares profoundly about the well-being of its customers, seeing them not as consumers but as flesh-and-blood human beings whom it is privileged to serve. It would no more mislead, mistreat, or ignore its customers than any thoughtful person would exploit loved ones at home. Its team members experience the joy of service, of enriching the lives of others.

Envision a business that embraces outsiders as insiders, inviting its suppliers into the family circle and treating them with the same love and care it showers on its customers and team members. Imagine a business that is a committed and caring citizen of every community it inhabits, elevating its civic life and contributing in multiple ways to its betterment. Imagine a business that views its competitors not as enemies to be crushed but as teachers to learn from and fellow travelers on a journey toward excellence. Visualize a business that genuinely cares about the planet and all the sentient beings that live on it, that celebrates the glories of nature, that thinks beyond carbon and neutrality to become a healing force that nurses the ecosphere back to sustained vitality.

Imagine a business that exercises great care in whom it hires, where hardly anyone ever leaves once he or she joins. Imagine a business with fewer managers, because it doesn't need anyone to look over peoples' shoulders to make sure they are working or know what to do, a business that is self-managing, self-motivating, self-organizing, and self-healing like any evolved, sentient being.

See in your mind's eye a business that chooses and promotes leaders because of their wisdom and capacity for love and care, individuals who lead by mentoring and inspiring people rather than commanding them or using carrots and sticks. These leaders care passionately about their people and the purpose of their business and little for power or personal enrichment.

Imagine a business that exists in a virtuous cycle of multifaceted value creation, generating social, intellectual, emotional, spiritual, cultural, physical, and ecological wealth and well-being for everyone it touches, while also delivering superior financial results year after year, decade after decade. Imagine a business that recognizes that while our planetary resources are limited, human creativity is unlimited and continually fosters the conditions in which its people can rise to their extraordinary, almost miraculous potential.

Such businesses—suffused with higher purpose, leavened with authentic caring, influential and inspirational, egalitarian and committed to excellence, trustworthy and transparent, admired and emulated, loved and respected— are not imaginary entities in some fictional utopia. They exist in the real world, by the dozens today but soon to be by the hundreds and thousands. Examples of such companies today include Whole Foods Market, The Container Store, Patagonia, Eaton, the Tata Group, Google, Panera Bread, Southwest Airlines, Bright Horizons, Starbucks, UPS, Costco, Wegmans, REI, Twitter, POSCO, and many others. In the decades ahead, companies such as these will transform the world and lift humanity to new heights of emotional and spiritual well-being, physical vitality, and material abundance.

Welcome to the heroic new world of Conscious Capitalism.

The Tenets of Conscious Capitalism

Conscious Capitalism is an evolving paradigm for business that simultaneously creates multiple kinds of value and well-being for all stakeholders: financial, intellectual, physical, ecological, social, cultural, emotional, ethical, and even spiritual. This new operating system for business is in far greater harmony with the ethos of our times and the essence of our evolving beings.

Conscious Capitalism is not about being virtuous or doing well by doing good. It is a way of thinking about business that is more conscious of its higher purpose, its impacts on the world, and the relationships it has with its various

FIGURE 2-1

The four tenets of Conscious Capitalism

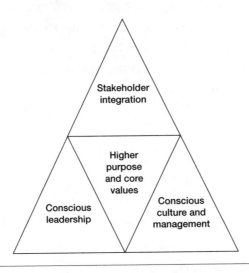

constituencies and stakeholders. It reflects a deeper consciousness about *why* businesses exist and how they can create more value.

Conscious Capitalism has four tenets: higher purpose, stakeholder integration, conscious leadership, and conscious culture and management (figure 2-1). The four are interconnected and mutually reinforcing. We refer to these as tenets because they are foundational; they are not tactics or strategies. They represent the essential elements of an integrated business philosophy that must be understood holistically to be effectively manifested.

Higher Purpose

Business has a much broader positive impact on the world when it is based on a higher purpose that goes beyond only generating profits and creating shareholder value. Purpose is the reason a company exists. A compelling sense of higher purpose creates an extraordinary degree of engagement among all stakeholders and catalyzes creativity, innovation, and organizational commitment.[11]

Purposeful companies ask questions such as these: Why does our business exist? Why does it need to exist? What core values animate the enterprise and unite all of our stakeholders? Higher purpose and shared core values unify the enterprise and elevate it to higher degrees of motivation, performance, and ethical commitment at the same time. As the figure shows, higher purpose and core values are central to a conscious business; all the other tenets connect back to these foundational ideas.

Stakeholder Integration

Stakeholders are all the entities that impact or are impacted by a business. Conscious businesses recognize that each of their stakeholders is important and all are connected and interdependent, and that the business must seek to optimize value creation for all of them. All the stakeholders of a conscious business are motivated by a shared sense of purpose and core values. When conflicts and potential trade-offs arise between major stakeholders, conscious businesses engage the limitless power of human creativity to create win-win-win-win-win-win (what we will refer to henceforth as Win^6) solutions that transcend those conflicts and create a harmony of interests among the interdependent stakeholders.

Conscious Leadership

You cannot have a conscious business without conscious leadership. Conscious leaders are motivated primarily by service to the firm's higher purpose and creating value for all stakeholders. They reject a zero-sum, trade-off-oriented view of business and look for creative, synergistic Win^6 approaches that deliver multiple kinds of value simultaneously.

In addition to high levels of analytical, emotional, and spiritual intelligence, leaders of conscious businesses have a finely developed systems intelligence that understands the relationships between all of the interdependent stakeholders. Their fundamentally more sophisticated and complex way of thinking about business transcends the limitations of the analytical mind that focuses on differences, conflicts, and trade-offs.

Conscious Culture and Management

The culture of a conscious business is a source of great strength and stability for the firm, ensuring that its purpose and core values endure over time and through leadership transitions. Conscious cultures naturally evolve from the enterprise's commitments to higher purpose, stakeholder interdependence, and conscious leadership. While such cultures can vary quite a bit, they usually share many traits, such as trust, accountability, transparency, integrity, loyalty, egalitarianism, fairness, personal growth, and love and care.

Conscious businesses use an approach to management that is consistent with their culture and is based on decentralization, empowerment, and collaboration. This amplifies the organization's ability to innovate continually and create multiple kinds of value for all stakeholders.

By embracing the principles of Conscious Capitalism, businesses can bring themselves into close harmony with the interests of society as a whole and align themselves with the evolutionary changes that we humans have been experiencing. Conscious Capitalism provides an ethical foundation that is essential but has been largely lacking in business. We believe that businesses should lead the way in raising consciousness in the world. The larger the company, the greater its footprint and therefore its responsibility to the world. Our friend Kip Tindell, cofounder and CEO of The Container Store, refers to this as the "power of the wake."[12] Just as a ship leaves behind it a large body of turbulent water, so too do individuals and companies leave a wake behind them. However, most of us are so focused on our destination that we never look around to appreciate the full impact we have on the world.

The Financial Performance of Conscious Businesses

Like all businesses, conscious businesses are subject to the discipline of the market, and they need to deliver strong financial results. Appendix A addresses the important issue of the financial performance of conscious businesses in detail, but here is a preview. In addition to creating social, cultural, intellectual, physical, ecological, emotional, and spiritual value for all stakeholders, conscious businesses also excel at delivering exceptional financial performance over the long term. For example, a representative sample of conscious firms outperformed the overall stock market by a ratio of 10.5:1 over a fifteen-year period, delivering more than 1,600 percent total returns when the market was up just over 150 percent for the same period.

As Bill George, former CEO of Medtronic and one of the foremost conscious leaders of our times, puts it, "Some people may interpret the phrase Conscious Capitalism to be soft. But it is not soft at all. It is tough; it is challenging. You've got to do both. You have to perform, and you perform for a purpose. It's like a sports team. You really care about working together as a team, but at the end of the game, you still want to win."[13] Conscious businesses win, but they do so in a way that is far richer and more multifaceted than the traditional definition of winning, in which others must lose for someone to win.

Doing What Is Right Because It Is Right

Conscious businesses have a simple but powerful belief: the right actions undertaken for the right reasons generally lead to good outcomes over time. If we allow ourselves to become too attached to what the Buddha called a "cherished outcome," we become more likely to engage in actions that seem to work in the short term, but may have harmful long-term consequences. Conscious businesses do what is right because they believe it is right.[14] They treat all their stakeholders well because that is the right, humane, and sensible thing to do—and because it is also smart business practice to do so. They operate with a sense of higher purpose because that is what gets their people excited about coming to work. The leaders of conscious businesses care about service to others because that is ultimately what leads to fulfillment and value creation.

We never actually fully control outcomes in our lives, but in business, we have created a deep-seated illusion that we do. What we can do is learn to control our actions and reactions. Traditional businesses give their managers hard targets for metrics like market share, profit margins, and earnings per share. Such metrics confuse cause and effect. To achieve those numbers—which are just abstractions—managers often knowingly undertake actions that are harmful to stakeholders, including, ultimately, shareholders. For example, managers might squeeze their team members or their suppliers. These actions may deliver the desired numbers in the next quarter, but they also plant the seeds for much bigger problems in the future. This is what happened to Toyota a few years ago, when the company started to set numerical goals for sales growth and market share. Managers throughout the organization soon shifted their focus to meeting the numbers and away from creating safe and reliable cars. The result: a spate of quality and safety problems that greatly tarnished the hard-won reputation of the company.

The lesson is to focus on the things we can control, which are our actions and our reactions, and trust that the right actions will lead to positive outcomes, not always immediately but in the long term. The positive outcomes may not be exactly what we had in mind. Depending on the quality of our actions and external factors, they could be different but far better.

Conscious Capitalism Is Not Corporate Social Responsibility

A good business doesn't need to do anything special to be socially responsible. When it creates value for its major stakeholders, it is acting in a socially responsible way. Collectively, ordinary business exchanges are the greatest creator of value in the entire world. This value creation is the most important aspect of business social responsibility.

The whole idea of corporate social responsibility (CSR) is based on the fallacy that the underlying structure of business is either tainted or at best ethically neutral. This is simply not the case. As we showed in chapter 1, free-enterprise capitalism has helped improve our world in numerous ways.

While businesses do not need to redeem themselves by doing good works in the world, there is nothing wrong with businesses focusing some of their attention on social and environmental challenges. Conscious businesses believe that creating value for all their stakeholders is intrinsic to the success of their business, and they consider both communities and the environment to be important stakeholders. Creating value for these stakeholders is thus an organic part of the business philosophy and operating model of a conscious business.

By contrast, firms that are primarily profit-driven tend to graft social and environmental programs onto a traditional business profit-maximization model, usually to enhance the firm's reputation or as defensive measures to ward off criticism. Many such efforts are really about public relations and have rightly been dismissed as "green-washing." What is needed is a holistic view that includes responsible behavior toward *all* stakeholders as a core element of the business philosophy and strategy. Rather than being bolted on with a CSR mind-set, an orientation toward citizenship and society needs to be built in to the core of the business.[15] Table 2-1 summarizes the key differences between Conscious Capitalism and CSR.

TABLE 2-1

How Conscious Capitalism differs from Corporate Social Responsibility

Corporate Social Responsibility	Conscious Capitalism
Shareholders must sacrifice for society	Integrates the interests of all stakeholders
Independent of corporate purpose or culture	Incorporates higher purpose and a caring culture
Adds an ethical burden to business goals	Reconciles caring and profitability through higher synergies
Reflects a mechanistic view of business	Views business as a complex, adaptive system
Often grafted onto traditional business model, usually as a separate department or part of public relations	Social responsibility is at the core of the business through the higher purpose and viewing the community and environment as key stakeholders
Sees limited overlap between business and society, and between business and the planet	Recognizes that business is a subset of society and that society is a subset of the planet
Easy to meet as a charitable gesture; often seen as "green-washing"	Requires genuine transformation through commitment to the four tenets
Assumes all good deeds are desirable	Requires that good deeds also advance the company's core purpose and create value for the whole system
Implications for business performance unclear	Significantly outperforms traditional business model on financial and other criteria
Compatible with traditional leadership	Requires conscious leadership

CONSCIOUS CAPITALISM AND THE HEROIC SPIRIT OF BUSINESS

A Way Forward

Every human being is born relatively undeveloped, but holds the potential for virtually unlimited personal growth. Likewise, business and free-enterprise capitalism can also evolve to richer purposes and extraordinary positive impact. Conscious Capitalism brings our rapidly evolving consciousness together with a keen appreciation for the core principles that animate capitalism. It enables us to better use this great system of social cooperation in ways that will transform our lives for the better and bring opportunity and hope to the billions on the planet still living with poverty and deprivation.

In the early years of the twenty-first century, we are becoming acutely aware that our natural resources are finite. But we are also coming to realize that there is no limit to our entrepreneurial creativity. When we learn how to manifest our creativity on a mass scale, when many more of the seven billion of us are enabled to blossom and empowered to create, we will discover there is no problem on earth that we cannot solve, no obstacle we cannot overcome.

Just as splitting the atom unleashed the awesome power hidden inside that seemingly inconsequential particle, Conscious Capitalism offers the promise of tapping into human potential in ways that few companies have been able to do. Businesses must view people not as resources but as sources.[16] A resource is like a lump of coal; you use it and it's gone. A source is like the sun—virtually inexhaustible and continually generating energy, light, and warmth. There is no more powerful source of creative energy in the world than a turned-on, empowered human being. A conscious business energizes and empowers people and engages their best contribution in service of its noble higher purposes. By doing so, a business has a profoundly positive net impact on the world.

We believe that the way forward for humankind is to liberate the heroic spirit of business and our collective entrepreneurial creativity so they can be free to solve the many daunting challenges we face. Our world does not lack for business opportunities: there are billions of people whose basic needs are not being adequately met, and we need to rethink how we can continue to meet the needs of the already-prosperous in a more sustainable manner. Companies that recognize this and unlock the natural human creative spirit to address these challenges and capitalize on these opportunities will flourish for a long time.

This journey starts with the discovery of a company's unique higher purpose, an idea that we will explore in the next two chapters.

PART ONE

THE
FIRST TENET

Higher Purpose

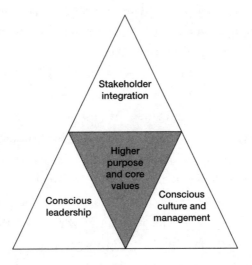

W hat are the two most important days of your life? Author Richard Leider asks this question of every audience he addresses. The first one is obvious: the day you were born. But the second is not so obvious. It is not the day you die; that is the end of the story, not a high point. It is not the day you graduate, get married, or have your first child—all significant milestones, of course, but not life defining for most. Richard's answer: it is the day you realize *why* you were born.

Not everyone experiences that day; many of us don't even know to ask the question. But for those who do, that day becomes a major fulcrum in their lives. Nothing is ever the same once you discover your true purpose, your calling. The complexion of daily life and of work changes. You are able to draw on reservoirs of energy and inspiration that you did not even know existed within you. Work becomes truly fulfilling, a source of satisfaction and joy.

One of the most successful books ever published is *The Purpose Driven Life*, by Arizona pastor Rick Warren. Since its publication in 2002, the book has sold tens of millions of copies. It has caught on in such a big way because it touched something very profound in people, a spiritual yearning and hunger for meaning and purpose in their lives. Meaning and purpose have always mattered to people, but they have taken on more urgent resonance with a growing proportion of us in the present times and will continue to grow in importance as society ages and we collectively become more conscious.

For companies, purpose matters because it energizes them and allows them to transcend the parochial concerns of individual stakeholders. When all stakeholders are aligned around a common higher purpose, they are less likely to care only about their immediate, narrowly defined self-interest. Having a higher purpose is the starting point of what it means to be a conscious business: being self-aware, recognizing what makes the company truly unique, and discovering how the company can best serve. Having a compelling purpose can also galvanize a company to strive for greatness. As Jeff Bezos, founder and CEO of Amazon.com, says, "Choose a mission that is bigger than the company. The founder of Sony sets the mission for the company that they were going to make Japan known for quality."[1]

Walter Robb, co-CEO of Whole Foods Market, speaks eloquently of our company's purpose: "We are not so much retailers with a mission as missionaries who retail. The stores are our canvas upon which we can paint our deeper purpose of bringing whole foods and greater health to the world."

Core values constitute the guiding principles the business uses to realize its purpose. Whole Foods Market's core values succinctly express the purposes of the business—purposes that include making profits but also creating value for all of the major constituencies. Our business talks and walks our values; we share them with our constituency groups and invite feedback in the form of dialogs. The core values are these: selling the highest-quality natural and organic products available, satisfying and delighting our customers, supporting team member happiness and excellence, creating wealth through profits and growth, caring about our communities and the environment, creating ongoing win-win partnerships with our suppliers, and promoting the health of our stakeholders through healthy eating education.

CHAPTER 3

Purpose: The Corporation's Search for Meaning

Voluntary exchange for mutual benefit creates the ethical foundation of business, and that is why business is ultimately justified to rightfully exist within a society. But what is its purpose? The cofounder of the medical devices company Medtronic, Earl Bakken, has long been a tireless evangelist for the company's reason for existing: "The story of Medtronic is one of men and women who have dedicated their lives and careers to helping real people overcome pain and disability to lead more normal, happy lives. It's a story I never tire of hearing or telling." Bill George was CEO of Medtronic for ten years, during which time the medical technology company's market capitalization grew from $1.1 billion to $60 billion. One of George's first actions was to bring the inspirational cofounder back to the company. In a conversation with us, George recalled the power of rediscovering the company's purpose:

> Earl used to do these mission events for employees that were just wonderful. He talked for an hour and then gave the employees a bronze medallion with the symbol of the company—a person rising off the

operating table and walking away to a full life. Medtronic's philosophy under Earl had always been that we were not putting a pacemaker into someone's body; we were restoring them to full life and health. After giving someone the medallion, he would say, "Your job here is not just to make money for the company; your job is to restore people to full life and health." At every holiday party, we would hear from six patients about how a Medtronic defibrillator or a stent or a spinal surgery with a stimulator had changed their life. That's what we all lived for. It was the backbone and the heart of the company.[1]

What Is Purpose?

Every conscious business has a higher purpose, which addresses fundamental questions such as: Why do we exist? Why do we need to exist? What is the contribution we want to make? Why is the world better because we are here? Would we be missed if we disappeared? A firm's purpose is the glue that holds the organization together, the amniotic fluid that nourishes the life force of the organization. You can also think of it as a magnet that attracts the right people—the right team members, customers, suppliers, and investors—to the business and aligns them. No matter its specific intent (see the sidebar "Examples of Higher Purpose"), a compelling purpose reduces friction within the organization and its ecosystem because it gets everybody pointed in the same direction and moving together in harmony.

EXAMPLES OF HIGHER PURPOSE

- Disney: To use our imaginations to bring happiness to millions.
- Johnson & Johnson: To alleviate pain and suffering.
- Southwest Airlines: To give people the freedom to fly.
- Pivot Leadership: Better Leaders = Better World.
- Charles Schwab: A relentless ally for the individual investor.

- BMW: To enable people to experience the joy of driving.

- Humane Society US: Celebrating animals, confronting cruelty.

- American Red Cross: Enabling Americans to perform extraordinary acts in the face of emergencies.

An excellent guide for discovering or rediscovering your higher purpose is *It's Not What You Sell, It's What You Stand For*, by Roy Spence and Haley Rushing, cofounders of the Purpose Institute. As they put it, "What is a purpose? Simply put, it's a definitive statement about the difference that you are trying to make. If you have a purpose and can articulate it with clarity and passion, everything makes sense, everything flows. You feel good about what you're doing and clear about how to get there. The more constituents that you have the more important it is to have a simple and clearly defined purpose that everyone and everything can report up to and a set of Core Values that animates the way people interact with one another."[2]

Purpose is most powerful when it taps into a "universal human truth." In other words, it is fully aligned with the higher aspects of what it means to be human (or as Abraham Lincoln elegantly put it, with "the better angels of our nature"). Such a purpose has an uplifting moral quality, appealing to people's highest ideals and motives and transcending narrow personal concerns.[3]

Purpose must come before formulating a strategy. It seems so obvious today, but it wasn't always so. Business academics and executives long ago bought into the notion that the purpose of all business is to maximize profits and shareholder value. In fact, most business school courses on strategy hardly mention the word *purpose* in any other context.

Purpose, *mission*, and *vision* are often used interchangeably. However, it is important to maintain a distinction among the three. Purpose refers to the difference you're trying to make in the world, mission is the core strategy that must be undertaken to fulfill that purpose, and vision is a vivid, imaginative conception or view of how the world will look once your purpose has been largely realized.[4]

THE FIRST TENET: HIGHER PURPOSE

Why Purpose Matters

A higher purpose gives great energy and relevance to a company and its brand. Google's original purpose was to organize the world's information and make it easily accessible and useful. As founders Larry Page and Sergey Brin said, "How can that not get you excited?"[5] REI's purpose is to reconnect people with nature. The Container Store helps people get organized so they can be happier.

Consider Southwest Airlines, perhaps the most successful airline in the history of the world. Southwest's animating purpose from day one was to democratize the skies, that is, to make air travel accessible to the average person. When Southwest came into being in the early 1970s, only 15 percent of Americans had flown on an airplane; today, more than 85 percent have flown, due largely to Southwest's pioneering efforts to offer low fares, bring air service to smaller markets, and market it in a fun way. Southwest has been consistently profitable since it started operations. It provides a great experience for customers. Team members love working there. The company is founded on having fun and radiating love (its stock symbol is LUV).

Whole Foods Market is passionate about helping people to eat well, improve the quality of their lives, and increase their lifespan. Our purpose is to teach people that what they put into their bodies makes a difference, not only to their health and to that of the people who supply the food, but also to the health of the planet as a whole. From our start in 1978 as Safer Way, Whole Foods Market has promoted organic food and the agricultural systems from which it derives. By helping to develop markets, customers, distribution networks, and even the national standards for labeling for organic foods, Whole Foods has also promoted the environmental benefits that accompany the increasing number of organic farms, dairies, ranches, and sustainable agricultural practices. For example, because organic farms utilize no synthetic fertilizers or pesticides, there is reduced usage of fossil fuels and less chemical contamination entering food chains and water supplies.

Purpose and meaning are now being embraced by large mainstream companies such as Unilever, PepsiCo, Inc., and Procter & Gamble which touch the lives of billions. At PepsiCo, Inc., CEO Indra Nooyi has been emphasizing

"Performance with Purpose" by investing heavily in drinks and food products that are healthier for customers. P&G CEO and chairman Robert McDonald is seeking "purpose-inspired growth." He has articulated the company's purpose as "touching and improving more lives, in more parts of the world, more completely."[6] Unilever CEO Paul Polman recognizes the importance of connecting the company to a purpose beyond profits and growth. "Having a deeper purpose to what we do as people makes our lives more complete, which is a tremendous force and motivator. What people want in life is to be recognized, to grow and to have made a difference. That difference can come in many forms; by touching someone, by helping others, by creating something that was not there before. To work for an organization where you can leverage this and be seen to be making a difference, that is rewarding."[7]

Purpose is something we can never take for granted; the moment we do, it starts to be forgotten and soon disappears. It has to be at the forefront of consciousness (and therefore decision making) literally all the time. When the purpose is clear, leadership teams can make quicker and better decisions. Clarity of purpose also leads to bolder decisions. Rather than adjusting decisions according to the winds of public opinion or changes in the competitive environment, decisions in a purpose-driven company take those things into consideration while also being informed by something more soulful and sturdy. This leads to superior overall performance. Purpose-informed decision making is a critical connection point between clarity of purpose and superior performance, financially and otherwise.[8]

Losing a Sense of Purpose

Every major profession has a higher purpose as its reason for being. This is true of medicine, which is about healing. It is also true for education, architecture, engineering, and the legal profession. Each is animated by service to a higher purpose, one that is aligned with the needs of society and that gives the profession legitimacy and value in the eyes of others. Each of these professions, of course, is also partly about making a profit and earning a living. However, when any profession becomes *primarily* about making money, it starts to lose its true identity and its interests start to diverge from what is good for society as a whole. As Einstein said, such a loss of higher purpose is not uncommon today: "Perfection of means and confusion of ends seem to characterize our age."

Consider two industries that have lately fallen in public regard. The pharmaceutical industry's drop in public esteem has been precipitous. It used to be a greatly admired industry with a clear sense of higher purpose; companies invested heavily to develop miracle drugs that saved, improved, and extended lives, and developed vaccines to prevent devastating diseases such as polio and cholera. As recently as 1997, 80 percent of Americans had a positive view of the industry; this plummeted to less than 40 percent by 2004.[9] The industry has long been extraordinarily profitable, but its relentless obsession with ever higher revenues and profits has obscured its essential purpose of preventing, curing, and containing diseases. The industry's loss of purpose has coincided with its declining reputation and a major increase in ethical lapses. In recent years, many drug companies have been spending much more on aggressive, often misleading advertising and less on R&D targeted at the serious illnesses that most afflict humankind.

The financial sector too has a clear inherent higher purpose: to provide people with attractive alternatives for saving and growing their money by investing that money in ways that are maximally beneficial to society. Each type of financing alternative has its own role and purpose: venture capital to fund risky early-stage businesses, debt capital to meet working capital needs and to prevent ownership dilution, equity capital to provide long-term financing for growth and expansion, and so on. But in recent years, the financial sector has become increasingly profit obsessed and short-term oriented. Compensation levels have soared to ridiculous heights as financial incentives have fueled the fire toward immediate, profit-only management, diminishing real value creation. Many banks started to trade on their own accounts in order to generate greater profits. This has led them into many well-documented risky ventures, while also compromising their integrity as financial advisers. No wonder the industry's reputation is in tatters.

By embracing the idea that their primary, even sole purpose is to make money, businesses sacrifice the great power that comes from having a higher purpose. Worthy, transcendent goals elicit greater levels of creativity, collaboration, diligence, loyalty, and passion from all stakeholders.

Happiness Cannot Be Pursued . . .

The great Austrian psychologist Viktor Frankl gave us a priceless gift of wisdom over sixty years ago, and it remains highly relevant today. As a psychiatrist in pre–World War II Vienna, he spent nearly two decades treating thousands of people who were depressed and prone to suicide. His quest was to go beyond helping people not be depressed and enable them to be truly happy. Eventually, he developed a comprehensive theory of human happiness firmly grounded in his own clinical work. In his classic book *Man's Search for Meaning* (cited by the Library of Congress as one of ten most significant books ever written), he wrote that happiness cannot be pursued; it *ensues* as the result of living a life of meaning and purpose.[10] The more directly you pursue happiness, the less likely you are to achieve it. Pursuing happiness directly may result in short-term hedonistic pleasure, but it does not lead to authentic, soul-satisfying happiness; that only comes from living a life of meaning and purpose.

Frankl taught that people can discover meaning and purpose in their lives in three ways: by doing work that matters, by loving others unconditionally, and by finding meaning in their suffering.

The last one may be Frankl's most profound teaching. All of us are guaranteed to experience loss and grief in our lives. But we can choose how to respond to that suffering. As Frankl put it, the last of the freedoms left to us under the most trying of circumstances is the freedom to choose how to respond.[11]

A simple equation captures this:

$$\text{Despair} = \text{Suffering} - \text{Meaning}$$

If we cannot derive any meaning from our suffering, if we think it's a random event or just our own rotten luck, we experience great despair. At the extreme, this can cause people to take their own lives. But if we can find some meaning, the level of despair goes down; if we can find a great deal of meaning, despair can disappear completely.[12]

Interned by the Nazis in 1942, Frankl was forced to test his theory (called logotherapy, after *logos*, Greek for "meaning") in the crucible of the Holocaust. He spent about three years in Auschwitz and various other concentration camps.[13] Over 95 percent of those who were sent to those camps died there. Frankl survived the ordeal and helped many others do so, because he believed that his own life had a purpose, which was to help others discover *their* purpose and thus find happiness. Though the only manuscript of his first book had been burned by his captors as soon as he was first arrested, he went on to write thirty-nine books and receive twenty-nine honorary doctorates before dying in 1997 at the age of ninety-two.[14] His work has transformed the lives of millions of people around the world.

. . . Nor Can Profits

Profits are an essential and desirable outcome for business. Indeed, it is socially irresponsible to run a business that does not consistently generate profits. Profitable companies can grow and continue to fulfill their higher purposes, and their profits fuel the growth and progress of our society. Through taxes, business profits help fund governments and the many public services people rely on.

Just as happiness is best experienced by not aiming for it directly, profits are best achieved by not making them the primary goal of the business. They are the outcome when companies do business with a sense of higher purpose, build their businesses on love and caring instead of fear and stress, and grow from adversity—Frankl's principles reinterpreted for business. The paradox of profits is that, like happiness, they are best achieved by not aiming directly for them.

If a business seeks only to maximize profits to ensure shareholder value and does not attend to the health of the entire system, short-term profits may indeed result, perhaps lasting many years, depending upon how well its competitor companies are managed. However, neglecting or abusing the other constituencies in the interdependent system will eventually create negative feedback loops that will end up harming the long-term interests of the investors and shareholders, resulting in sub-optimization of the entire system. Without consistent customer satisfaction, team member happiness and commitment, and community support, the short-term profits will prove to be unsustainable over the long term.

The most common objection to the above argument is that many businesses are highly profitable and are not actively managed to optimize the value for all stakeholders. Instead, they put the interests of their investors first. Doesn't this disprove our argument? Not at all. Most businesses are simply competing against other similar businesses that are organized and managed with the same overall values and goals—maximizing profits. The real question is, how does a traditional profit-centered business fare when it competes against a stakeholder-centered business? As we detail in appendix A, there is compelling evidence that conscious businesses significantly outperform traditional businesses over the long run.

If business leaders become more aware that their business is not a machine but part of a complex, interdependent, and evolving system with multiple constituencies, they will see that profit is one of the important purposes of the business, but not the sole purpose. They will also begin to see that the best way to maximize long-term profits is to create value for the entire interdependent business system. Once enough business leaders come to understand and accept this new business paradigm, Conscious Capitalism will reach a take-off point and the hostility toward business will start to dissipate.

Work and Purpose

Everyone craves meaning and purpose in life, but few people find such fulfillment at work. The oral historian Studs Terkel wrote movingly about American workers struggling to earn a living and to create a life and legacy: "It is about the search, too, for daily meaning as well as daily bread, for recognition as well as for cash, for astonishment rather than torpor; in short, for a sort of life rather than a Monday through Friday sort of dying."[15]

George Bernard Shaw wrote of the joy of meaningful work in this famous passage: "This is the true joy in life, the being used for a purpose recognized by yourself as a mighty one; the being thoroughly worn out before you are thrown on the scrap heap; the being a force of Nature instead of a feverish selfish little clod of ailments and grievances complaining that the world will not devote itself to making you happy."[16]

THE FIRST TENET: HIGHER PURPOSE

Unfortunately, the level of personal and emotional engagement people have with paid work today is abysmally low. The absence of purpose results in work that is devoid of meaning and that therefore does not tap into our higher human capacities. Team members feel disconnected and become indifferent toward their work. Gallup conducts team member engagement surveys every year and has found the level of engagement with paid work has been shockingly low for the past ten years. In 2010, only 28 percent of team members were found to be engaged in (or emotionally connected to) their work. About 53 percent were indifferent, and 19 percent were actually hostile.[17] This reflects an appalling, almost tragic waste of human potential. The difference in business impact and personal happiness between a team member who is inspired, passionate, and committed and one who merely shows up for a paycheck is enormous. The blame for this does not lie with "lazy and unmotivated" workers, but with companies that fail to create purposeful workplaces in which people are given the opportunity to find meaning, purpose, and happiness in their own lives by contributing to the valuable work of the company. To us, this represents the "shame of management," in the same sense that Peter Drucker referred to the rise of the consumer movement as the shame of marketing.

While engagement with paid work at for-profit businesses has remained abysmally low, involvement with volunteer and paid work at nonprofits has grown dramatically. In *Blessed Unrest*, Paul Hawken estimated that there were approximately two million nongovernmental organizations (NGOs) in the world and showed that their numbers are growing rapidly.[18] People are devoting enormous amounts of time, effort, and money to causes that usually have nothing to do with their narrowly defined self-interest. The reason is that these activities nourish people in ways that working for most businesses simply does not.

To tap this deep wellspring of human motivation, companies need to shift their emphasis from profit maximization to purpose maximization.[19] By recognizing and responding to the hunger for meaning that is a quintessential human condition, companies can unlock vast sources of passion, commitment, creativity, and energy that lie largely dormant in their team members and other stakeholders.

Purpose-driven motivation is *intrinsic* motivation and is far more effective and powerful than extrinsic financial incentives. Companies that primarily use financial incentives to motivate their team members soon discover that it is a double-edged sword. It can work reasonably well as long as the company's financial performance is outstanding. But when financial performance lags, such companies inevitably experience a crisis of morale. For publicly traded companies, the stock price becomes a barometer of the morale of team members and executives. These firms have a hard time pulling out of slumps, whereas purpose-driven companies recover faster. They remain true to their purpose even when times are bad, and the best ones become even more committed to their core purpose.[20]

Matching Individual Passions with Business Purpose

People are most fulfilled and happiest when their work is aligned with their own inner passions. Personal passion, corporate purpose, and business performance all go together. For a passionate foodie, working for Wegmans or Trader Joe's or Whole Foods Market can be truly fulfilling. For outdoors enthusiasts, Patagonia, REI, and L.L.Bean are wonderful places to work. In such settings, work becomes so much more than a job. It even goes beyond having a satisfying career. It becomes a calling—something we were born to do.

It is therefore critical for purpose-driven organizations to hire, at every level of the company, people who align strongly with the purpose of the enterprise. If the business hires people who think the purpose is silly or irrelevant, they will not align with it and will be—literally—at cross purposes. The good news is that when an organization has a strong purpose and communicates it clearly and consistently, the organization naturally attracts people who align with the purpose.

Having a sense of purpose and deriving joy from their work help companies overcome obstacles in their path and the objections of naysayers. Biz Stone, the cofounder of Twitter, recalls, "When Twitter was just starting out, our biggest challenge was friends and colleagues telling us, 'This is not useful.' We overcame that challenge because we found joy in our work. When you love what you do, when you are what I call emotionally invested in your work, then you can overcome almost any challenge with ease."[21]

Companies also must take into account personal alignment with purpose when promoting anyone into a higher leadership position. Any enterprise that hires senior leaders from outside the company risks the subversion of its purpose by either indifference or hostility. Many companies in recent years have made the mistake of bringing in highly paid, high profile outside leaders who didn't align with the purpose or the values of the enterprise. A great example is The Home Depot, which brought in a former top executive from General Electric (Bob Nardelli) who wasn't aligned with its purpose or culture. Eventually, this led the cultural "immune system" of The Home Depot to reject his leadership style. The organization declined under his leadership until he was removed and replaced by someone who was better aligned with the company's purpose and culture.

In the next chapter, we look at how companies can discover and grow their unique purpose.

CHAPTER 4

Discovering and Growing Purpose

Some companies are born with a sense of higher purpose. Others are created because their founders see a market opportunity they can profitably exploit. As such companies reach maturity, they often find themselves in a sort of existential crisis, much in the same way that many adults start asking questions about meaning and purpose when they reach midlife.

Higher Purpose Discovered: A Heartwarming Story About Trash

An example of a company whose founders saw a market opportunity to exploit is Waste Management, the leader in the mundane but essential business of disposing of our trash. Founded in 1968, the company had a growth strategy of "rolling up" the fragmented trash collection business by acquiring local trash haulers around the country. Until a few years ago, its tagline was utilitarian and uninspiring: "Helping the world dispose of its problems."

According to financial analysts, the company's most valuable assets were its 271 landfills, enough to bury over forty years' worth of trash at its current rate of growth.

As the sustainability movement gained speed, it presented major challenges to the company. People and companies started throwing fewer things away. For example, Walmart made a commitment to eventually reduce the amount of trash it sends to landfills to zero, threatening a core revenue stream for Waste Management.

Under CEO David Steiner, Waste Management has turned these challenges into opportunities and discovered a higher purpose for itself: as a company that looks for innovative ways to extract value (in the form of energy and materials) from the waste stream. It has set up a consulting division that helps companies like Alcoa and Caterpillar reduce their waste, in effect cannibalizing its own landfill business. It is moving capital investment away from landfills and into materials recovery facilities that use sophisticated technologies to separate comingled recyclable materials. It has invested in over a hundred waste-to-energy projects that already generate enough clean energy to supply 1.1 million homes (more than the entire U.S. solar industry). The company sees huge potential in treating waste as a valuable asset rather than a problem to be buried for future generations to deal with. It generates about $13 billion in revenues annually but estimates that the waste it handles contains about $10 billion of value, most of it not yet extracted. The company may soon start paying customers for certain kinds of waste (such as organic waste) even as its competitors charge them to haul it away. Steiner says the future of the company lies in joining and leading the sustainability movement.[1]

Not surprisingly, financial analysts firmly wedded to the traditional trash business model see all this as a distraction. A Credit Suisse First Boston analyst downgraded the stock in 2009, saying the company "does not want to be a trash company but instead a one-stop 'green' environmental services shop, and that transformation requires both a lot of patience and capital."[2] The company's new tagline is "Think Green," and it now describes itself as "North America's leading provider of integrated environmental solutions." That's a long way from just hauling your trash and putting it "out of sight, out of mind." You can bet the company's team members are now a lot more excited about going to work in the morning.

Great Companies Have Great Purposes

There is no "right" purpose for every business; there are as many potential purposes as there are enterprises or organizations. Each business must strive to find and fulfill the purpose that is embedded within its own collective DNA. Just as each individual person is unique and valuable, so too can every business be unique and valuable. But just as some individuals set great purposes for themselves and eventually achieve greatness, we believe that the best companies in the world have great purposes too. These great purposes are usually discovered or created by the founders and endure at the core of their business philosophy. Great purposes are transcendent, energizing, and inspiring for all the interdependent stakeholders.[3]

While great purposes have unique expressions at each business, we find it helpful to group them into a set of well-known and timeless categories (table 4-1). There's no intrinsic reason why business should be different from any other human endeavor. The same enduring ideals that animate art, science, education, and many nonprofit organizations can and should also animate business. These were articulated by Plato as the transcendent ideals of the Good, the True, and the Beautiful. Humankind has been seeking to create, discover, and express these transcendent ideals for thousands of years.

TABLE 4-1

Four categories of great purposes

The Good	Service to others—improving health, education, communication, and quality of life
The True	Discovery and furthering human knowledge
The Beautiful	Excellence and the creation of beauty
The Heroic	Courage to do what is right to change and improve the world

THE FIRST TENET: HIGHER PURPOSE

Plato considered these three ideals ends in themselves, not as means to other higher ends. Those who pursue the Good want to serve others because it is intrinsically rewarding to do so, not because they anticipate some favorable consequences from doing so. The pursuit of Knowledge or Truth is its own reward, whether or not that knowledge is ever used in a particular way. The creation of Beauty is an intensely soul-satisfying, uniquely human experience. People create beauty because their desire to do so arises from deep within. Their creation need not be seen or experienced by anyone else to make it worthwhile; it need only please its creator.

To these three, we have added the Heroic to complete a framework of higher purposes that we find most great businesses seek to express in some form. The following examples illustrate how these four enduring ideals are being expressed by great businesses in the world today.

The Good

The first great purpose that great businesses often express is the *Good*. The most common way this ideal manifests itself in business is through service to others. This is a deeply motivating purpose that is emotionally very fulfilling to individuals who truly embrace this ideal. Authentic service is based on genuine empathy with the needs and desires of others. Genuine empathy leads to the development, growth, and expression of love, care, and compassion. Businesses dedicated to the great purpose of service to others seek ways to grow the emotional intelligence of their organizations so they can nourish and encourage love, care, and compassion toward customers, team members, and the larger community.

While any category of business can be motivated by the heartfelt purpose of service to others, we find that service and retail businesses that depend greatly on the goodwill of their customers are most likely to express this particular purpose and devote themselves to it wholeheartedly. An excellent example is The Container Store, which creates value for its customers by providing excellent service and quality products that help people better organize their lives. The company thinks of itself as a business that helps people have a higher quality of life, expressed in the statement "Get organized, be happy."

Zappos defines its purpose as "delivering happiness." It does this through great customer service, high-quality products, competitive prices, and fast delivery. In a sense, the quest for delivering happiness is a fairly accurate synonym for the pursuit of the Good. Other examples of service-oriented businesses that exemplify the great purpose of the Good include Amazon.com, Nordstrom, JetBlue, Wegmans, Bright Horizons, Starbucks, The Motley Fool, and Trader Joe's.

The True

The second great transcendent purpose that animates many great businesses is the *True*, which we define as the "search for truth and the pursuit of knowledge." Think about how exciting it is to discover and learn something that no one has ever known before, which advances humankind's collective knowledge. Through such advancements, the quality of human life is improved, the cost of our lifestyles declines, and we can live healthier and more fulfilling lives. We are collectively better off as a result of that pursuit of knowledge.

This great purpose is at the core of some of the most creative and dynamic companies in the world today. Google is an excellent example of a company with this kind of purpose, expressed early on in the company's history as "to organize the world's information and make it universally accessible and useful." This purpose statement is clear and simple, yet profound. It makes clear why the company exists and how it creates value. The statement also provides managers with a great deal of strategic direction. Google started out by simply indexing the Web and allowing for fast searches of textual information. Over time, it has expanded into books, audio information, video content, still images, personal picture collections, maps (recently adding indoor maps for shopping malls and airports), the skies, the ocean floor, medical records, your own desktop, company Web sites, and so on, all the while remaining true to its original purpose. Few of us can get through a day without googling at least once and usually multiple times. Google makes us feel like the entire knowledge of the world is available to us whenever and wherever we want it, with the touch of a few buttons or clicks.

Wikipedia is another organization that has enabled people to pursue knowledge quickly and efficiently. Companies like Intel and Genentech have invented new and incredible technologies such as the microprocessor and biotechnology, furthering humankind's potential in numerous ways. In fact, many businesses in biotechnology or computer hardware and software are good examples of companies whose highest purpose is the discovery of new knowledge that enhances, extends, or otherwise improves our lives. Amgen and Medtronic are other examples of great companies motivated by the excitement of discovery and the pursuit of knowledge. These companies have greatly benefited humankind through their successful pursuit of this great purpose.

The Beautiful

The third great transcendent purpose at the core of great businesses is the *Beautiful*, which can be expressed in business through "the pursuit of beauty and excellence, and the quest for perfection." A company that expresses beauty in the world enriches our lives in numerous ways. While we more commonly experience the Beautiful through the work of creative artists in music, painting, film, and handicrafts, we also see it expressed through certain special companies that have tapped into this powerful purpose as they pursue perfection in their chosen field. True excellence expresses beauty in unique and inspiring ways that make our lives more enjoyable.

An excellent example is Apple, with its single-minded focus on creating "insanely great technology" that has made our lives better. People love the beauty of Apple's products (such as the iMac, iPod, iPad, and iPhone), not just in their appearance and the value they create for us, but also in the simplicity and fun of the interactions we have with them.

Four Seasons and BMW are other businesses that are motivated by excellence to create beautiful things and experiences that approach perfection.

The Heroic

The fourth type of purpose is the *Heroic*, describing businesses that are motivated by a desire to change the world, not necessarily through service to others or through discovery and the pursuit of truth, or through the quest for perfection, but through a powerful Promethean desire to really change things—to truly make the world better, to solve insoluble problems, to do the really courageous thing even when it is very risky, and to achieve what others say is impossible. When Henry Ford first created the Ford Motor Company, it was a heroic company whose purpose was "Opening the highways to all mankind." At a time when only the wealthy could afford cars and the freedom they provided, Ford truly changed the world in the early part of the twentieth century.

A hero is defined as "a person of distinguished courage or ability, admired for brave deeds and noble qualities." A heroic company takes risks and perseveres in the face of enormous odds. It maintains and strengthens its human qualities while doing so, all in service of changing the world for the better in some tangible way.

One of the best examples of a truly heroic enterprise is the Grameen Bank, started by Muhammad Yunus, in Bangladesh. His brilliant and beautiful vision was to help end poverty and transform the world by empowering the poorest of the poor. As we highlighted in chapter 1, the world has seen tremendous progress in ending poverty through free-enterprise capitalism. Yunus likes to say, "Someday poverty will be something that's only seen in museums." Yunus's heroic dedication to ending poverty in Bangladesh and throughout the world resulted in his winning the 2006 Nobel Peace Prize. His book *Banker to the Poor* is an inspiring tale of heroic enterprise.[4]

Over time, our higher purposes at Whole Foods Market have evolved toward the heroic category. As the company has grown, our purpose also has grown in both meaning and complexity. Every three years, approximately eight hundred store team leaders, coordinators, and star performers from all over the company come together in a "Tribal Gathering" for a long weekend dedicated to networking, education, and inspiration. At our 2011 meeting, the executive leadership articulated several higher purposes we wish to realize:

1. We want to help evolve the world's agricultural system to be both efficient and sustainable. This includes a much higher level of livestock animal welfare, seafood sustainability, and upgraded efficiency and productivity of organic agriculture.

2. We want to raise the public's collective awareness about the principles of healthy eating: a diet that is centered on whole foods, is primarily plant based, is nutrient dense, and includes mainly healthy fats (minimal animal fats and vegetable oils). We believe this diet will radically improve the health of millions of people by helping prevent and reverse the lifestyle diseases that are killing so many of us—heart disease, stroke, cancer, diabetes, and obesity.[5]

3. Through the Whole Planet Foundation, we want to help end poverty around the world by making microcredit working-capital loans to millions of impoverished people to help them create and improve their businesses.

4. We want to help make Conscious Capitalism the dominant economic and business paradigm in the world to spread human flourishing.

The purpose of a business does not have to be confined to only one of the four great ideals. Many businesses straddle multiple purposes. In some ways, Whole Foods Market is pursuing the Good, the True, the Beautiful, and the Heroic simultaneously. Ultimately, all four of these ideals are connected. When something is Good, it is also True, Beautiful, and Heroic in its own specific ways. Similarly, when something is Beautiful, it can also be seen as Good, True, and Heroic. There is always unity within the diversity if our minds are able to see the integration.

Searching for Purpose

Purpose usually exists when a company is first created. The entrepreneurs who create the company may not always make it explicit, but there is generally a tacit purpose that animates the entrepreneur. As a company grows, the founding entrepreneurs sometimes make the purpose explicit and articulate the company's core values. That is part of becoming a more conscious business, a business that gradually becomes aware of its reason for being.

REI went through this a few years ago. CEO Sally Jewell describes the process the company used:

> We spent time as a large leadership group, 150 people, asking, "Why does REI exist?" Then we asked ourselves five times, "Why is that important?" And two more questions: "What would happen if REI went away?" and then, "Why do I devote my creative energies to this organization?" We took those couple hundred sheets and came up with our core purpose: to inspire, educate, and outfit for a lifetime of outdoor adventure and stewardship. While we make money by being an outfitter, what we really do is inspire people to do things they aspire to do—educate them so they can try something that they've been uncomfortable trying before. And if we do that well, it works its way into their everyday lives and they begin to give back, and that's the stewardship component.[6]

Unfortunately, many businesses over time become so preoccupied with surviving, growing, reacting to marketplace changes, or just making money that they forget their purpose. The leadership of such an older business may need to go back and rediscover the company's purpose, much as an archaeologist seeks to discover what brought about a city or a civilization.

At some point in their evolution, companies that started as opportunistic, money-making enterprises need to discover or create their higher purpose beyond profit maximization in order to realize their full potential. They can do this through a process we call *purpose search*. The process includes representatives of all the stakeholder groups: the senior leadership of the company and some board members, team members, customers, investors, suppliers, and members of the community. All have a stake in the flourishing of the business, and all have a vision of what the purpose of that enterprise could be. When we bring these major stakeholders together to discover or create a higher purpose, some amazing things can happen. The exchange of information, values, and unique perspectives about the business can result in the rediscovery or creation of the company's higher purpose in a fairly short time—usually within a few days, and sometimes even in a single day if it is a really engaged process and is facilitated by a skilled consultant.

Once the purpose is articulated, it must live and breathe in the organization. This does not happen automatically; it requires strong determination by the senior leadership of the organization, especially the CEO. Conscious leaders have to embody the purpose in their own lives and lead by example. They must talk about the purpose at every opportunity when they engage with different stakeholder groups such as team members, investors, and customers.

Another key is perseverance. Some stakeholders are naturally skeptical; they may view the search for a purpose as just another management fad. To succeed, the business must work on the implementation of purpose on an ongoing basis. The work must involve all levels of the organization, so that the entire company feels invested and energized. The purpose must be integrated into orientation processes and new team member training programs. It also needs to be explained to customers and to the media. Leaders must take purpose into account in making all important decisions. For example, purpose should be integrated into performance evaluations, R&D, and strategic planning.

The Hero's Journey

Many conscious businesses start out with a definition of purpose that aligns with one of Plato's ideals: the Good, the True, and the Beautiful. But in some ways, the Heroic purpose is the ultimate destination for all conscious businesses.

As a company starts to fulfill its purpose more completely along the lines of the good, the true, and the beautiful and becomes a successful business, it finds that its impact on the world becomes larger and ultimately transformational. Southwest Airlines sought to deliver great service at affordable prices; in the process, it transformed the airline business and helped bring the benefits of air travel within the reach of hundreds of millions of people on the planet. Google pursued its truth-seeking purpose of organizing and making easily accessible the world's information with such single-minded devotion and achieved such enormous success that the company has transformed and enriched our daily lives. Apple has created products as objets d'art that are beautiful to behold but also incredibly useful and functional. In doing so, it has had a transformational impact on the lives of hundreds of millions of people and on not one but six industries: computing, music, telephony, retail, publishing, and entertainment.

As a company grows and evolves, its purpose, too, deepens and expands. All worthy purposes eventually take on a heroic character, because at some point, vision combines with scale to transform the world. In many cases, the purpose, too, becomes explicitly heroic, far grander in its scope and ambition than anything that could have been imagined at the company's birth.

In the next part of the book, we turn our attention to the centerpiece of the conscious business philosophy: taking care of all the stakeholders and treating them as an integrated whole rather than as competing claimants on a fixed pool of value.

PART TWO

THE
SECOND TENET

Stakeholder Integration

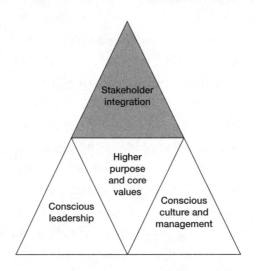

very business has stakeholders, whether or not it thinks of them that way. Conscious businesses understand this thoroughly. They treat satisfying the needs of all their major stakeholders as ends in themselves, while traditional businesses often treat their stakeholders other than investors as the means to achieving their ultimate goal of profit maximization.

THE SECOND TENET: STAKEHOLDER INTEGRATION

Conscious Businesses and Trade-Offs

A key difference between a traditional business and a conscious business is that in the former, managers routinely make trade-offs among stakeholders. A good manager is seen as one who makes trade-offs that are more advantageous to the investor stakeholders than to others. Conscious businesses understand that if we look for trade-offs, we *always* will find them. *If we look for synergies across stakeholders, we can usually find those too.*

As Ed Freeman and his colleagues write, "Managing for stakeholders is not about trade-off thinking. It is about using innovation and entrepreneurship to make all key stakeholders better off and get all of their interests going in the same direction."[1]

Another way to describe trade-offs is *zero-sum thinking*, the idea that if somebody wins, somebody else has to lose. Conscious Capitalism recognizes that business is the ultimate positive-sum game, in which it is possible to create a Win[6] for all the stakeholders of the business. No one has to lose, not even competitors; if competitors see each other as potential teachers and allies in helping each other improve, they can all become better and less antagonistic or complacent.

Adam Smith's "invisible hand" works fairly well at the market level to align what companies do with what people need. At the company level, however, it is essential that the "conscious mind" of management create a system in which all major stakeholders are aligned with the purpose of the organization and with each other. All should function as organs of a single body (indeed, the word *corporate* comes from *corpus*, or "body"), and all should be respected, valued, and integrated into the functioning of the enterprise. If any one major stakeholder is elevated and put in a different category (i.e., one group's interests are treated as an end while others are treated as means), it sets in motion a dynamic that can destroy the harmony and sense of oneness in the system. Rather than looking to create value for each other and for the system as a whole, participants then retreat into a me-first mode. They start to make myopic trade-offs, placing their own short-term self-interests ahead of others and the whole. As we discuss later, this results in a kind of stakeholder cancer that, left unchecked, can destroy the organization.

THE SECOND TENET: STAKEHOLDER INTEGRATION

Organizations thrive on human commitment and creativity. Conscious organizations motivated by purpose and governed by the stakeholder model elicit extraordinary amounts of creative human energy, because their team members are passionately engaged, customers are ardently loyal, suppliers are treated as part of the family, and so on. Since everyone is aligned in the same direction and moving in harmony, friction in the system is minimal. All that creativity and commitment is channeled toward shared ends, generating great value for all stakeholders.

Casey Sheahen, CEO of Patagonia, sees little distinction between the company's stakeholders: "We try to make all our stakeholders feel like they're part of the tribe. Transparency, great customer service, highest quality, environmental activism—all of those things matter to employees and customers and all of our other stakeholders. We really don't see any difference across our stakeholders, and [we] treat them all as one."[2]

Sometimes, individuals literally take on multiple roles. Most team members of Whole Foods Market are also regular customers, something we encourage by offering team members generous store discounts from 20 to 30 percent. As with most conscious businesses, many team members began working for Whole Foods Market because they were happy and satisfied customers. Most are also investors through stock option grants, and many buy stock in the company on their own. They are all part of the local community of each store.

The team member stakeholder thus has the greatest degree of multi-stakeholder identity. More than any other stakeholder, team members experience the company from multiple perspectives, making them even more important to the success of the business than one might initially think.

The Whole Foods Market Stakeholder Interdependence Model

The diagram presented here is a visual depiction of how we think of our major stakeholders at Whole Foods Market and their connections to each other and to the company. At the center of the diagram are our purpose and core values. Surrounding the central purpose are the various constituencies: customers, team members, suppliers, investors, the community, and the environment. All are linked interdependently. Management's responsibility is to hire the right people, train them well, and ensure that those team members flourish and are happy while they are at work. The team member's job is to satisfy and delight customers. If we have happy customers, we will have a successful business and happy investors. Management helps the team members experience happiness, team members help the customers achieve happiness, the customers help the investors achieve happiness, and when some of the profits from the investors are reinvested in business, you end up with a virtuous circle. We are continually astounded at how few businesspeople understand these simple but powerful linkages.

This visual representation only approximates the reality, however. The web of relationships that exist among the stakeholders is actually much richer and more complex than can be depicted in a simple diagram.

Stakeholders *as* the Essence of the Company

Stakeholders make up a company. They include all the people who impact and are impacted by a business. We must honor them as people first before treating them according to the role they happen to be playing. They all contribute to the creation of value, and it is therefore vital that they share fairly in the distribution of that value.

In chapters 5 through 10, we will look at how companies can create value for each of their major stakeholders—those with whom they have a direct trading relationship. In chapter 11, we will discuss how companies can relate to their secondary, or outer-circle, stakeholders. We conclude this part of the book in chapter 12 by looking at the interdependent relationships between stakeholders and how companies can leverage those interdependencies to create even greater value.

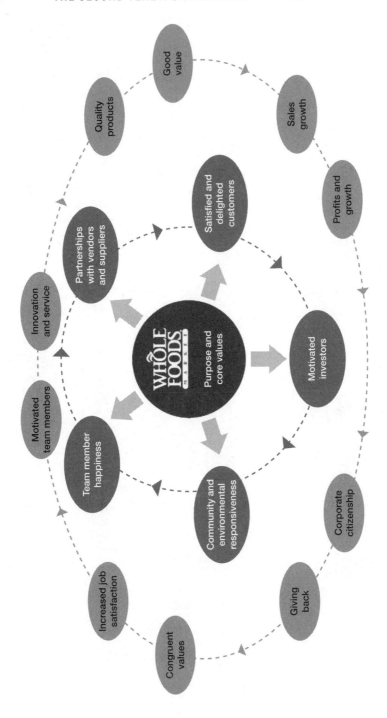

CHAPTER 5

Loyal, Trusting Customers

The purpose of every business ultimately revolves around creating value for customers. As the great management thinker Peter Drucker said, "There is only one valid definition of business purpose: to create a customer."[1] Most conscious businesses consider either their customers or their team members their most important stakeholder, but whichever one they consider their highest priority, the other is almost always a close second. Doug Rauch, former president of Trader Joe's, views team members and customers "as two wings of a bird: you need both of them to fly. They go together—if you take care of your crew members, they'll take care of your customers. When your customers are happier and they enjoy shopping, it also makes your employees' lives happier, so it's a virtuous cycle."[2]

At Whole Foods Market, we think of customers as our most important stakeholders because we know that without enough satisfied and happy customers, we have no business at all. After all, customers trade with the business voluntarily. In a competitive market, unhappy customers always have the option of trading someplace else.

Customers are clearly critical to every business, but surprisingly they are often forgotten. It is easy to get caught up in the internal processes of a company and lose sight of the primary reason for the company to exist. Jeff Bezos of Amazon.com points out, "In a typical company, if you have a meeting, no matter how important it is there is always one party who is not represented: the customer. So it's very easy inside the company to forget about the customer."[3] He started putting an empty chair in every meeting to remind participants of this.

As with all stakeholders, the well-being of customers must be treated as an end and not just as a means to profits for the business. Businesses that think of customers as a means to the end—profits—do not have the same level of empathy, commitment to service, and understanding of customer needs as do businesses that treat customers as ends. Customers know when someone genuinely cares about their well-being. Businesses must think of their customers as human beings to be served, not as consumers to be sold to. In fact, the very word consumer objectifies people, suggesting that their only role is to consume.

Developing Closer Relationships with Customers

While some customers only care about getting a quality product for a good price, many increasingly want to trade with businesses whose purpose and values align with their own. Such customers can develop closer relationships with the company; they are not passive, disinterested traders. Every business benefits if its customers care about it and invest in it emotionally. Many such customers become advocates on behalf of the business and have a vision about how the business should be. They care enough to tell the business when it needs to change and evolve, learn and grow.

When a business lacks a clear purpose and simply tries to understand what customers want, it fails to honor what is important to itself. It can act soullessly, bowing down to and even "spinning" to customers. Customers, in turn, have no passion for the company and feel as if the company is trying to sell to them rather than serve them. But if a company starts with a clear purpose, it is much more able to form authentic customer relationships and attract like-minded customers, those who share its passion. Now more than ever, in this age of information democracy and social media, such authentic relationships blossom while shallower ones fade.[4]

Trust is critical to having a good relationship with customers and is developed by dealing with them with authenticity, transparency, integrity, respect, and love. When we develop a high-trust relationship with someone, he or she becomes like our friends and family. Whole Foods Market does not think of our customers as consumers or even as clients; we prefer to think of them as our friends and our guests when they are in our stores.

The Home Depot cofounder Bernie Marcus describes how he feels about customers: "Arthur [Blank] and I actually love the customers. When I would go into stores, I would hug and kiss customers because I recognize that everything I had in my life came from them. That is the difference between me and Jack Welch. With Jack, the bottom line was the most important thing. With us, we said if we treat the customer right, we eventually would have the bottom line."[5]

Leading and Educating Customers

Businesses have to serve their customers and look out for their best interests. Often, this means that we need to educate them, not just respond to what they are asking of us. But this is only possible if they trust us. When they do, customers implicitly give us permission to influence them. Without trust, we can push them or pull them, but we cannot lead, educate, or influence them.

This is a big issue for Whole Foods Market. Often, what customers desire to eat and what they actually need for their health are not the same things. A person who is obese and at risk for diabetes doesn't need more candy bars, ice cream, or sugary sodas, but may be addicted to them. How should conscious businesses deal with customers facing such a conflict between needs and desires? This question is more urgent today because such situations are becoming increasingly common. A high percentage of people are addicted to substances that are fundamentally bad for them. These addictions are often created and fed by clever marketing campaigns backed up by huge advertising and promotional budgets.

Responsibilities to Customers

Educating customers is not the same as preaching to them. If the business is able to see unarticulated or latent needs that customers don't yet recognize, it has a responsibility to educate them about the potential value they are not yet seeing. For example, at Whole Foods Market we believe we have responsibilities to our customers regarding healthy eating and wellness. We have recently launched a Wellness Club program in some stores to help educate our customers about dietary patterns and choices that lead to optimal health and well-being. We can only do this knowing that customers ultimately decide what is valuable to them. They express their preferences every time they trade with our business. We have to satisfy those customers in terms of what they want in the moment, while steering them toward better choices over time. The challenging art of our business is to educate customers to want what's good for them, but at the same time to give them the freedom to still choose the products they want even if the choices aren't good for them. If we do our job well, over time customers will start to choose differently.

We have seen this play out with the growth of organic food over the years. When we started over thirty years ago, organic was less than 5 percent of our total sales. But after years of educating our customers and talking with them as well as working closely with our supplier partners, more than 30 percent of the food we sell is now organic. People are getting the message; it just takes time, trust, patience, and continuous communication.

Any business that forgets that customers are ultimately in charge and that it must work to serve them is making a potentially fatal mistake. Customers can always find someone else willing to satisfy their needs and desires. As their trust in us has grown, our customers increasingly look to Whole Foods Market to be their "editors," as we carefully examine and evaluate the products we sell. For example, we do not offer tobacco products, foods with artificial ingredients, hydrogenated oils, meat produced with low animal-welfare standards, or fish that are being fished beyond sustainability. The decisions were made not just because of customer concerns, but because we study health trends of humans, animals, and the environment.

When Responsibilities Conflict with Customers' Wants

Often, people ask us, "Why does Whole Foods Market sell some foods that aren't particularly healthy?" This is a good question because we have both high-quality standards that prevent us from selling many products and a desire to satisfy our customers by providing them with the foods they want to buy. The answer is that our company is in a never-ending dialogue internally and with our customers, trying to strike the right balance between being so restrictive that we no longer have a viable business and so permissive that we are no longer true to our core value concerning healthy eating. We have not found a right answer once and for all, but our intent is always to educate and lead our customers toward healthier eating habits, while simultaneously listening to their feedback and providing them with the products they want to buy. Ultimately, our customers "vote with their money" every time they shop. Just as, over time, they have voted for more and more organic foods, we hope they will gradually vote the unhealthiest foods out of our stores by choosing not to buy them.

Customer-Focused Innovation

One of the beauties of free-enterprise capitalism is that it motivates businesses to provide greater value, higher quality, and better service all the time. Competition forces us to continuously improve, innovate, and to be more creative—or be left behind. To thrive, we have to offer customers new products, services, and value that our competitors don't. What makes it even more challenging is that customer expectations about quality and value rise continuously. What might have satisfied them twenty-five years ago doesn't satisfy them today. As the Red Queen says in *Through the Looking Glass*, "It takes all the running you can do, to keep in the same place. If you want to get somewhere else, you must run at least twice as fast."[6]

Now, having to run twice as fast sounds like a rather draining proposition! But that is what we would need to do if we just keep doing the same things we have always been doing. The only way to escape from that trap is through creativity and innovation, by creating superior products and services that competitors have not yet thought of or cannot easily duplicate. Conscious businesses have an advantage because they are inherently more creative. Instead of getting trapped into a never-ending efficiency and productivity competition, conscious businesses innovate by thinking of the unmet needs and desires of their customers. This is challenging and fulfilling at the same time.

If Whole Foods Market, for example, had to compete with Walmart strictly on the basis of supply chain efficiency or distribution economies of scale, it would be impossible for us to win. But what we *can* do is be more nimble, more creative, and more innovative and provide higher-quality service while creating a better store environment. By the time Walmart figures out what we are doing, we will have moved on to newer and better innovations that create new value for our ever-evolving customers.

The Higher Purpose of Marketing

Conscious businesses take a different approach to marketing than traditional businesses do. Most people today are pretty cynical about marketing; the very word is seen by many as a pejorative term. Marketing is widely seen as trying to manipulate people by persuading them to do something not in their best interest. At Whole Foods, we think of marketing as enhancing the quality of our relationship with our customers. To us, everything that develops and deepens the relationship and builds trust is good marketing. Anything that detracts from that is bad marketing.

Trader Joe's is another great example of a company that takes a conscious approach to marketing and advertising. It spends less than 1 percent of its revenue on advertising, much below the industry average. Rather than having frequent sales, as most retailers do, Trader Joe's offers customers great value every day. Its primary advertising vehicle is a highly entertaining and informative publication called *The Fearless Flyer*, which customers actually look forward to receiving and reading. As Doug Rauch, former president, puts it:

> Since conscious businesses are purpose-driven organizations that are aligned with their stakeholders, they do not need to use marketing as a way to stimulate or create interest that otherwise wouldn't be there. They can honestly share what's true about their product or service. They don't try to create demand artificially and temporarily; they just authentically communicate and connect with people around their common values. Trader Joe's has a clear sense of purpose and a strong focus on the customer experience. Over time, this has resulted in customers becoming raving fans and highly effective unpaid ambassadors and marketing agents for the company. Not only do their employees, but even their vendors become marketers for them![7]

Businesses have a lot of power to shape the popular culture and to influence the tastes and preferences of customers, primarily through their marketing efforts. This persuasive power is backed up by about $1 trillion of spending every year on marketing in the United States alone, or more than $3,200 per man, woman, and child.[8] With this power comes great responsibility. All of that spending has a large impact on the popular culture. The culture, in turn, is a very powerful force in shaping people's behavior. Unfortunately, the huge resources being spent on marketing today are having impacts that are not always conducive to living a healthy, meaningful, and fulfilling life.

Marketing can make customers aware of wonderful new offerings and guide them in a favorable direction, but it also can try to persuade them to do things not conducive to their well-being. Most advertising overpromises benefits and tries to induce customers to buy the company's products whether or not the products are a good fit with their needs. Normally, this would only work in the short run, because people would soon realize that the company is leading them astray. The problem is that many customers get hooked on bad things and can't easily quit (cigarettes, alcohol, sugar, caffeine, junk food, and some pharmaceutical drugs come to mind).

In many ways, the marketing profession has lost sight of its higher purpose: to understand customer needs thoroughly, align what the company does with the satisfaction of those needs, and thereby improve the quality of life for customers and financial performance for the business. Smart marketing aligns customer needs and desires; it helps customers to want that which is also good for them. Great marketing is about truly making customers better off by understanding and satisfying their most important life-affirming needs, even needs that people may not consciously recognize. It is about providing real value rather than engaging in self-serving hucksterism. It is, in a sense, about healing.[9]

HEROIC SELLING

The idea of selling has a bad connotation in many people's minds, bringing up the image of a pushy or overzealous salesperson. But when selling is linked to real needs that customers have but cannot articulate, it provides a valuable service and can be almost heroic. The way Kip Tindell, cofounder and CEO of The Container Store, puts it, team members sometimes "wimp out" and give customers only what they ask for rather than searching for additional ways to add value. That hurts the company as well as the customer. Kip illustrates this lesson with a story he calls "man in the desert":

> The man in the story has been stranded in the desert for days, he's near death, and he's crawling to an oasis. You live in this oasis, and you see this man, who is hoping you're not a mirage. What most businesspeople would do is to rush out and give the man a glass of water. They would pat themselves on the back, thinking that what they have done is sufficient and wonderful. But of course, there's so much more that can be done for this man. He probably has heat exhaustion or sunstroke; he obviously needs a hat and sunscreen; he needs to be re-hydrated. You could call his wife and family and let them know he's okay, since he's been missing for

days. What you're doing is intuiting the many needs of this stranger you come across in the desert. In our Houston, Texas, store, they would say that after a few hours the man in the desert should be swimming in a pool with a margarita, so thoroughly have we taken care of him! The man in the desert is much happier with everything that's been done for him. That's what we call "heroic" selling: it's sticking entirely with what the customer truly wants and needs, and doing something that's good for the customer and good for the company.[10]

Customers as Advocates

Conscious companies recognize the power of putting customers' interests ahead of their own and communicating authentically and transparently with people. They provide customers with honest and complete information and help them find products that best fit their needs—even if those products are made by competitors. The value of strengthening the relationship and building trust with customers far outweighs the cost of losing an occasional transaction. Research by Glen Urban at MIT has found that when companies demonstrate such genuine commitment to the well-being of their customers, customers reciprocate in multiple ways: they become much more trusting, increase their future purchases, and become advocates on behalf of the company—unpaid but very effective salespeople, in effect.[11]

The most effective marketers for any business are truly delighted customers. They market the business for you. If you have enough such customers, you really don't need to do much advertising. This is why Whole Foods Market does very little advertising. We might take out a few ads when a new store opens, but that's about all. For us, marketing is about satisfying, delighting, and nourishing our customers, creating good relationships with them and building trust. If we do that, customers reciprocate by giving back to the business through loyalty and through positive word-of-mouth communications to their friends and people they know.

THE SECOND TENET: STAKEHOLDER INTEGRATION

Social media has become an accelerant and an amplifier; it gives those people who love a business a bigger voice to communicate about it. Moreover, the fragmentation of media away from the Big Three networks, not to mention technology that makes it easy to skip commercials, has made it much more difficult to reach the larger market through traditional advertising. This has given a real marketing advantage to companies that have a higher purpose and that are adept at using the tools of marketing not to sell, but rather to add value among people who share their beliefs.[12]

The Nexus Between Customers and Team Members

The relationship between customers and team members is crucial, especially in a service business like retailing. For Whole Foods Market, it is impossible for us to create value for customers except through our team members. Team members provide quality service and create a rich customer experience. That's why our stakeholder philosophy teaches that "happy team members result in happy customers." If we truly care about our customers, we also must really care about our team members.

Next, let us look at the other wing that makes the bird of free enterprise soar: team members.

CHAPTER 6

Passionate, Inspired Team Members

Is it possible to build a business on love and trust instead of fear and stress? That is the question the founders of Whole Foods Market asked back in our early days. We looked around at the businesses we knew, and saw that there was a huge amount of fear and stress among the team members in many of those businesses. Hardly anybody we knew actually looked forward to going to work.

Here is a rather depressing little fact about work life today: the rate of heart attacks goes up dramatically on Monday mornings across the world![1] The sad reality is that many people hate their work and are stressed out by their jobs. The workplace is frequently a pressure-cooker environment, working conditions are often poor, team members are not valued as human beings, and colleagues view one another as competitors and threats. No wonder the restaurant chain named TGIF for "Thank Goodness It's Friday" has struck such a chord with so many. Most people see their job as just a burden they have to bear and somehow get through until they can really enjoy themselves in the evenings, on weekends, and during vacations. They live for their time outside work.

Does it have to be this way? Must work equal drudgery? Far from it. The observation that most people are unhappy in their work doesn't mean that work is unimportant or cannot lead to happiness. The reality is that work is central in the lives of many people. As Sigmund Freud said, "Love and work are the cornerstones of our humanness."

Work, Meaning, and Happiness

Most people in the twenty-first century (especially those who are well educated and reasonably affluent) want to work for more than just a paycheck. They crave work that is stimulating and enjoyable. They're looking for meaning; they want their work to make a difference, to make the world a better place. They're looking for a community of friends. They're looking for opportunities to learn and to grow and to have fun.

A few years ago, Gallup conducted a study of human happiness in 155 countries. The Gallup World Poll revealed that the leading determinant of happiness is not wealth; beyond a certain level, its effect plateaus. It is not health; most people in good health take it for granted. It is not even family. The number one determinant of happiness is "a good job": work that is meaningful and done in the company of people we care about. Jim Clifton, chairman and CEO of Gallup, writes, *"What the whole world wants is a good job. This is one of the most important discoveries Gallup has ever made . . .* Humans used to desire love, money, food, shelter, safety, peace, and freedom more than anything else. The last 30 years have changed us. Now people want to have a good job, and they want their children to have a good job."[2]

This should not surprise us. After all, most of us spend about a third of our waking hours working at a paying occupation. If our work is inherently satisfying and we like and respect our colleagues, we feel fulfilled and happy. If we find the work to be a drudgery or worse, and if we are surrounded by unhappy and cynical people or people looking to get ahead at our expense, we are bound to be miserable.

Work does not have to be grim and boring. Working effectively and having fun are not an either-or situation. Our work should be where we find meaning and purpose, but also community and enjoyment. We can be intently focused on our work, and we can have fun doing it. A fun workplace is actually one of the keys to creating a dynamic, innovative culture.

A great example of a company that is both a fun place to work and highly innovative is Southwest Airlines. Herb Kelleher, the longtime CEO who built the company, is a creative maverick who wanted to create a fun workplace where everybody really loves to come. He personally set the norm by engaging in numerous outrageous stunts that have become legendary in the company and the industry. As Robert W. Baker, a vice president at the company's much less successful arch-rival American Airlines, ruefully said, "That place runs on Herb Kelleher's bullshit."[3] As it turns out, it runs pretty darn well!

Job, Career, Calling

Our work can exist at three levels: job, career, or calling.[4] If it is "just a job," it is a pure transaction: we put in a certain number of hours a week in exchange for a certain salary and set of benefits. We decide whether the transaction makes sense for us or not. But we have no emotional connection with the work. It means nothing to us beyond our needing the money to survive. We live our actual lives on the evenings and weekends.

More ambitious people think of their work as a *career*, offering them opportunities to attain higher levels of responsibility and reward by doing more than the bare minimum necessary to keep the job and shrewdly navigating the corporate hierarchy. But many such people are not emotionally invested in their work or value any rewards beyond the material. At the extreme, overly ambitious career-minded people can engage in self-serving behavior that is damaging to the organization and their colleagues.

Work also can be a *calling*—so meaningful to us that we would continue doing it even if we win the lottery and became independently wealthy. Such work offers us value and satisfaction beyond the paycheck. It relates to something we are passionate about, something the world really needs. We feel most alive, most ourselves, when we are doing that work. Ultimately, this is what we need to strive for, as team members and employers: that as many people as possible are engaged in work that feels like a calling.

Whole Foods co-CEO Walter Robb describes the importance of value alignment between the company and team members: "I always ask new Team Members how and why they have chosen to come to work for us. After what at this point are thousands of individual conversations, I can tell you that besides our reputation for being a good place to work, the single most important reason is that we line up with their own personal values, and that they truly feel we are a place where they can make a difference in the world. That is the language of purpose."[5]

Management thinker Gary Hamel considers team member engagement as critical to competitive advantage: "In a world where customers wake up every morning asking 'what's new, what's different, and what's amazing?' success depends on a company's ability to unleash the initiative, imagination and passion of employees at all levels—and this can only happen if all those folks are connected heart and soul to their work, their company, and its mission."[6]

Intrinsic Versus Extrinsic Motivation

The evolutionary and societal changes of the past several decades have made traditional approaches to influencing and motivating team members much less effective. In his recent book, *Drive: The Surprising Truth About What Motivates Us*, Daniel Pink reviews the research on human motivation for the past forty years and concludes that most businesses are ignoring what the scientific evidence clearly suggests they should do.[7] They continue to manage by relying heavily on extrinsic motivators, symbolized by the proverbial carrot-and-stick approach—the use of incentives and threats. But extrinsic motivators are only effective when the work lacks inherent meaning and the potential for creativity and satisfaction, such as with assembly lines where simple rote tasks must be repeated without end.

When team members find their work to be inherently meaningful and enjoyable, they operate from the much more powerful *intrinsic* motivation.

To tap into that, companies must first ensure that they hire the right people for the right job. This means hiring talented and capable people who are also personally committed to the company's purpose and their work. Companies must also redesign work to make it more meaningful. This means increasing the opportunity for people to grow and develop mastery in a particular domain. Finally, companies must empower people so they have more autonomy. These three elements—mastery, purpose, and autonomy—together lead to high levels of intrinsic motivation, which is key to creativity, engagement, performance, and satisfaction.

Conscious Hiring and Retention Practices

Conscious companies take great care in the initial hiring. It's much harder today to remedy hiring mistakes than it used to be, so companies should invest a great deal of time and effort to make sure they hire people who are a good fit with the organization—those who believe in the purpose of the business and resonate with its values and culture. For example, The Container Store puts candidates through eight interviews with eight people. The company primarily looks for good judgment and sound integrity; everything else, it believes, is a commodity or can be taught.

At Whole Foods Market, everyone is hired into a particular team on a probationary basis for thirty to ninety days, at the end of which a two-thirds positive vote by the entire team is required before a new hire is granted full team member status. The logic is simple: anyone is capable of fooling a team leader for a while, but it is much more difficult to deceive the entire team. Probationary team members who have poor attitudes or bad work habits or who don't fit the Whole Foods Market culture are not elected to their team. When this happens, they have to try to find a new team to join (again on a probationary basis) or leave the company.

Once hired, most team members at conscious businesses tend to stay. As Kip Tindell says, "One of the things about The Container Store that makes me proudest is that people join this company and never leave. Our team member turnover is less than 10 percent per year, in an industry that's over 100 percent."[8] At Whole Foods Market, our voluntary turnover for full-time team members (who make up over 75 percent of our workforce) is also less than 10 percent per year. Because team members stay for a long time, conscious companies can afford to invest in training them. Few companies take this as far as The Container Store, which recently increased the amount of formal training it gives each employee from 240 to 270 hours. The retail industry average is 16 hours.

An employment practice based on fear became quite well known over the last two decades, with the financial success that Jack Welch experienced as the longtime CEO of General Electric until 2001. Rooted in its rating system for team members, GE's policy was to fire the bottom 10 percent of its workforce every year (Enron had a similar policy).[9] The rationale is that people are so scared of being in the bottom 10 percent that they work really hard to make sure they're not. But even if people are working hard and think they are doing okay, they can't be sure. People can be so afraid of being in the bottom 10 percent that they begin to see coworkers as rivals rather than as fellow teammates. They try to do what they can to make sure they're ahead of the next person on the team. Viktor Frankl wrote with shame of the relief he and other inmates felt in the concentration camps when someone else was selected for termination: "better him than me" was the feeling. We think such a policy is very damaging to workplace morale, because it creates a climate of fear and pits people against each other. Fear *can* be an effective short-term motivator; in a crisis situation, it can elicit extraordinary efforts for a short time. But as an ongoing policy, it's a disaster. Why create an arbitrary 10 percent turnover? If everyone is doing well, everyone should stay.

Conscious firms count even former team members as supporters. Some, like consulting firm McKinsey and Australian law firm Gilbert & Tobin, have formal alumni programs for former team members. At most firms, laid-off team members have very hostile attitudes toward the company. At conscious businesses, this is usually not the case. For example, many people who had to be let go when The Motley Fool was forced to shrink rejoined the firm later when it started growing again.

Promoting Teamwork

It is no coincidence that many conscious businesses organize their people into teams. Working in teams creates familiarity and trust and comes naturally to people. Humans evolved over hundreds of thousands of years in small bands and tribes. It's deeply fulfilling for people to be part of a team, where their contributions are valued and the team encourages them to be creative and make contributions. A well-designed team structure taps into otherwise dormant sources of synergy, so that the whole becomes greater than the sum of the parts. The team culture of sharing and collaboration is not only fundamentally fulfilling to basic human nature, it is also critical for creating excellence within the workplace. It's also a lot more fun. Over time, the best teams develop a sense of identity. At Whole Foods Market, for example, teams often adopt imaginative names such as the Rocking Richardson Grocery Team or the Green Produce Monsters.

Most of our teams at Whole Foods have between six and one hundred members; larger teams are subdivided into subteams. The leaders of each team are also members of the store leadership team, and store team leaders are members of the regional leadership team. This interconnected team structure continues all the way up to the executive team at the highest level of the company. Teams make their own decisions regarding hiring, the selection of many products, merchandising, and even compensation. Teams have profit responsibilities as well. Most of our incentive programs are team-based, not individual. For example, gain-sharing bonuses are awarded according to team performance.

Teams allow people to feel safe and have a sense of belonging. The creative ideas of individuals bounce around within the team and get improved upon. Especially in the United States, there is a myth of the lone genius coming up with brilliant ideas that change the world. While that occasionally happens, the more common scenario is that an individual comes up with an idea and shares it with other members of his or her team; they become excited and improve upon it. The spirit of collaboration allows the idea to evolve and mature.

It is natural for people to both collaborate and compete. At Whole Foods, we have found it very effective to have different self-managing teams compete with each other in a friendly way. For example, the produce team in one store strives to increase its productivity and sales compared with other produce teams within the same geographical region, as well as other produce teams throughout the company. It is a matter of great pride to be recognized as the best produce team or the best meat team in a region or for the entire company. This is the opposite of Jack Welch's model, where team members compete not to be terminated. Here, they compete as part of a team to be rewarded, but no one is necessarily cut from the team.

Our experience at Whole Foods Market shows that trust, cohesion, and performance are optimized in this type of small-team organizational structure. Each person is a vital and important member of the team. The success of the team depends on the invaluable contributions of everyone on the team; no one is invisible, and no one can be a free rider because the team effectively self-polices.

A Conscious Approach to Compensation

In any workplace, team members pay a great deal of attention to how the compensation system works. No matter what an organization says about its values and its purpose, how it compensates is a form of "walking the talk." Nothing saps motivation more quickly than the perception that the compensation system is unfair and rigged. If an organization talks about higher purpose, exemplary customer service, and other ideals but its compensation system is inconsistent with those ideals, it's not going to be very successful.

At Whole Foods Market, we have adopted certain compensation policies that have been quite effective. Perhaps the most radical one has been to have total transparency on compensation; everyone who works at the company can know what everyone else is paid. This transparency is an essential part of our culture, and it ensures that the compensation system is fair. Because it is transparent, team members can give feedback on what they find to be unfair, giving the company an opportunity to change and evolve it.

Some type of team compensation is helpful to reinforce the nature and cohesion of the teams. At Whole Foods Market, we use a protocol called gain-sharing. When a team increases its labor productivity, everyone on the team shares in the bonuses, which are paid in proportion to the individual's hours worked. This reinforces solidarity within the team by aligning the interests of individuals together. In our experience, this type of team compensation doesn't undermine intrinsic motivation, because it is intrinsically rewarding to be part of a successful and winning team.

Everyone in our executive leadership team (the seven top executives) is paid exactly the same salary, bonus, and stock options. There is great solidarity and a high degree of trust within the group, and we want that to continue. You could make the case that some leaders are a little more valuable than others. But small differences in compensation can, over the years, stoke envy and erode trust in people. Our leaders also have a strong sense of calling, which supersedes the need to have their relative self-worth validated by money.

Internal Versus External Equity

Related to the issue of fairness, we have also adopted a policy at Whole Foods Market that caps the total cash compensation, including bonuses, for any team member at nineteen times the average pay of all team members. In publicly traded companies of a similar size, this ratio, including equity awards and other incentives, can be as high as four hundred to five hundred times.[10]

In setting compensation, companies consider internal equity (where the compensation system is perceived internally to be fair) and external equity (where the compensation for any particular position is competitive with the external market). Most companies focus primarily on external equity when it comes to executive pay. If they find that a competitor is paying its CEO or chief financial officer a certain amount, they think their pay has to be comparable or higher. Few companies are content to be average; many strive to be at the 75th percentile or beyond. This has created a ratchet effect that has led to rapidly rising executive compensation in recent decades.

If external equity is not tempered with internal equity, it can lead to a system that is perceived to be unfair internally, which is a huge de-motivator. At Whole Foods, our salary cap has been in place for about twenty-five years (the ratio has risen gradually over the years to its current nineteen-to-one level to stay reasonably competitive with the external market), and inadequate compensation has never caused us to lose any senior executives we wanted to retain.

There is another rationale for the salary cap. We want leaders who care more about the purpose and people of the company than they do about power or personal enrichment. Our senior executives are well compensated, but they are clearly not making the most money they could. If they simply want to maximize their personal compensation, they could certainly make more than they do at Whole Foods Market. Indeed, many of them routinely receive offers that are considerably larger. But our leaders believe that their compensation at Whole Foods is reasonable and fair compared with others within the company. Although most would not turn down more if offered more (human nature being what it is), by any reasonable standard they are wealthy and can do what they want in life.

This reflects a third reason we believe a salary cap is good: it attracts people with a higher degree of emotional and spiritual intelligence. At some point, people have enough money to have financial security, live a comfortable, adventuresome lifestyle, and fulfill most of their aspirations in life. It is a mark of emotional and spiritual maturity to be able to say, "I have enough." Past a certain point, it is not healthy to want more; actually, it is a kind of sickness.[11]

Egalitarian Benefits

Most companies have a distinct class system when it comes to benefits. Executives are given an array of special perks unavailable to everyone else. They have more attractive retirement packages and better health insurance, they fly first class or in private jets and stay in better hotels, they have tax advisers helping them, and so on. At Whole Foods Market, everyone from the CEO to entry-level team members has the same benefits. The only differences are based on tenure with the company—the longer someone has been with the company, the greater his or her paid time off and the larger the company contribution toward health-care premiums and company-funded health-care reimbursement accounts. A cashier who has worked for the company for several years enjoys the same benefits enjoyed by the two co-CEOs of the company. It's very powerful to be able to tell people about this practice. It creates a sense of solidarity throughout the organization. From time to time, we have had to resist the efforts of certain leaders in the company who felt they deserved better benefits than others because they're in a higher position. Eventually, those leaders left the company for better financial opportunities elsewhere and in every case we were happy to see them go. We were able to replace them with more capable leaders who aligned better with our culture. For Whole Foods Market, the issue is nonnegotiable.

At Whole Foods, team members vote every three years on the benefits they want. We started this practice because team members would frequently ask about new kinds of benefits, such as pet bereavement insurance! We realized that we were not smart enough to figure out the best benefits that people should have. So we decided to let the team members themselves decide. Every three years, we open up all the benefits for a mass vote. The leadership decides what percentage of the total revenue will go toward benefits for the company, and then assigns a cost for every potential benefit. Team members prioritize and vote on the benefits that they most prefer. This process results in benefits that reflect the needs and desires of the majority of the team members in the company. Team members often select benefits that the leadership did not necessarily think were good decisions. For example, they got rid of a benefit that paid people for community service hours, opting instead for more paid time off.

Team Member Health and Wellness

Providing team member health care has become a real challenge for businesses, especially in the United States, where costs keep rising inexorably. Here is a telling statistic: fifty years ago, Americans spent approximately 16 percent of their disposable income on food and 5 percent on health care. In 2010, they spent 7 percent on food and 17 percent on health care.[12] Yet, conscious businesses do not compromise on the need to provide their people with good health insurance. Most of them extend this to part-time team members as well, provided the person meets a threshold number of hours per week. One such company is Trader Joe's. As Doug Rauch, former president, says, "When people come to work, they bring their worries, their sickness, their anxiety or their sadness, and customers feel that. For us, it's a win–win: you pay for these crew member benefits, and the crew member is grateful, appreciative, and happier—and when they're happier, customers will feel that happiness and enjoy being in your store more."[13]

Most companies think of team member health only in terms of health-care costs. But health care should not be just about containing costs; it should be about helping people lead healthy, vibrant, fulfilling lives. Whole Foods Market has created innovative health-care and wellness plans that have made a big difference to the morale of our organization. As a self-insured company, we spent over $200 million in fiscal 2011 on health care for our team members. We are always looking for ways to provide good benefits to our team members while containing costs—no easy task, given the extraordinary rise in health-care costs in the United States in recent decades. Our health insurance plan is based on two programs working together: a high-deductible health-care plan to pay for catastrophic needs, and personal wellness accounts (funded by the company as either a health reimbursement account or a health savings account for day-to-day needs). The fact that we are self-insured makes us more prudent about health-care costs. We are always explaining this to our team members—that the company itself, not an outside insurance company, ultimately pays their health claims.

Beyond our innovative health insurance plan, we now place a huge emphasis on improving the health and well-being of our team members. This is a great example of a Win^6 strategy that leverages the interdependency of stakeholders. We know that when our team members are healthy, they have more energy to do their jobs and give better service to our customers, and the company, in turn, needs to spend less money on their health care. So it's a win for team members, customers, investors, and other stakeholders.

To help improve the health and wellness of team members, Whole Foods Market offers a voluntary Healthy Discount Incentive Program, based on each team member's degree of wellness. The program offers additional store discounts beyond the standard 20 percent that all team members receive. The extra discount is based on meeting certain biometric criteria for cholesterol levels, body mass index, height-to-waist ratio, and blood pressure, along with being nicotine free. Once a year, we bring a mobile lab to our stores and other facilities. The company pays for the voluntary testing, which costs about $78 a person, and each team member's score determines the level of the additional store discount he or she can receive. There are four additional levels, ranging from 22 percent to 30 percent: bronze, silver, gold, and platinum. Within our culture, it has become a matter of pride for team members to move up to higher levels. As a result, people are paying more attention to their diet and are exercising more, and many have quit smoking (smokers aren't eligible for any level of higher discount). In the second year of this program, we saw a nearly 20 percent increase in the number of team members qualifying for some type of incentive discount. It's early, but we're very encouraged by our progress so far.

The second program is called Total Health Immersion. We offer our sickest team members and those most at risk for getting ill—those who are obese, have heart disease or diabetes, or have very high cholesterol or blood pressure levels—the opportunity to attend the program if they wish. These are highly motivated people, often with various food addictions, who want to be healthier. The goal is to help them gain control of their lives, maybe for the first time ever. Many of them had despaired that they could ever make lasting changes with their health. At the company's expense (over $3,000 per person), these team members have the opportunity to go into a one-week medically supervised program in which they receive intensive education about healthy eating and healthy living. In that week, people who are obese lose on average about ten pounds; their total cholesterol can drop forty points or more and their blood pressure can drop thirty points. The food is fresh and healthy, they feel full, and it tastes good. They see so much progress in seven days that they realize that they can actually take control of their health for the rest of their lives. It gives them great joy, because they learn that they don't have to be fat or sick any longer.

The results of this program have been simply stunning. We had no idea people could make such great progress so quickly! About thirteen hundred people have gone through the program in its first two years. Dozens have lost over a hundred pounds each in less than a year. Heart disease and diabetes have been reversed. Doctors say that type 2 diabetes is not curable; it may not be curable by pharmaceutical drugs, but it's definitely curable through changes in diet and lifestyle. In fact, it can be cured quickly. In thirty to ninety days, people can stop taking insulin and reverse type 2 diabetes (always under the supervision of medical doctors trained in this type of nutritional therapy). In most cases, this requires radical dietary changes to a whole-foods, plant-strong, nutrient-dense, and healthy-fat diet. Team members willing to make those lifestyle changes have made amazing gains in their health, and fairly quickly. In fact, we're so excited about this program that we have extended the opportunity to the spouses and domestic partners of team members and plan to offer the program to the public in 2013.

The Joy of Work

Conscious businesses create purposeful work environments that challenge and encourage their team members to learn and grow. They understand the importance of creating self-managing work teams that are both empowered and collaborative. The conscious business organizes itself around intrinsic motivators such as purpose and love and creates a work environment that enables its team members to flourish as self-actualizing human beings. The benefits from this are shared by all the stakeholders, including investors. In the next chapter, we discuss the importance of treating your investors responsibly and consciously.

CHAPTER 7

Patient, Purposeful Investors

Financial capital (the money invested in businesses) serves an indispensable role in free-enterprise capitalism. For free-enterprise capitalism to evolve successfully, financial stakeholders must become more conscious and reconnect with their higher purpose.

Rediscovering the Higher Purpose of Capital

True investors have an important purpose to their work and collectively create great value for society. Debt capital (loans that must be paid back with interest) provided by banks and other investors is essential because it helps businesses grow without diluting equity ownership. Equity capital (investments made in exchange for a percentage of ownership in the business) provided by venture capitalists is invaluable for young and innovative, but higher-risk businesses to grow, as is private equity capital and public equity capital for larger and more mature businesses. Without such funding, most businesses simply cannot reach their full potential, and it is far more difficult for them to innovate, grow, and create value for their stakeholders.

Investor stakeholders don't receive enough credit for the good they do, but they often hurt their collective reputation in society by wearing their identity as no-nonsense, bottom-line people as a badge of pride. When they portray themselves as only interested in money, they fall into the trap that the critics and enemies of capitalism created, the notion that business is all just about profit and nothing else. Accusations of greed and selfishness quickly follow.

Unfortunately, the caricature that business is all about greed and money and profit is sometimes accurate regarding the financial part of capitalism. More than any other sector of the economy, Wall Street is characterized by remarkable short-term wealth creation and extraordinary levels of compensation that are sometimes difficult to defend as fairly earned and deserved. During the financial crisis of 2008–2009, it appeared that the great wealth produced on Wall Street had come from short-term speculation, trading, and gambling rather than through investing, with the gains pocketed by the speculators and traders, but the losses absorbed by the government and the tax payers. Wall Street, and its philosophy that only profits and maximizing shareholder value really matter, has in many ways become disconnected from the real economy in which everyone else works and lives. Regrettably, this has tainted people's views of all of business and all of capitalism.

It sometimes seems that the values and philosophy of Wall Street has become a type of cancer that is corrupting the healthier parts of the larger business system. The economic meltdown in 2008 resulted in unprecedented governmental bailouts of those in the financial sector deemed "too big to fail." Not only did hundreds of billions of tax-payer dollars go to bail out profligate Wall Street banks and government-sponsored enterprises such as Fannie Mae and Freddie Mac, but the Federal Reserve has maintained artificially low interest rates for several years now that enable these same financial institutions to make very high and virtually risk-free profits on the interest rate spreads—a prime example of crony capitalism run amok.[1]

Treating Investors Responsibly and Consciously

Having been entrusted with the capital of investors, businesses have an ethical and fiduciary responsibility to make money for them. They should strive to cultivate relationships with their investors that are based on mutual respect and trust, just as they do with their customers, team members, and suppliers. Many businesses use the rhetoric of shareholder value maximization, but then act as if they have no special obligation to their investors. A company should no more take its investors for granted than it should its customers. Think of how you would treat investment capital if it came from your parents or close friends.

A great example of someone who treats his investors with respect and transparency is Warren Buffett at Berkshire Hathaway. Better than any business leader we know, he views investors as true stakeholders and partners. He cultivates long-term relationships with them and has always been transparent about what Berkshire Hathaway is trying to do when it makes investments. Buffett has worked diligently to communicate the company's business and investing philosophies to his investors. Indeed, he has helped educate at least two generations of long-term value investors through his famous annual Letter to Shareholders. With his open and long-term approach, Buffett has created amazing shareholder value for several decades, earning a compounded annual gain of 20.2 percent between 1965 and 2010, compared with 9.4 percent for the S&P 500. The overall gain over those forty-five years has been a mind-boggling 39,419 percent, compared with 5,699 percent for the S&P 500.[2]

Just as a business is selective in choosing its team members and vendors, it should also be selective in choosing its investors. With a publicly traded business such as Whole Foods Market, people are free to buy and sell the stock, so the company can't prevent anyone from doing so. But if you communicate consistently who you are, what your values are, and what your business philosophy, purpose, and strategy are, you will attract and build a following of shareholders and other investors who most align with your philosophy and vision of the business. You want investors who align with your purpose and understand your philosophy about stakeholders, so that when times become tough, they don't pressure you to abandon your philosophy. In other words, you want investors who treat you the way T. Rowe Price treated Whole Foods Market during the Great Recession, as we describe below.

Jeff Bezos of Amazon.com describes his perspective on investors: "With respect to investors, there is a great Warren Buffett–ism. You can hold a rock concert and that can be successful, and you can hold a ballet and that can be successful, but don't hold a rock concert and advertise it as a ballet. If you're very clear to the outside world that you're taking a long-term approach, then people can self-select in."[3] As Buffet has said, you get the investors you deserve.

Investors Versus Speculators

Ideally, investors should commit to a business for the long haul. But the average shareholding period in the United States has dropped steadily over the years. It used to be about twelve years in the 1940s, declined to about eight years in the 1960s, and is now well below one year.[4] The trends are similar in other countries. Nowadays, too many investors go into an investment with an *exit strategy*. This phrase came into the language through venture capitalists and private equity investors who invest capital in a business and have a strategy for when and how they are going to exit the investment. We think the idea of going into an investment with a predetermined exit strategy is rather noxious.[5] We don't have an exit strategy with our husband or wife or children or with our close friends. We don't have an exit strategy with our customers or team members or suppliers or the communities where we live. Why should investors have an exit strategy? Of course, in a free-enterprise system based on voluntary exchange, investors are free to exit a relationship when they feel it is no longer creating value. But ideally, investors should stay invested in companies they value for many years, perhaps indefinitely.

Tom and David Gardner, founders of the investment advice company The Motley Fool, have strong views on this:

> Long-term investing is a tautology, because that is what investing is.
> Short-term investing is a contradiction in terms. The synonym for

that, trading, has become the great focus for many. If you are going to be a long-term investor, you have to make sure the companies you are investing in have principles and rewards that are linked to long-term excellence . . . The way you lose is by getting worried about a great company's short-term hiccup rather than buying on the dip and being a partner with that business for years and decades.[6]

Companies should make a clear distinction between those who just place short-term bets on their stock and those who invest for the long term because they want to see the business grow and flourish over time. You should feel a higher level of obligation to long-term investors than to short-term speculators, just as you do in your personal lives with your friends and family compared to strangers.

At Whole Foods Market, we talk to investors who are long-term holders of our stock at least every quarter, after we announce our earnings results, to ensure that they understand the evolving purpose of our business, our business strategies, and what we are trying to accomplish. We strive to be as transparent as possible with them.

Whole Foods Market did an initial public offering (IPO) of our stock in 1992, and we have been able to create a great deal of value for our investors over the years. Our stock price steadily increased from $2.17 on a split-adjusted basis up to a high of $79 in late 2005. However, beginning in 2007, we saw our business growth begin to steadily slow down and then fall off a cliff when the financial crisis of 2008–2009 hit. In the fall of 2008, same-store sales (defined as sales from stores open for longer than twelve months) began to decline for the first time in our company's history. We had averaged same-store growth of about 8 percent for 25 years through all types of economic environments. However, this economic downturn was unlike anything we had ever experienced. Our stock price dropped from $79 down to just $8 over a period of three years. It was fascinating and frightening for the company to experience that. It was like living through a slow-motion earthquake. To use another metaphor, we felt as though a riptide was pulling us away from the shore, out to sea, and we had no idea when it would stop or what we should do to find safe waters.

Yet, we were fundamentally the same company; nothing tangible had changed. The one comforting thing was that some of our long-term investors were very patient and understanding. In fact, they increased their investment as the stock price declined. The best example of that is the mutual fund company T. Rowe Price, which has been one of our largest shareholders for many years. We met with this shareholder regularly and talked about what was happening with the company. T. Rowe Price told us over and over again that it really believed in the business and in its long-term potential. To paraphrase, "Don't become discouraged. Don't do anything now that you will regret later. We believe that if you keep doing a good job, eventually this recession will end, and the stock is going to bounce back up." Sure enough, the stock came roaring back and is trading at over $95 per share as we write this. To us, this represents the kind of relationship a public company should strive to have with its investors—one based on mutual respect, transparency, honesty, support, patience, and trust.

T. Rowe Price invested in Whole Foods Market because they hoped we would successfully grow our business over the long-term. We entered into a long-term relationship together, because that is what we each sought. Of course, a company needs to deal with speculators with integrity as well; they have certain rights too and they do create value in markets by providing liquidity for trading. But it is a waste of time to try to develop a relationship with somebody who's not going to be there. This is true not only in personal relationships, but in business relationships as well.

Bill George, whose ten-year record of shareholder value creation as CEO at Medtronic was extraordinary, has strong views on which investors management should pay attention to: "I believe to serve shareholders best, you should listen to long-term shareholders. Listen to the founders, the owners, people who are really committed to building the enterprise, not the short-term traders hoping to make a quick profit."[7]

Analysts and Their Models

Wall Street firms such as Goldman Sachs, JPMorgan Chase & Company, and Citigroup provide research on virtually all large public companies. Their company analysts tend to be very quantitatively oriented and look at businesses primarily through the lens of financial models. However, these models, no matter how sophisticated, can never fully capture the complex strategies, opportunities, and challenges of the companies being followed. But since these are usually the only tools an analyst has, he or she tends to rely on them heavily. It appears that the models are often more real to an analyst than the actual businesses they represent!

Using their financial models, many analysts award each company they cover a quarterly grade based on the company's financial performance and outlook. They revalue each company according to what their models tell them. This creates some unhealthy consequences, as many public-company CEOs start managing their companies to try to deliver the financial results that Wall Street and financial analysts expect. That approach may work in the short term, but in the long term, it can cause companies to move away from fulfilling their purpose and creating long-term value for all of their stakeholders. Companies can become obsessed with trying to raise their numbers for the next quarter so that they will look good in the analysts' financial models and receive a good grade, giving a boost to the stock price. But those grades do not always reflect the best long-term strategic positioning of the business. The models also put pressure on the company to *revert to the mean*, that is, to operate its business in the same way its competitors do.

Here is an example of how chasing after good short-term grades from financial analysts can be dangerous to a conscious business. Every quarter, analysts predict the gross profit margin (i.e., sales minus cost of goods, divided by sales) for the company. They also typically ask the company how it is going to increase its gross profit margin, as though that should be some type of goal in and of itself. If a company delivers a higher-than-expected gross profit margin, it is considered good, and the company receives a higher grade. The issue is how that is accomplished. Companies can increase their overall profit margin in the short term by cutting jobs, wages, or benefits, raising prices, or squeezing suppliers, but these actions could have negative long-term consequences by alienating team members, customers, and suppliers, respectively.

Strategically, a company produces the gross profit margins it does based on the intensity of competition in the marketplace, what customers are willing to pay, what the company thinks the optimum markup and the right sales mix are, and so on. The factors that go into the gross profit margin are subtle and multidimensional, while the analysts' models are relatively simple. A good business executive thinks of all these factors in the context of a complex interconnected system, while analysts look at things in a more linear and mechanical way.

Consider labor costs. No doubt, increasing labor productivity is usually a good goal to strive for because it can result in increased value creation for all stakeholders, including team members. But companies can also temporarily lower labor costs and raise profits by not paying team members as well, cutting back on hours worked, or reducing total headcount. But then labor turnover is likely to go up, resulting in higher training costs, lower morale, degraded customer service, and less-capable team members. Disgruntled team members might also start thinking about organizing a union. So cutting labor expense is not necessarily always a good thing. Analysts may love the short-term results, write glowing reports, and issue "buy" recommendations. But if such actions are taken without careful consideration of all the likely long-term consequences, they are likely to harm the company's competitiveness and impede its ability to generate profits in the future.

We have learned at Whole Foods Market that the best strategy is to be aware of the models the investment community uses for our company, but never to manage the business just to score well on those models. We simply refuse to compromise on our goal of optimizing long-term value creation for the business as a whole.

Stock Options and Investors

Some businesses get lured into managing for short-term financial objectives because of the way the stock option game is played. The main issues with stock options are concentration and timing. At most public companies, options are given by the millions to just a few executives and mostly expire within a few years. At the average public company, 75 percent of stock options are given to the top five executives.[8] Executives have very strong incentives to try to push the stock price up in the short term when their stock options are vested and can be sold for large profits. When so much compensation is linked to short-term or intermediate-term incentives, it can lead CEOs to make decisions that are not in the best long-term interests of all the stakeholders, investors included. We don't think stock options should be eliminated, but boards of directors need to be acutely conscious of the dangers of stock option concentration among just a few executives.[9]

While stock options can be quite dangerous if misused, they can be valuable if treated as just one useful tool in the overall compensation package. At Whole Foods Market, stock options are widely distributed, with 93 percent going to nonexecutives. Everyone at Whole Foods is eligible for them, so everyone has a little bit of a stake in having the company grow and create more value for all stakeholders. No senior executive receives large stock option grants; the typical executive grant is two thousand to six thousand shares per year, so the incentives to try to increase the stock price over the short term are not that great.

Can Public Companies Be Conscious?

One of the assertions we frequently hear is that you can only manage a business consciously if it is small or privately owned, but that once it becomes a large public company, it is difficult if not impossible to do so. This is clearly a fallacy; we have cited several examples of highly conscious public companies. Whole Foods Market, Southwest Airlines, Google, Panera Bread Company, Costco, Nordstrom, UPS, and several other large publicly traded companies that are managed by the principles of Conscious Capitalism outlined in this book. There is no inherent reason why *any* large public company cannot become more conscious and be managed by the same principles. As environmental scientist Amory Lovins has said, "If something exists, it must be possible."[10]

THE SECOND TENET: STAKEHOLDER INTEGRATION

This misconception is based on the pervasive belief that big corporations are all dedicated to the sole purpose of maximizing profits and shareholder value and that the legal deck is stacked against anyone trying to change this. The consequences of this narrow view that many large publicly traded companies have of their responsibilities are reflected in the disturbing observation that only about 19 percent of Americans have confidence in big companies, while about 64 percent trust small businesses.[11]

Some people believe the only way to change this is to change the laws of incorporation so that public companies can escape from the legal fiduciary requirement to maximize profits and shareholder value.[12] But this view reflects a mind-set that trade-offs between stakeholders are inevitable. It fails to recognize the holistic nature of the business enterprise: that all stakeholders are interdependent and that the best way to optimize long-term profits and long-term shareholder value is to simultaneously create value for the other stakeholders too.

Once we commit to a long-term perspective and creating value for all stakeholders, the conflicts and trade-offs that supposedly exist between investors and other stakeholders start to disappear. No laws need to be changed to enable businesses to create value for stakeholders other than investors. Every single publicly traded company can begin operating in a more conscious way right now. It is a question of raising the consciousness of the firms' leadership and summoning the will to change.

We are not suggesting this is easy. Large corporations have to overcome a lot of inertia and decades of legacy thinking. But the barriers that prevent them from changing are not legal ones; they are the outmoded mental models with which companies have operated in the past.

Investing in the Future

Much of the animosity toward capitalism today comes from the distortions that crony capitalism has created. In no place is crony capitalism more evident than in the financial sector of the economy. No sector of capitalism more urgently needs to become more conscious and discover its higher purposes and the importance of stakeholder value creation than the financial sector. The sector's philosophy of maximizing short-term profits and personal compensation while ignoring all other stakeholders is a proven failure with extremely harmful consequences for all of us.

It doesn't have to be this way, however. The investor stakeholder can help create tremendous value throughout American society. Indeed, for much of American history, it has done just that. Wall Street and all financial investors need to collectively rediscover their higher purposes and begin serving all of their stakeholders responsibly. The world's future prosperity depends on it.

CHAPTER 8

Collaborative, Innovative Suppliers

It is virtually impossible to be successful in any business without a network of strong suppliers. Whole Foods Market has tens of thousands of suppliers, most of which supply food. We buy a large amount of local foods in every community where we operate, which is one reason we have so many suppliers. Suppliers also include landlords, telephone service providers, electric utilities, garbage collection companies, and everyone else the business trades with for goods and services. One could even think of team members and investors as falling into the supplier category, as they supply labor and capital. However, it is better to classify team members and investors as important stakeholders in their own unique categories.

Recognizing the Importance of Suppliers Today

No business can be good at everything, so smart businesses focus on what they do well and leave the rest to suppliers and other partners.[1] Whole Foods Market excels at retailing high-quality natural and organic foods, creating wonderful store environments, and providing good service to our customers. But we are not very good at product innovation, and we're certainly not good at farming or manufacturing. These are not our core competencies, so we need a strong, innovative supplier network to help us develop and provide the products our customers want to buy.

Companies that don't have good collaborative partnerships with their supplier network can become competitively vulnerable. One of the reasons Whole Foods Market has been so successful is that we've maintained a philosophy of collaboration and partnership with our suppliers. This has enabled us to offer our customers many products that no one else can. Our suppliers are highly innovative, continuously improving the quality and selection of products we can offer our customers.

A good example is the recent trend toward locally sourced foods, which became popular in the mid-2000s. Within a few years, local foods became a huge growth category at both food stores and restaurants. Whole Foods Market has partnered with literally thousands of new businesses that started up to meet the exploding customer demand for these products. Now we're seeing our competitors such as Safeway, Walmart, and Kroger starting to participate in this trend. However, the fact that we are heavily decentralized and started earlier in creating an extensive network of local suppliers has given us an innovation edge in this category.

Having great suppliers and maintaining healthy relationships with them is critical for competitive advantage and long-term business success. Today, as much as 70 to 80 percent of the value the average company provides to its customers is created by suppliers.[2] Many businesses today can be described as a mile wide and an inch deep; they offer a broad range of products and services to their customers but add less value themselves than they used to, relying more heavily on their suppliers. Their competitive advantage thus depends greatly on the quality and capabilities of their suppliers.

The bottom line is this: having weak suppliers leads to a relatively weak business. Strong suppliers are an integral part of the foundation for a strong and competitive business. We must never take our suppliers for granted.

Treating Suppliers with Respect

Despite their great importance, however, suppliers remain the most neglected of the major stakeholders at most companies. Every successful business knows the value of customers and investors; increasingly, people are seeing how important team members are, and many businesses are now attempting to be more socially responsible to their communities and environment. But for the most part, suppliers are still taken for granted and not treated with the same courtesy and respect other stakeholders are given.

Whole Foods Market provides a good example of how a business can easily neglect or not fully understand the value of suppliers. In theory, we always have considered suppliers important stakeholders. But in practice, we sometimes neglected them. We discovered this to our chagrin when we brought some of our suppliers together in 2007, and one supplier told us, "We don't feel you treat us as well as you treat your other stakeholders; we're not even mentioned in your core values or your purpose statement." We were surprised to hear this, but it turned out these suppliers were right. It was a blind spot for us, even though we pride ourselves on being a conscious business. We certainly weren't conscious enough in this area. We knew we had to correct this right away. The realization led us to articulate our sixth core value: "Creating win-win partnerships with our suppliers." By making this core value explicit and working diligently to actualize it in our company, we've improved our relationships with our suppliers immensely over the past few years.

A good supplier can be selective about the customers it does business with. Any customer that does not treat its suppliers well, that is, as a true partner with a win-win approach, will not earn the supplier's loyalty. At the first opportunity, good suppliers will channel more of their business to their better customers and reduce or cease doing business with an abusive customer.

Every company should strive to have such a good relationship with its suppliers that it becomes their favorite customer. Most companies would love to be on *Fortune* magazine's list of the one hundred best companies to work for, be recognized as having superior financial returns, or be known for providing the highest level of service to their customers. Your company should also strive to be the best at how it relates to its suppliers. You would then end up with the best suppliers and a more competitive business. To accomplish this, start thinking of suppliers as though they are customers. This means treating them fairly, understanding their needs, ensuring that they are able to make a profit while doing business with you, and looking for ways to enhance the relationship over time.

Partnering with Suppliers

Companies can operate with their suppliers in a transaction mode or a relationship mode. Those operating in a transaction mode seek the most favorable terms for themselves on every occasion; however, in doing so, they sacrifice many of the benefits that could be obtained if both parties adopted a long-term win-win relationship mind-set. Conscious businesses seek mutually beneficial lasting relationships of integrity with their suppliers. Benefits include lower costs over time, higher quality, a better fit with the company's requirements, greater resilience in bad times, reduced risk for both parties, and more opportunities to innovate. By developing better relationships with suppliers, a business creates more value for itself, its suppliers, and its other stakeholders.

Whole Foods Market is in direct and daily communication with our customers, and we can give feedback to our supplier network regarding exactly what our customers like or don't like about their products, whether the products are too expensive, when their differentiation is valuable, and when it is not. At the same time, our suppliers are constantly innovating, creating new products and improving existing ones. Our partnerships lead to win-win mutually beneficial relationships where Whole Foods Market flourishes, as do our customers and the tens of thousands of suppliers with whom we trade.

While all suppliers are valuable, some are more critical to business success than others and should be treated as partners. When the suppliers are critical to competitive advantage, the business should strive to make them stronger and more robust. When building a supplier network, ask questions such as, "Which of these suppliers is giving us competitive advantage? Which relationships are most critical to our success? How can we better partner with them? How can we create more trust? How can we be more transparent? Do they share our commitment to a long-term relationship?"

Even supplier relationships you may currently think of as not critical to the business can become so. For example, buying electricity from the local utility seems like a routine transaction. But in fact, it can become a valuable relationship. Whole Foods Market has deepened our relationships with a number of our electricity suppliers because we've embraced various green energy technologies such as fuel cells, solar power, and wind energy. A number of our stores now are powered primarily by fuel cells; this has come about primarily through our partnerships with utility companies and other energy suppliers.

How Not to Treat Suppliers

A partnering mind-set is in sharp contrast to the more common view of suppliers as adversaries from whom the business tries to extract as much value as possible for the lowest price. Each side tries to take as much as it can from the other. Negotiations are a power struggle—a tug-of-war in which the stronger party ends up with a disproportionate share of the benefits. This mind-set is harmful and threatens the well-being of both parties and their other stakeholders. Businesses need to cooperate and collaborate with suppliers to create value for customers. Excellent communication, trust, and mutual innovation with suppliers create superior value for customers and lead to competitive advantage in the marketplace.

Numerous companies have suffered and many have perished because of their poor supplier relations. If suppliers are squeezed and bullied to give discounts beyond what they can financially absorb or believe to be fair, they may acquiesce in the short term because they have no other choice, but their trust in the relationship is severely undermined. Over time, they may try to recoup their profit margin by lowering quality, reducing service, or cutting corners on safety—all of which harm their customers' businesses.

THE SECOND TENET: STAKEHOLDER INTEGRATION

One of the best known examples of poor supplier relationships is General Motors in 1992–1993 under its global purchasing czar José Ignacio Lopez de Arriortua. Lopez's method of dealing with suppliers was described as unorthodox and brutal. When GM was struggling to meet its profit goals, he made a unilateral decision to cut payments to suppliers, who were told if they did not accept the price cuts, GM would no longer do business with them. In the short run, most suppliers had no choice; GM represented a high percentage of their total sales, and it would devastate them financially to walk away from that business immediately. This tactic saved GM about $4 billion in the short term, elevating Lopez to cult status in the company and industry (and Wall Street's financial analysts loved it too). However, GM's suppliers greatly resented the way they had been treated. In succeeding years, the best of them started to wean themselves off GM's business and focus on better customers. The net result was that GM lost many of the best suppliers in the automotive industry and was left with only those offering low prices, but also poor quality and little if any innovation.

Such shortsighted approaches, unfortunately, are all too common. In fact, Lopez was viewed within the industry as such a hero that a bidding war erupted between Volkswagen and General Motors for his services.

The Whole Foods–United Natural Foods Partnership

Cultivating and strengthening relationships with the most innovative suppliers providing the most critical services and products is essential for competitive advantage and sustained success as a business. Our most important supplier at Whole Foods Market is the publicly traded company United Natural Foods, Inc. (UNFI), which accounts for about 30 percent of our total purchases. Whole Foods is UNFI's biggest customer, at about 36 percent of the supplier's net sales. UNFI also warehouses and distributes much of Whole Foods' private-label inventory. Over the years, we have worked steadily to deepen our relationship with UNFI. We have a 10-year contract with this supplier but actually negotiate a new contract every five years. We do this because we want to sustain our high-trust collaborative partnership in perpetuity, and want UNFI to be confident that we won't try to take advantage of them.

This approach helped us improve what was honestly not a very healthy relationship for many years until we both made a commitment to be full partners. The investment community was always nervous that as UNFI's largest customer, Whole Foods Market could at any time decide to self-distribute and cut the company out. This would have been quite harmful to UNFI's business and stock price. Regretably, we used to hint periodically at that possibility to negotiate better deals. The distrust and fear this created was harmful to the spirit of a win-win partnership. Developing a richer, more collaborative, high-trust relationship has been very beneficial for both UNFI and Whole Foods Market. It gives UNFI the security and certainty that its largest customer is fully committed, and the improved relationship has enabled us to turn more of our distribution business over to UNFI, which has enhanced our competitive advantage in the marketplace.

Adopting Conscious Supplier Practices

Companies have many opportunities to create win-win outcomes with their suppliers. Here are some examples of approaches taken by conscious firms.

Finding Opportunities to Create Value

Companies should continually look for creative ways to craft mutually beneficial relationships with suppliers. For example, The Container Store studied its suppliers' businesses and found that many of them have slow seasons when much of their machinery is idle and workers are laid off. The company now tries to place large orders during such slow times. This doesn't cost The Container Store much but has a significant positive impact on the supplier's business.

THE SECOND TENET: STAKEHOLDER INTEGRATION

Paying on Time

One of the biggest complaints suppliers have is that their customers don't pay them on time. Ironically, the larger the customer, the more pronounced this problem. This common but unfair practice creates a ripple cash-flow problem throughout the supply chain, as suppliers are often unable to pay their own suppliers in time. Conscious businesses make it a point to always pay on time or earlier. Retailers especially have a great advantage in that they have high liquidity but their suppliers do not. Small manufacturers often find that the more they sell, the worse their cash flow becomes.

The South Korean company POSCO is the most admired steel company in the world, according to *Fortune*, and the fourth-largest steelmaker in the world.[3] POSCO has excellent relationships with all its stakeholders, but is particularly noteworthy for its orientation toward suppliers. The company makes it a point not only to pay all its suppliers on time, but to actually pay in cash within three days, a policy it started in 2004. Its purpose in doing so is to help the financial flexibility of its partners so they in turn can pay their own suppliers on time, enhancing the health of the whole business system.[4]

Treating Suppliers Fairly

Fairness is an essential quality in dealing with all stakeholders, especially suppliers. W. L. Gore & Associates CEO Terri Kelly says, "We're not a company that is the cutthroat, saving-a-penny type and moving on to the next supplier; that becomes very disruptive to the business. For our associates on both the supplier side as well as on the customer side, there's kind of a natural value system that we have in terms of being fair to all of them. At the end of the day, our reputation is at stake."[5]

Helping Suppliers Survive and Flourish

Conscious companies often help suppliers through difficult times. REI CEO Sally Jewell describes the company's philosophy: "Some of our suppliers are quite small, and we represent a large part of their business. During the downturn, there were instances where their banks would not support them. So we prepaid for inventory and held it in our warehouse, because they really needed the cash flow to survive. We didn't do it without thinking about, 'Is this a company that's going to survive? Is this a supplier that is really critical to our customers? Are they producing a product that really needs to thrive over the long term?' So we weren't irresponsible about it, but tried to be thoughtful."[6]

Conscious companies invest in their suppliers to help them grow. The Container Store sometimes buys machinery for its suppliers to use to manufacture the products it sells. POSCO provides its suppliers with focused long-term support intended to help them become world-class businesses. It has established a Win-Win Growth Bureau with twenty-three members to oversee and coordinate these activities, running about sixty-seven programs—including technology assistance, low-interest financing, and assistance with human resource development—to support suppliers.

POSCO also has a certified-partner program for suppliers who meet its high standards on criteria such as leading-edge technology, cost effectiveness, delivery schedule, and continuous improvement. Certified partners receive preferential treatment for contracts, a waiver of financial deposits, invitations to overseas steelmaker visits, and chances to participate in POSCO's top management education programs.

At Whole Foods, it has been very gratifying for us to see so many of our suppliers start as little mom-and-pop businesses and grow into substantial enterprises, largely, although of course not entirely, due to their partnership with us. In many cases, Whole Foods Market is their largest customer, the one essential customer they needed. Many of our suppliers start out with the dream of getting into one store, and then multiple stores, and then eventually all the Whole Foods stores, and thereby growing into a national company that does business with us throughout the country and perhaps internationally as well. An excellent example of this is Honest Tea, the organic bottled-tea company that began selling in a couple of our Washington, D.C., stores back in 1998. The company's teas were quite successful in these stores and quickly spread throughout our mid-Atlantic region. Within just a few years, Honest Tea products were in all our stores. As a result of Honest Tea's success at Whole Foods Market, many of our competitors began to sell the products in their stores as well. In 2008, The Coca-Cola Company purchased a 40 percent interest in Honest Tea for $43 million and began a national rollout of Honest Tea products through its distribution network.

Sharing the Wealth

POSCO created a benefit-sharing program for its tier one suppliers in 2004, the first in Korea. Since then, 459 partners have received approximately $70 million as their share of increased profits generated through hundreds of innovations. In December 2010, POSCO expanded the program to include tier two through tier four partners.

Growing Together from Tough Times

Forging win-win relationships is easier when times are good. The test of a true partnership is what happens when the business declines due to an economic downturn, unexpected competition, or some other unfortunate event. Many companies come down hard on their suppliers when times are tough. However, it is harmful and unfair to try to pass the burden disproportionately to the supplier network. This weakens and damages the relationship and undermines the competitive positioning of the business. Companies with an attitude of partnership and collaboration work with their supplier network in a conscious way to stay competitive and survive the adversity.

Tough times come with a silver lining: they are an opportunity to make the business more efficient by reducing waste and redundancy. Companies can collaborate with their suppliers and ask, "What are the added costs here that aren't really creating value for either one of us, or for our customers?" When times are good, the old cliché applies: "If it ain't broke, don't fix it." However, in a downturn, things *really are* broken; a downturn offers an opportunity to improve things, because people are less resistant to change and improvements. The streamlined business model results in stronger cash flows and profits when business conditions improve.

After Howard Schultz came back to Starbucks in early 2008, he found that the company had become quite inefficient during its boom years: "We took out $580 million of costs in 2008. Some 90% of it has been permanent. None of it is customer facing. That was there for many years. Why did it take a crisis to allow us to have the courage to do that?"[7]

Spreading Consciousness Throughout the Value Chain

As conscious businesses change the parameters of their relationships with suppliers, these changes can have a ripple effect throughout the supply chain. Companies should encourage their suppliers to adopt similar approaches in their relationships with their own suppliers. Similarly, suppliers that start seeing the benefits of a win-win relationship with a conscious customer should take this philosophy to their other customers and educate them. In this manner, a conscious collaborative approach to customer-supplier relationships can spread widely, to the benefit of all the companies affected as well as their stakeholders.

CHAPTER 9

Flourishing, Welcoming Communities

Does business have a social responsibility? To a conscious business, this is an odd question, because the answer is obvious; *of course* business has a social responsibility. The community stakeholder is one of the core constituents for a conscious business. Businesses exist within local communities, national communities, global communities, as well as virtual communities of common interests. It is unthinkable for a conscious business to see itself as separate from the rest of the human community.

Too many people equate social responsibility with philanthropy. Philanthropy is actually just a small part of the social responsibility of business. If a business is responsible to its investors, employees, customers, suppliers, and the environment but refuses to contribute toward philanthropic organizations, it would be neglecting the important community constituency. Such a business would be considered a stingy neighbor, but the fact is that it still creates value in the world through the value it creates for its other stakeholders. Conversely, a business could be very philanthropic to its communities, but if it creates shoddy or harmful products, exploits its employees, cheats its suppliers, and does significant damage to the environment, it can hardly be considered an ethical or socially responsible business.

Is Business Philanthropy Theft from Investors?

While ordinary business exchanges create important social value for communities, most conscious businesses want to do more. They see the community as an important stakeholder worthy of conscious thought and deliberate actions to create additional value and help solve social and environmental challenges. Indeed, for many conscious businesses, this is part of their intrinsic purpose. They donate time, money, and their unique capacities to support their communities in numerous ways.

Some people view this type of philanthropy as a form of theft from investors. They say, "If you feel altruistic toward other people, you should exercise that altruism with your own money, not with the assets of a corporation that don't belong to you." This view was famously articulated by Milton Friedman in 1970 in his essay "The Social Responsibility of Business Is to Increase Its Profits": "There is one and only one social responsibility of business—to use its resources and engage in activities designed to increase its profits so long as it stays within the rules of the game, which is to say, engages in open and free competition without deception or fraud."[1]

At first glance, this position sounds reasonable. A company's assets do belong to the investors, and its management does have a duty to manage those assets responsibly. In our view, this argument is not wrong so much as it is myopic. That is because when engaged in wisely, corporate philanthropy is simply good business and works for the long-term benefit of investors and other stakeholders as well.

The argument that philanthropy is theft from the investors assumes that there are inherent conflicts and trade-offs between the investors and the other stakeholders, including the community stakeholder. This need not be the case. However, if corporate philanthropy does not create any value for investors, they would certainly be within their rights to object to the irresponsible use of corporate resources. Management has to be held accountable for its results and for using the capital of the business responsibly.

Of course, there has to be a limit to corporate philanthropy. Whole Foods Market has long had a policy of donating 5 percent to 10 percent of its profits to nonprofit organizations. But if donating 10 percent of profits is good, wouldn't 20 percent be even better? Why not donate 100 percent of profits for the betterment of society? Obviously, there comes a point where being too philanthropic would kill the business. A company's sense of responsibility to its communities doesn't mean that it doesn't also have compelling responsibilities to its investors and other stakeholders. As always, companies must seek to optimize value for all of the stakeholders.

Corporate philanthropy ultimately requires the legitimacy of investor approval. Smart corporate philanthropy can be beneficial to the corporation, its stakeholders, and society. Done wisely, what appears at first to be theft actually turns out to be the exact opposite.

Businesses as Citizens

A good metaphor for the appropriate role of business in society is citizenship. A conscious business behaves like a responsible citizen in its communities. This means that it helps tackle some of the problems that communities are struggling with on a local, national, and potentially global basis. Most businesses have certain infrastructure capabilities and intellectual capital that can be leveraged to help the communities where they are doing business. Conscious businesses routinely work with nonprofits in the communities where they trade, especially nonprofits engaged in activities related to their core business. They encourage their team members to become involved in community activities.

This voluntary sense of responsibility can be misunderstood and abused. Business does not exist to be a servant or tool of social activists or the government. Some people would like businesses to act like a dog on a leash and do whatever the government wants them to do. That's been tried; it's called corporatism or fascism. It is about dominating and controlling business to make it serve the goals of political rulers.

THE SECOND TENET: STAKEHOLDER INTEGRATION

Being a good citizen creates a healthy relationship between business and its communities. It is a Win[6] approach, because if a company fulfills its citizenship obligations appropriately, it creates value for the community that its customers, team members, suppliers, and investors all support and benefit from. This helps the business flourish.

The manner in which companies approach community involvement matters. Some companies exhort their team members to give back to the community by working on service projects over the weekend. This can be off-putting because many team members don't feel that they have taken anything that needs to be given back and resent being asked to give up what is rightfully theirs—their weekend. When companies approach community service in this manner, the participation rate can be quite low. It works far better if two conditions change. First, the community service should take place on a workday, so that the company would be contributing its team members' work time, and they would be contributing their effort. Second, the projects should come out of genuine, ongoing, shared concerns, rather than being dictated to team members from the top down. Otherwise, the work feels contrived and self-serving, designed more to make the company look good than to serve a genuine need in the community.[2]

Local Citizenship

Writing a check for a worthy cause is one way of being a good citizen, but there are more creative ways. At Whole Foods Market, we take our local and global citizenship responsibilities very seriously. Locally, each store is empowered to do three to four "5 percent days" every year, when 5 percent of the gross sales (not merely profits) is donated to various local nonprofit organizations. The team members and local store leadership decide which nonprofits within the community to support. When we do these 5% days, we ask the nonprofits we're supporting to encourage their members to shop with us that day, since 5 percent of the day's sales will go to the nonprofit. This creates a win-win; we support the nonprofit, which in turn supports Whole Foods Market. The event creates goodwill with the members of the

HOW A CONSCIOUS BUSINESS RESPONDED TO A TRAGEDY

The venerable 144-year-old Tata Group of India, one of the world's most admired and conscious businesses, consists of more than one hundred operating companies in over eighty countries. It had revenues of $84 billion in 2010–2011 and employs over 425,000 people worldwide.

The true mettle of an individual or a company is tested in times of crisis, not when things are going well. In November 2008, the Tata Group's iconic Taj Mahal Palace & Tower Hotel in Mumbai was the epicenter of a horrendous terrorist attack that killed 164 people and wounded at least 308 in the southern part of the city.[*] Eleven hotel team members were killed, most while helping approximately 1,500 guests escape from harm. For the entire duration of the attack, not a single team member abandoned his or her post. Many repeatedly guided guests to safety before they themselves were shot by the terrorists. Some even stood in front of guests to take bullets.

The dedication of its team members is exemplified most powerfully by the hotel's general manager, Karambir Singh Kang, who lived with his family in an apartment in the hotel. In the midst of the terror and panic, Kang calmly supervised the evacuation of hundreds of trapped guests. Ratan Tata, chairman of the Tata Group, later told CNN, "The general manager lost his wife and two sons in one of the fires in the building. I went up to him today and I told him how sorry I was, and he said, 'Sir, we are going to beat this. We are going to build the Taj back into what it was. We're standing with you. We will not let this event take us down.'"[†] Indeed, in an act of defiance, the hotel reopened for business a mere twenty-one days after the attack, even though two-thirds of it was very badly damaged. Though it took two

---

[*] The discussion of Tata Group in this chapter comes from Sam K Life Is Beautiful Blog, "How Tatas Responded After Mumbai Terrorist Attacks," March 16, 2012, http://karmarkars. net; and other published accounts.

[†] Taylor Gandossy, "Taj Mahal Hotel Chairman: We Had Warning," CNN.com Asia, November 30, 2008, http://edition.cnn.com/2008/WORLD/asiapcf/11/30/india.taj.warning/index.html.

more years for the rest of the hotel to be repaired and reopened, not a single team member was laid off during that time.

Ratan Tata and other senior company leaders attended all eleven funerals and visited the families of all eighty team members who were killed or injured. Within twenty days, Tata established a new trust to provide assistance to all those who were injured and to the families of those killed. Tata set up a psychiatric center in collaboration with the Tata Institute of Social Sciences to counsel those needing help, as well as outreach centers to provide food, water, sanitation, first aid, and counseling for team members and others in their South Mumbai neighborhood.

The company assigned a mentor for every affected team member to serve as a single point of contact to ensure that the person received any help needed. For team members living alone in the city, their family members were flown in from outside Mumbai and accommodated in the Tata-owned Hotel President for up to three weeks.

Tata provided compensation to the families of every deceased member, ranging from $80,000 to $187,000. In addition, Tata did the following:

- Guaranteed that deceased team members' residences would be provided to the family, through the lifetime of the next of kin.

- Waived all loans and advances, regardless of amount.

- Committed to paying the team member's last full salary for life.

- Took complete responsibility for the education of children and dependents through college—anywhere in the world.

- Provided full health-care coverage for all dependents for the rest of their lives.

- Provided a counselor for life for each person.

Tata even extended relief and assistance to the families of those who were killed in the vicinity of the hotel and at the railway station a few miles away. For Tata, these people were their neighbors, and the company felt a responsibility to help them. Railway employees, police staff, street vendors, and pedestrians *who had nothing to do with the company* were offered assistance of 10,000 Indian rupees (about $200) per month for six months. Street vendors who lost their carts were given new ones. A four-year-old granddaughter of a street vendor had been shot with four bullets during the attack. She was removed from the government hospital and taken to Bombay Hospital. The Tata family spent several hundred thousand rupees on her treatment. Even the employees of competing hotels were looked after.

When the company's HR leaders presented this plan to Ratan Tata, his response was not "How much will this cost? Can we afford it? Are we setting a bad precedent?" Instead, he asked, "Are we doing enough? What more can we do?" The Tatas knew that they would be spending millions on rebuilding the hotel. How could they not pay even more attention to help rebuild the lives of their people—especially the families of those who gave their lives so that guests would survive?

How do you build a culture in which team members are willing to pay the ultimate price to look after guests? It was certainly not written down as a requirement or an expectation in an employee manual. As Kang says, "Every team member at the Taj felt that their house was being attacked. When your house is attacked, what do you do? You defend it and whoever is there inside. The family values that we all believe in are part of our corporate culture in the Tatas . . . The Tatas truly exhibit that the organization has a soul. I am very very proud that I work for them."

nonprofit; they may come in and shop our store for the first time, decide they like it, and begin shopping with us regularly in the future.

Such a philanthropic strategy creates value for multiple stakeholders. Team members like it because they can contribute their effort and see immediate results without having to give up their own time and money. Because team members are involved in selecting the nonprofits that local stores support, they derive a sense of satisfaction from that. Nonprofits that are featured often set up tables inside the store. Interested customers are able to engage with people from the nonprofit. That can be a win for the customers, because they may discover a great community nonprofit they didn't know about and decide to get involved with it. The goodwill from customers, team members, and the local community also creates value for investors over the long term through increased sales and profits.

Global Citizenship

At Whole Foods Market, we feel a responsibility to all the communities in the world where we trade. We have created two global nonprofits with ambitious goals: the Whole Planet Foundation, created in 2005, and the Whole Kids Foundation, created in 2011.

We've concluded that the best way for us to support the communities we trade with is to work to alleviate poverty through micro-lending programs. Initially, we worked exclusively with Mohammed Yunus and his pioneering microcredit lending institution, the Grameen Trust. The Whole Planet Foundation now works with many local microfinance organizations that are already offering microcredit in a community. We engage in thorough research and due diligence to find partners most aligned with our values. We are now in fifty-plus countries and have provided more than $35 million in capital to fund over two hundred thousand microcredit loans. The average first loan size is about $133, and 92 percent of the loans have been made to women. The money recycles back and is loaned out again and again; it stays permanently in those communities. It is never paid back to the Whole Planet Foundation. Considering the multiplier effect of repaid loans and the leverage the foundation's funding gives local partners to find additional funding, the impact is now well over $130 million in total loans. In just seven years, we've improved the lives of an estimated 1.2 million-plus poor people in more than countries. We currently trade in ninety-one countries, seventy-nine of which are eligible to participate in our microlending program. Our goal is to be in all eligible countries within the next five years. Eventually, as Whole Foods Market grows larger, our trading network will expand, and we hope someday to make loans in every country in the world with a microcredit industry.[3]

Conscious Philanthropy and Stakeholder Value

The Whole Planet Foundation is a good example of how conscious philanthropy can work for the benefit of the investors. Probably nothing we have done in our history at Whole Foods Market has raised the morale of the organization more than the work of this foundation; our team members are so excited and proud of what we're doing to help end poverty. It is a great example of philanthropy that creates value for every one of our major stakeholders.

Once a year, we conduct a "prosperity campaign" that lasts six weeks. We give our customers the opportunity to donate to the Whole Planet Foundation to fund microcredit loans. We promote the campaign in our stores with brochures and posters. Customer support has been amazing. In 2012, the prosperity campaign raised $5.6 million in six weeks. Many customers who learn about what the Whole Planet Foundation is doing become excited about it. Our stores compete to raise the most money within a region and in the whole company.

Our team members also love it. We have created a program where our team members can now go to six countries where we do microcredit lending—Guatemala, India, Kenya, Peru, Ghana, and Brazil—to volunteer for two to four weeks. This has become our own little Peace Corps. We pay for their housing, food, and transportation; they donate their time. Most members are in their early twenties, haven't traveled widely, and have seldom seen serious poverty up close. But they're idealistic, and they want to make a difference. The trip is usually a transformative experience. When they come back, they become ambassadors for the program to the rest of our team member base. The impact has been huge. Team members feel immensely proud of this higher purpose of Whole Foods Market. They feel that we're walking the talk and really trying to make a difference in the world. The program has had a positive impact on all our team members, not just those selected to go on the trips. It enhances their commitment and energy to know that they are part of a company that is making a positive impact on the world in this way. This program has been so successful that it has caused our purpose to evolve. We now think that one of Whole Foods's higher purposes is to help end poverty. We did not think that five years ago, but this program has altered our thinking and expanded our horizons.

Our suppliers also win with this program. In certain designated categories, suppliers compete to be a member of what we call a Suppliers' Alliance, which means they commit to donating an agreed-upon amount of money to the Whole Planet Foundation. In exchange, we offer them special recognition in our stores. Their products are featured prominently and given better shelf placement. We only feature one supplier in a category. It's a significant win for our suppliers because their sales go up and new customers are introduced to their products. It's a win for the Whole Planet Foundation because of the additional donations it receives. In addition, the suppliers' team members are also able to participate in our volunteer programs, so they become more engaged as well.

So how is all this good for investors? It has created tremendous goodwill with our other stakeholders. It has also generated a great deal of positive publicity, leading to greater goodwill toward Whole Foods Market in the larger world community. Although it's difficult to quantify, the amount of money Whole Foods Market is investing in this program is generating perhaps a 1,000 percent return to our investors, factoring in goodwill, positive publicity, enhanced brand recognition, and higher morale, which result in higher sales, profits, and market capitalization.

Of course, we are hardly alone in approaching philanthropy consciously. For example, IBM has launched its own version of the Peace Corps, a program called Corporate Service Corps, which sends IBM team member volunteers to emerging countries to trigger socioeconomic growth by applying their technology and business skills. The program is part of IBM's Global Citizen's Portfolio initiative. The company uses Corporate Service Corps as a way to develop leaders while helping address important socioeconomic issues. IBM received five thousand applications within three weeks after announcing the program, and selected one hundred top-notch team members to work in countries such as Ghana, the Philippines, and Romania. Selected team members come from thirty-three countries and have an average of ten years of experience at IBM.

According to Stanley Litow, vice president of Corporate Citizenship and Corporate Affairs, the program offers "a triple benefit: a benefit to these communities by solving problems on the ground that benefit the community, a benefit to the individual by providing them with an exemplary form of leadership training and development, and a benefit to the company by developing a new generation of global leaders."[4]

At Whole Foods, we have recently created a new foundation we're very excited about: the Whole Kids Foundation. This is another good example of our purpose evolving. As we started going deeper into our healthy eating initiatives, we were often asked, "What are you doing about nutrition in our schools? It's appalling how bad the food our children eat is; what is Whole Foods Market going to do about it?" Our first response was, "Why do you think that's our responsibility? We're already doing a lot." But our customers and team members pointed out the opportunity to go further and do more. They kept asking, "Can you please get involved in this?" Finally, we realized we had to listen to our stakeholders, and so we created the Whole Kids Foundation.

The foundation's activities will evolve over time, but the initial focus of this nonprofit is to support schools in providing more nutritious food to children. We're doing that by installing salad bars, giving out school garden grants, and educating teachers about healthy eating. The Whole Kids Foundation, together with its partners, has already funded more than a thousand salad bars and hundreds of gardens in schools throughout the United States. Our goal is to provide a salad bar to any U.S. school that wants one and to work with these schools on their supply chains to increase the amount of fresh fruits and vegetables available to our children. Sadly, most schools don't offer students anything fresh; almost everything comes frozen or in cans and boxes. Our children need fruits and vegetables the most, and they're not getting them in the current system, which has been largely captured by special interests such as the dairy, meat, and processed-food industries. (This is an example of crony capitalism, with companies using the power of government to promote their business interests at the expense of the health and well-being of children.) Schools have to change their procurement practices to replace those cans and boxes with fresh foods. We are working with interested schools on recipe development to take greater advantage of local produce, connecting schools with fresh food suppliers and more.

Another responsibility we're taking on is to provide nutritional education for teachers and for their students. We're putting together programs and curricula for schools to teach the principles of healthy eating. The Whole Kids Foundation is also working with Let's Move, First Lady Michelle Obama's initiative to tackle the epidemic of childhood obesity. We will work with other nonprofits and the government to try to improve the nutritional quality of the food and nutritional education in our schools.

Conscious Businesses and Nonprofits

Nonprofits play a vital role in society, addressing areas that business is unable to do profitably and that government can't do competently. Governments are too bureaucratic, too slow, and overly politicized. Business, too, is unable to serve some of society's needs effectively, because it can't create an acceptable financial return on investment.

Nonprofits are by definition mission driven, so they understand the "purpose" part of Conscious Capitalism very well. They have stakeholders just like any other business. But instead of having investors seeking a financial return on capital, they have donors who are looking for a psychic return on their donations, usually defined as progress toward fulfilling the mission of the nonprofit.

Unfortunately, many nonprofit organizations operate with a mentality that creates inefficiencies, stagnation, and ineffectiveness. The vast majority depend on donations from the business sector or private citizens to exist; in other words, they're not sustainable on their own. Conscious businesses can help address this sustainability challenge.

A False Wall

Many people believe that there's a substantial ethical difference between the purposes of nonprofits and government and those of businesses. In their minds, a metaphorical wall separates these entities. They see nonprofits and the government as having purposes that are dedicated toward serving the common good; because these entities are not trying to make a profit, they are seen as unselfish and dedicated to public service and thus "good." Business, on the other hand, is seen as bad, because it is supposedly motivated by selfishness and greed and cares only about money. In reality, this depiction is untrue of most businesses, particularly conscious businesses.

In many ways, conscious nonprofits and conscious businesses are quite similar; they are based on voluntary, noncoercive exchanges; have higher purposes; serve all their stakeholders; and have conscious leadership. Conscious businesses and conscious nonprofits both create value for their stakeholders. The wall separating them needs to be taken down. We need both to create a prosperous and flourishing world.

Natural Partners

Business is a natural ally of the nonprofit sector, and the two should work hand in hand. Conscious businesses seek ways to be more effective in serving their community stakeholders. Conscious nonprofits can leverage this desire to help fulfill their own purposes within communities. In a typical partnership, the business provides money, operational expertise, and intellectual capital, while the nonprofit provides purpose, highly motivated workers, and a network of relationships. Such partnerships are a win-win-win for both the nonprofit and the business because they more efficiently produce greater value for the communities both entities seek to serve.

For example, the Whole Planet Foundation has worked with dozens of nonprofits around the world to grant microcredit loans more effectively. Those nonprofits have an infrastructure in place; they have a higher purpose and dedicated people. Whole Foods Market can offer the money they need in order to be more effective in fulfilling their mission. The Whole Planet Foundation only affiliates with nonprofits that are aligned with us on values and purpose and are very effective at what they do. This careful selection process has led to effective partnerships with a number of international nonprofits that are expanding along with the foundation into different regions around the world. These nonprofit partnerships are very similar to our supplier partnerships. By working collaboratively, total value creation is greatly enhanced for all participating organizations and for the millions of poor people we are collectively serving.

THE SECOND TENET: STAKEHOLDER INTEGRATION

It is also natural for a conscious business committed to the community stakeholder to create its own nonprofit organizations and foundations, applying some of its business skills to those nonprofits. In addition to the Whole Planet Foundation and the Whole Kids Foundation, we also started the Animal Compassion Foundation, which has since been converted to a public nonprofit known as the Global Animal Partnership, focused on improving livestock animal welfare practices. We will discuss this nonprofit further in the next chapter.

Taxes

One way business supports its communities is through the many different taxes it pays to governments. Taxes on business are much greater than almost anyone realizes. Not only does the United States now have the highest corporate taxes in the entire world at over 39 percent (state and federal combined), but business also pays many other taxes such as property, employer, franchise, and various excise taxes.[5]

To put taxes into perspective, consider this: in fiscal 2011, Whole Foods Market had profits after taxes of approximately $343 million, but we paid over $825 million in total taxes to all jurisdictions.[6] Our taxes were twenty-four times greater than the money we spent on philanthropy ($34 million, about 10 percent of our net profits) and more than twice as high as the profits we were allowed to keep. If business taxes were lower, all the other stakeholders would have more—lower prices for customers, higher wages and benefits for team members, and higher net profits for investors, and the amount of money we could give to support the nonprofit sector would also be proportionately greater.

Creating Value for Society

For much too long, business has been viewed as less noble than either nonprofits or the government because it pursued profits, while they pursued social good. This fallacy needs to be shattered. Business creates tremendous value for all of its stakeholders and therefore also for society.

Collectively, business is the greatest creator of value in the world, much more than the nonprofit and government sectors combined. Both nonprofits and governments depend on the prosperity and wealth business creates, as business is the ultimate source of all taxes and donations.

We will close this chapter by returning to the Tatas, the extraordinary business group that has been a conscious business for longer than any other that we know of. From its beginnings 144 years ago, Tata has been about the community and nation building. The company states its purpose as follows: "At the Tata Group, we are committed to improving the quality of life of the communities we serve. We do this by striving for leadership and global competitiveness in the business sectors in which we operate. Our practice of returning to society what we earn evokes trust amongst our consumers, employees, shareholders and community. We are committed to protecting this heritage of leadership with trust through the manner in which we conduct our business."[7]

The business is not "owned" by the family. Two-thirds of the shares of the parent company, Tata Sons, are owned by charitable trusts. Through them, Tata run the two largest cancer hospitals in India, where half the patients are treated for free. The Indian Institute of Science, Tata Institute of Fundamental Research, and Tata Institute of Social Sciences are all funded by these trusts. Social responsibility is part of the group's DNA; it is not an afterthought or a stunt. It is deeply engrained in the Tata culture as a matter of principle. It is not seen as an additional burden but as an essential cost of doing business.[8]

As Karambir Singh Kang says, "You will not find the names of our leaders among the names of the richest people in the world. We have no one on the Forbes list. Our leaders are not in it for themselves; they are in it for society, for the communities they serve. Our founder Jamshedji Tata was a true patriot who believed in nation building. Whether it was steel, hydroelectric power, civil aviation or locomotives, he wanted to invest in building the bones of the nation, the foundation on which the nation stands."[9]

Tata operates on the premise that a company thrives on social capital. As executive director R. Gopalakrishnan says, "We think and act as citizens first, rather than as corporations. Our corporate credo is that in a free enterprise, the community is not just another stakeholder in the business. It is in fact the very purpose of its existence."[10]

CHAPTER 10

A Healthy, Vibrant Environment

Conscious businesses think caringly, creatively, and strategically about the environment. They consider it one of the company's key stakeholders and treat it with the same respect and attention they give to the others.

The environment is the only stakeholder that is silent. Customers can speak for themselves, as can team members, suppliers, investors, and communities, but who speaks for the environment? Generally, only self-selected activists who often have their own biases and filters and may not accurately represent what the environment, if it could speak, would say it needs most.

For some companies, such as Patagonia, the environment or planet is the ultimate stakeholder. It is integral to the company's higher purpose. To safeguard the environment, Patagonia takes the life cycle of its products very seriously, from conception to ultimate disposal. As CEO Casey Sheahen says, "We take complete responsibility for every product we make. We repair our products, recycle them, help people sell them when they no longer need them. We are trying to protect all of the embodied energy in the product and not have it end up in a landfill."[1]

THE SECOND TENET: STAKEHOLDER INTEGRATION

There is no question that we face serious environmental problems today. While some are natural phenomena, most are the unintended consequences of the rapid industrial growth and greater prosperity we have achieved over the last two hundred years. These include freshwater scarcity and pollution, energy uncertainty, depleted fisheries, rapid deforestation, and climate change.

The Challenges We Face

The environmental challenges of the twenty-first century are radically different from those we faced 125 years ago. Certain aspects of the environment have improved, especially for people living in advanced economies. We have developed better ways to generate energy and handle our waste. Before the advent of electricity and gasoline-powered cars, most large cities were stinky, smoky, grimy, and covered in soot. Streets were littered with horse dung, and human waste was never far from sight or smell. Public water purity was highly suspect in most places. Forests were being cut down for fuel and farm-land at a rapid rate. Whale blubber was the principal source of fuel for lamps, and whales were consequently being hunted to near extinction. Fortunately, and in the nick of time, we discovered how to use petroleum for energy, and soon thereafter, the electric light bulb and internal combustion engine were invented. The streets became cleaner, and homes and buildings became far healthier and more comfortable.

Our challenges today are vastly different. In 1800, there were fewer than a billion of us on the planet, and each individual produced and consumed on average about $650 worth of goods and services a year.[2] Given the ways in which we met our needs for food, fuel, and shelter, even that seemed more than the planet could easily support. Today, there are over seven billion of us, each producing and consuming an average of about $8,000 worth of goods and services a year (in 1990 international dollars).[3] That is approximately $56 trillion in annual economic activity, compared with about $650 billion in 1800—an eighty-six-fold increase!

Let's look forward fifty years. If global per-capita GDP grows at 3 percent a year and if there are 9.6 billion of us on the planet by then, as the United

Nations projects, total economic activity would amount to over $300 trillion a year in 1990 dollars.[4] Looking forward a hundred years and assuming the population stabilizes (as many demographers expect) at about 10 billion, global GDP in 2110 would be more than $1,500 trillion, or twenty-seven times what it is today.[5] It is impossible to imagine our planet supporting that much production and consumption if we continue doing things the same way we have been doing them.

Of course, we won't continue doing things the same way, because we humans never do—provided we are afforded the freedom to find new solutions to old problems. To solve the numerous environmental challenges we will collectively face over the next hundred years, we will need to be even more creative and innovative than we have been in the past. This means we must become better at creating the conditions in which human ingenuity can flourish on a mass scale.

The Environment as a Stakeholder

We are all part of the environment. We live in it, it affects us and we affect it. The environment literally courses through our bodies every moment we are alive, in the air we breathe, the water we drink, and the food we eat. Many of the impacts we have on the environment don't disappear; they continue into the future. If we pollute our water and air, we have to breathe that air and drink that water. If we deforest the planet, we create devastating impacts for our children and grandchildren, as well as for all the other species that share the planet with us.

Businesses must to take full responsibility for their environmental impacts and start devising innovative ways to alleviate them. When we treat the environment as a major stakeholder, we start to seek Win[6] solutions, just as we do with all our other stakeholders. A mind-set focused on developing Win[6] strategies is essential, rather than one that views environmental responsibility and stewardship as some sort of burden or sacrifice. Conscious businesses refuse to accept trade-offs for the environment, just as they do for other stakeholders. A conscious business seeks to minimize its environmental impact even as it improves its relationships with customers, raises the morale of team members, and lowers the cost of doing business, all of which are terrific for investors. Here are two simple examples: as a business becomes more energy-efficient, it saves money; as a business reduces its waste, it spends less money on packaging and disposable products. Both are good for the business, good for the environment, and good for all the other stakeholders.

A Conscious Approach to the Environment

The first step after recognizing the environment as a major stakeholder is to become more conscious of the full impact we have on it and take responsibility for our actions. This is a fundamental attribute of what it means to be conscious. Once we become conscious of all of the consequences of our actions, it is unacceptable to ignore the negative ones or to continue to justify them as the inevitable side effects of creating other kinds of value.

Most of the environmental harm that has occurred on the planet has not been done deliberately. Too often, the critics of business and capitalism frame what has happened as a morality tale in which evil, greedy corporations are deliberately spoiling the environment in a malicious, premeditated way. This is untrue 99.99 percent of the time. Framing the issue that way is not only wrong and unfair, it is also counterproductive. Instead, we must see that most environmental harms have been the unintended consequences of actions that were well intended: creating desired goods and services for customers, providing jobs for team members, purchasing needed materials from suppliers, and so forth.

We need to address key environmental issues creatively and in an integrated way. While global warming or climate change gets a lot of attention, we have collectively focused on it so strongly in recent years that it has taken attention away from other important environmental challenges. These include critical concerns such as freshwater availability, air purity, seafood sustainability, environmental livestock impacts and welfare, deforestation, and desertification.

Whole Foods Market and the Environment

Whole Foods Market is involved with a number of important environmental initiatives, including supporting more sustainable forms of agriculture such as organic and local products; radically reducing our energy footprint; green building initiatives; and moving toward zero waste in our stores. We don't have space here to discuss all of our environmental initiatives in detail, so we will focus on three of the most important: more sustainable livestock production, animal welfare, and seafood sustainability.

Sustainable Livestock Production

Many of the most serious environmental issues the planet faces are intimately connected to global livestock production. In 2006, the United Nations Food and Agriculture Organization (FAO) produced *Livestock's Long Shadow*, a lengthy report on these impacts. This report documented some startling statistics:

- 30 percent of the entire earth's land area is now being used for animal production.

- 33 percent of all grains harvested are fed to livestock animals.

- 70 percent of all soy beans harvested are fed to livestock animals.

- 70 percent of all deforested Amazonian rain forest is used for pasture.

- 33 percent of all water pollution in the United States is due to livestock production.

- 18 percent of all greenhouse gases come from livestock production— more than all forms of transportation combined (14 percent).[6]

Other research has found that raising animals for food consumes more than half of all the water used in the United States. It takes about 2,400 gallons of water to produce a pound of meat, but only 25 gallons to produce a pound of wheat.[7] The average American consumes 273 pounds of meat each year. Animals raised for food in the United States produce 130 times more excrement than does the human population.[8] Since 1980 the global production of pigs and poultry has quadrupled and the production of cattle, sheep, and goats has doubled. The FAO predicts that by 2050, livestock production will again double.[9]

In addition, the cost to human health from heavy consumption of animal products has been well documented, demonstrating high correlations with obesity, diabetes, heart disease, and cancer.[10] Whole Foods Market is doing a number of things to try to lessen the high environmental and human health impacts from heavy meat eating:

1. We are educating our customers and team members about the health advantages of eating primarily a whole-foods, plant-based diet. While not directly advocating a vegan diet, we are encouraging everyone to eat far fewer animal foods and more whole-plant foods and to concentrate on vegetables, fruits, whole grains, legumes, nuts, and seeds. Research has now shown that eating primarily a whole-plant foods diet can prevent and reverse many of the lifestyle diseases that are killing people.

2. We are continually developing sources of animal foods that have been raised in non-factory-farm conditions, especially 100 percent grass-fed beef and lamb and pasture-raised pork and poultry. We believe that animals raised in these ways cause far less environmental damage and are also better for human health.

3. We have made improving animal welfare conditions a high priority and describe this effort in some detail below.

Animal Welfare

Whole Foods Market is intently focused on the treatment of livestock animals. There are more livestock animals in this world than there are people, by several orders of magnitude. Every year, about ten billion land animals (nine billion of which are chickens) and about fifty-one billion sea animals are killed for food, for Americans alone. Worldwide, nearly sixty billion land animals are killed for food each year.[11] The great majority of these animals are not allowed to live what anyone could objectively describe as a good life. Livestock animals are seen as meat and milk machines rather than as sentient creatures with whom we share the planet. The whole focus of factory farming has been to lower costs and increase productivity. The animals' welfare, unless it affects productivity in some way, has been completely ignored.

Whole Foods Market considers this a serious ethical and environmental issue. We refuse to sell commercial veal from tethered calves, foie gras from force-fed ducks, pork using gestation crates, and eggs from caged hens. Whole Foods is strongly committed to helping create alternatives to the factory-farm methods of raising livestock. Over the past eight years, after much research, we have developed step-rated animal welfare standards for a number of livestock animals. We set up a company nonprofit (which we later converted into a public nonprofit) called the Global Animal Partnership (www.globalanimalpartnership.org) to oversee the certifications. Six levels can be attained, ranging from step 1 (no crates, no cages) to step 5+ (animal welfare is a primary concern, no physical mutilations are permitted, animals spend their entire life on the same farm, and slaughter is done on-farm).

This is a good example of a Win[6], because we've created a system that has triggered a race to the top to improve animal welfare. Suppliers want better ratings because that leads to positive publicity, brand enhancement, and potentially higher prices for their products. Being naturally competitive, they want the best rating they can earn and strive to upgrade their animal welfare practices. It's beneficial for our customers, who know they can buy products made from animals raised under safer, healthier, and more humane conditions than the usual conditions for animals raised for typical supermarkets. It's good for the animals, because they are treated much better and lead less stressful and healthier lives. Our investors also benefit, because we offer meat products that are better differentiated and that enhance our competitive position. Our team members feel good about the company's commitment to improving animal welfare.

THE SECOND TENET: STAKEHOLDER INTEGRATION

Seafood Sustainability

Whole Foods also believes that seafood sustainability is a serious environmental issue. Many key seafood species are being fished beyond sustainability. We are working with the Marine Stewardship Council (MSC) to buy seafood that's been certified as sustainable (i.e., it comes from fisheries harvesting fish in a sustainable way). We also are working with the Monterey Bay Aquarium (MBA) and Blue Ocean Institute (BOI) to raise the consciousness of our customers and team members, as well as the media, about which species are the least sustainable. We label all of our seafood with MBA, BOI, and MSC ratings, using a color-coded system based on the degree of sustainability. In 2012 we eliminated all red-rated species (indicating dangerously low sustainability) from our stores.

Interestingly, after we began to focus on seafood sustainability, we were able to locate several sustainable alternatives relatively quickly. This illustrates the maxim that people tend to discover or create what they concentrate on. A great example is Atlantic cod, once the most abundant species of fish in the Western Hemisphere in the pre-Columbian era. New England and Eastern Canada built their fishing industries largely around the abundance of cod. But cod stocks have fallen 95 percent in the last four hundred years, and the fish is now considered a red-rated species by both the MBA and the BOI.[12] This is a big challenge for our stores, particularly those in the Boston area. New Englanders have been eating cod for hundreds of years. They want and expect it. After we eliminated all red-rated species from our stores, our purchasing and seafood teams have made a concerted effort to find sustainable fisheries for cod. Happily, at least one fishery is now being certified by the MSC. In the future, as consciousness rises about these issues, we're going to see more fisheries managed in a sustainable way.

Environmental Success Stories

Businesses have a major role in helping solve many environmental issues. In fact, most environmental challenges cannot be solved unless businesses fully commit to addressing them through entrepreneurial innovations. Not long ago, big businesses were considered enemy number one by the environmental movement.

Today, many big companies represent a beacon of hope at a time when governments and civil society seem unable to make much progress. As businesses become more conscious, this trend will only accelerate, and we are confident that humankind will start to replenish and restore earth's natural habitat over time.

Here are some examples of businesses moving ahead with innovative initiatives that are showing the way forward and inspiring others to follow their lead:

3M

3M has long been a pioneer in lowering the environmental impact of business. Many of 3M's businesses create products that have in the past been harmful for the environment. To deal with this challenge proactively, 3M introduced its Pollution Prevention Pays initiative, known as 3P, in 1975. The program was designed to prevent pollution in products and manufacturing and was well ahead of its time. The company estimates that its 3P program has prevented three billion pounds of pollution and saved the company nearly $1.4 billion. 3M uses approaches such as product reformulation, process modification, equipment redesign, and recycling and reuse of waste materials. Team members voluntarily participate in 3P programs and have completed over 8,100 projects in thirty-five years. The program has won numerous awards and is supported worldwide, regardless of pollution regulations in specific countries. Interestingly, the company has found that the processes arising from this program often create more functionally acceptable products. For example, a new process for creating abrasive backing, implemented at 3M's Alexandria, Minnesota, facility, improved product performance and reduced air emissions and costs. Environmentally friendly products are also easier and less costly to dispose of.[13]

UPS

UPS has long been highly conscious about its impact on the environment and has reaped many business benefits through its leading-edge sustainability practices. It is constantly advancing the state of the art in using every available technology to make its operations more efficient. In 2010, using telematics and GPS technology, the company delivered 350,000 more packages a day than the year before while driving 53,000 fewer miles per day. Its famous no-left-turns policy lowers accident risks and traffic delays, while also saving twenty million miles of driving a year. UPS also works with customers to shrink their product-to-package ratios; smaller boxes mean less nonsustainable packing fillers and fewer delivery trips.[14]

POSCO

Since its founding, South Korean steelmaker POSCO has been committed to minimizing its environmental impact. It has planted more than two million trees within the boundaries of its steel complex in Pohang, where the air quality is as good as it was before the plant was built. The sign over the entrance to their main plant is inspiring: "Resources are limited; creativity is unlimited."

Low-carbon, green growth is a huge challenge for companies like POSCO that use vast amounts of energy and produce a large quantity of carbon dioxide in the manufacturing process. POSCO has tried to turn this potential threat into an opportunity, publicly committing itself to becoming a "Global Green-Growth Leader" and vigorously pushing strategic carbon management throughout the world.[15] Notably, POSCO has developed a new steel producing process called FINEX, which reduces the generation of pollutants such as sulfur dioxide and nitrous dioxide by more than 95 percent and lowers costs by 15 percent (including lower energy consumption), compared with traditional blast furnaces. To its credit, the company has announced it will license the technology to its competitors so that the whole steel industry can become less polluting and more energy efficient.

Walmart

One of the most encouraging developments on the environmental front comes from Walmart. An effort that was originally seen as a way to insulate the company from environmental criticism has evolved into something much broader. The company has launched numerous initiatives that have not only had a positive impact on the environment, but also saved it huge amounts of money and, in some cases, generated new revenues. Earlier than most large companies, Walmart realized that a strong business case can be made for taking measures to enhance environmental sustainability—measures that do not depend on government subsidies or other incentive programs. The company is using its vast scale and power to change not only its own practices, but also those of its suppliers and many of its competitors.[16]

Here are some of Walmart's initiatives:

- Since 2005, it has reduced the carbon footprint of its stores by more than 10 percent and that of its truck fleet to a much greater degree. It has done so by installing energy-efficient lighting and refrigeration, using better fuel, streamlining its trucks, and planning better routes.

- The company has helped its suppliers in the United States and China reduce their carbon emissions and energy bills by 20 to 60 percent.

- A major initiative to reduce packaging has saved hundreds of millions of dollars in shipping and material costs. The company plans to continue to shrink its product packages and make them mostly recyclable, an effort expected to save $3.4 billion. For example, Walmart required its laundry detergent suppliers to shrink the detergent bottles, saving huge amounts of water, plastic, cardboard, and diesel fuel.

- Walmart has set itself an ambitious goal of sending zero waste to landfills; it has already reduced its waste by 81 percent in California in a pilot program. It is finding new uses for things that used to be sent to landfills, such as converting plastic waste into dog beds and food waste into compost. The company now earns about $100 million a year from waste it previously paid to have hauled away.

Where There Is a Will . . .

Of course, we do have many serious environmental challenges ahead of us. They can feel overwhelming; the consequences of a large, growing, and increasingly prosperous human population on the planet seem so dire that many of us become disheartened at the prospect of being able to arrest, let alone reverse, the decline in the quality of our environment.[17]

However, there is cause for optimism. Most people don't recognize how much progress has been made to improve our environment in the past hundred years. The air in the United States is far cleaner today than it was a hundred years ago, or even thirty years ago. Air quality in Los Angeles has improved dramatically in the past thirty years due to smart government policy. Regulations eliminated certain car exhausts by mandating the use of catalytic converters and phasing out the lead in gasoline. This was an appropriate property-rights issue for the government to take on, since the air belongs to everyone.

So the good news is that we *can* make progress and, in fact, have done so in the recent past. Here is another example. Many readers will remember the serious concerns that existed in the 1970s and 1980s about a phenomenon called acid rain. Sulfur dioxide, emitted by power plants, combined with other gases in the atmosphere to produce rain that was more acidic than normal. Many plants and fish began to die, and the fear was that acid rain would destroy ecosystems around the world.

To combat this, the United States passed a law setting up a sulfur dioxide trading system. Though many companies and environmentalists protested, the system created a market-based mechanism that aligned the incentives in an effective way. Each company was allowed a certain level of pollution as its "right" of doing business. Beyond that, it would have to pay a fine. If it installed antipollution equipment (called scrubbers) to reduce its emissions, a company could sell its unused pollution rights to those that had not invested in the equipment. As more companies started to install scrubbers, the resulting economies of scale caused the cost of scrubbers to decline, leading more companies to install the equipment—a virtuous cycle. Eventually, the cost was only one-tenth of what had been anticipated! Sulfur dioxide emissions have been cut by more than half and ecosystems that had been damaged by acid rain are recovering nicely.[18]

Another success story is the renewal of forests in the United States. Most of the deforestation in the United States occurred in the eighteenth and nineteenth centuries as forests were cleared by the pioneers to create farms. Between 1920 and 1990, forest cover in the United States remained stable. Since that time, forest cover has been increasing steadily, as about two million acres of land are being returned to forest each year. There is now 40 percent more wood in U.S. forests than there was fifty years ago. Because of the increased forest cover, some scientists estimate that the United States now absorbs as much in carbon emissions as it emits.[19]

Globally, of course, deforestation is still a huge issue. However, the experience of the United States shows that it can be effectively addressed. The experience around the planet is that as countries become more prosperous, environmental conditions improve. The pattern is that economic growth is detrimental to the environment when per-capita income is between $2,000 and $8,000, but becomes beneficial beyond that point. This is because people with higher living standards expect and demand a cleaner environment, and this generally is accomplished.[20]

Replacing Environmental Fear with Love

Some environmentalists refuse to acknowledge such positive evidence about the impact of business on the environment. They are firmly wedded to their message of environmental Armageddon and are unwilling to open their minds and change their views. Many also believe fear is the most effective motivator and think that they have to keep people scared to keep them from becoming complacent. However, fear short-circuits creativity and inhibits innovation and problem solving. When we rely on fear, people eventually start to emotionally contract and tune out. This has already happened with many environmental issues.

In the long term, as with all stakeholders, businesses must operate out of love and care for the environment. Operating out of fear, we can do very little. Care and love are far better strategies for solving environmental issues than continued fear and guilt.

We will solve our environmental challenges in the same way we solve all challenges: by raising consciousness, encouraging creativity and innovation, and recognizing and rewarding virtuous behavior. The government's role is crucial. It must enact sound, scientifically validated environmental regulations and ensure that unscrupulous operators are not able to prosper at the expense of more conscious and conscientious companies. We need to develop a societal immune system that isolates and rejects harmful, unsustainable environmental practices.

We have the ability to reverse our environmental problems on this planet. It is time to stop despairing and finger-pointing and start acting in a conscious and more caring way toward our shared planet.

CHAPTER 11

The Outer
Circle of Stakeholders

All the stakeholders of a business matter, but some are more critical to the success of the organization than others. How a company prioritizes its stakeholders varies depending upon the type of business. Major stakeholders for one business might be minor stakeholders for another. However, the primary identifying characteristic of the most important stakeholders, those we call major or inner-circle stakeholders, is that they engage in voluntary exchange with the organization for mutual benefit.

Customers, team members, investors, suppliers, communities, and the environment are thus generally considered major stakeholders. It could be argued that the environment doesn't exchange "voluntarily" and therefore shouldn't be included in the inner circle; we leave it there, however, because of its clear importance to all of us. Competitors, activists, critics, unions, the media, and government should also be viewed as stakeholders because they have an impact on the organization and can also influence the inner-circle stakeholders. Since they don't routinely engage in voluntary exchange with the organization for mutual benefit, we characterize them as outer-circle stakeholders. For some companies, unions and governments may be considered major stakeholders and grouped in the inner circle.

Competitors

Most companies do not think of their competitors as stakeholders; they view them as enemies to be crushed in the marketplace. Companies commonly use war metaphors in thinking about competitors. But a more constructive way to think about competitors is as *allies* in striving for mutual excellence. Good competitors help a business to improve and evolve because they offer its stakeholders choices. They can coax a company out of its complacency and away from suboptimal behaviors. Competitors create and innovate, coming up with ideas, strategies, products, and services that we may not have thought of on our own.

This constructive view is built on thinking about competitors in terms of what we can learn from them. Potentially, we can learn more from strong competitors than from anyone else, as they can from us. Most companies tend to look critically at competitors and focus on what they do poorly. No doubt, many competitors do things that are foolish or strategically unwise. But when they adopt a critical stance towards their competitors, business leaders can become arrogant and complacent. With such a mind-set, it is impossible for them to learn anything.

A far better attitude to have toward competitors is to zero in on what they're doing *right*, what they do better than us. It takes high emotional intelligence, self-awareness, and humility to recognize when a competitor is actually superior and can teach us and help our organization become better.

Every good business improves through its own innovations as well as through creative imitation. It is just smart business. At Whole Foods Market, we actually become excited when a competitor does something better than we do. We don't find it threatening to think that they are better than us in some ways; we see it as an opportunity for improvement. We like to go into our competitors' stores and see what they do particularly well. Often, we are able to assimilate our competitors' innovations and spread them faster than they can themselves. This is because we have developed a strong organizational capacity for taking ideas, growing them, improving on them, and spreading them throughout the company fairly rapidly. It doesn't matter where the idea originates: our team members, customers, suppliers, or competitors.

Sam Walton, the iconic founder of Walmart, was famous for frequently visiting his competitors to learn what they were doing well and for using what he discovered to improve Walmart. He would tell Walmart managers to visit other stores and not come back until they had identified one thing the competitors were doing better. In his autobiography, he wrote that he had probably spent more time in Kmart stores than the CEO of that company had.[1] Kmart never had the same orientation toward learning from Walmart, which is one reason why Walmart became so successful while Kmart faded away.

Their potential to help us learn and grow is the primary reason competitors should be seen as stakeholders. In this sense, they have a stake in our business, as we do in theirs. Like sports teams in the same league, we push each other to excel and fulfill our potential. If we view each other as offering opportunities to learn and grow, it becomes a win-win relationship; both companies can reap benefits, as do their customers and other stakeholders.

If their broader purposes start to align, competitors can also become fellow travelers on the same journey. We are often asked about Walmart's entry into the organic foods business. On the one hand, of course, this makes life more difficult for us. Walmart is a formidable competitor. The company has forced us not only to get better, but also to innovate quicker, differentiate ourselves, and come up with products we know Walmart will not be selling. We have to evolve in ways that allow us to flourish.

From another perspective, Walmart's entry into the organic business can be seen as a validation of our purpose; in fact, it helps us better fulfill that purpose. Our higher purposes include spreading sustainable agriculture and making healthier foods a bigger part of people's diets. If someone had told us twenty-five years ago that Walmart would one day be selling organic foods, we would not have believed it. That Walmart is now doing so is a testament to how far our company and the organic sector have come and tells us that we've successfully penetrated into the mainstream. Seen in this light, Walmart's embrace of organics is a great thing for us and the world.

Activists and Critics

Activists and critics can also be thought of as competitors to an organization; they compete with different ideas and values. A conscious way to view activists and critics is to recognize that they see things about your business that you don't or can't see. They offer an alternative vision of the way your business could be. You don't have to embrace those ideas; in fact, you may reject them outright as being just plain wrong, impractical, or contrary to your higher purposes. But it is still important to engage with activists just as you engage with competitors and other stakeholders. They too offer a potential opportunity to learn and grow. As Ed Freeman puts it, "Behind every activist is a new business idea."

We are not suggesting that it is fun to engage with hostile activists and critics; it is unpleasant to listen to harsh criticism from people who don't care at all about your business. They may not like or love you; they may even consider you bad and evil. Nevertheless, they often have valuable insights that can help move your business forward.

In 2003, animal rights activists showed up at the Whole Foods Market annual meeting and picketed, trying to coerce us to stop selling duck meat from one of our suppliers. They were handing out pamphlets that we believed contained inaccurate information and were saying bad things about our company to anybody who would listen. Initially, we were quite offended they were there; after all, this was our annual meeting with stockholders, and the activists were trying to hijack it. These people didn't care about Whole Foods Market. They may have bought a share or two as a ticket to get into the annual meeting, but they were there for their own agenda. They were trying to bully and coerce us, and no one likes that.

Nonetheless, as CEO, I began a dialogue with one of the activists, Lauren Ornelas, after the meeting ended. At the time, I believed Whole Foods Market already had the best animal welfare standards of any food retailer in the United States. Our dialogue continued by e-mail over the next few months. Lauren told me she could see I was well intentioned and idealistic, but she also said that I was also grossly uninformed when it came to animal welfare. She challenged me to learn more: "You need to be better informed. You're the CEO of a large corporation, and frankly you don't know what you're talking about." I was taken aback; I thought that was a rather harsh thing for her to say. But I accepted her challenge. That summer, I educated myself by reading a dozen books about the livestock industry and animal welfare. By the end of the summer, I realized she was absolutely right, that I had been quite ignorant. I was horrified by what I had learned. It became clear to me that many of the accusations she had been making about the meat industry were accurate. I personally changed my diet as a result of this experience and became a vegan. But I also wanted Whole Foods Market to begin to collectively engage with these animal welfare activists so they could help us improve our welfare standards. I felt we had a responsibility to do a better job finding suppliers who took better care of their animals.

That was the beginning of a conscious evolution in our company toward greater concern for animal welfare, as described earlier. Whole Foods Market has embraced the animal welfare rating program from the Global Animal Partnership, as have our customers. We have competitors interested in doing business with the Partnership as well. We are seeing the beginnings of a possible revolution in the welfare of livestock animals; this would not have happened if the activists had not come to our annual meeting and made a nuisance of themselves and confronted us, or if we had asked the police to throw them out as troublemakers. Instead, by engaging with them in a proactive, open way, our company evolved. We learned, we grew, and we're a better company as a result.

Labor Unions

Labor unions are an interesting category of stakeholders. As with activists, there has been a long history of adversarial relationships between companies and unions. These conflicts usually have been very harmful over the long term to all the stakeholders of the company, including unions and the team members they represent. To fully flourish, companies must evolve to form Win[6] partnerships that create value for all stakeholders. This requires the leadership of the company and the union to both become more conscious and adopt a spirit of cooperation and partnership.

THE SECOND TENET: STAKEHOLDER INTEGRATION

Labor unions began to grow in the early to middle part of the nineteenth century in response to the poor working conditions that often prevailed in the early stages of the industrial revolution. Workers had few rights then, and business owners were reluctant to give them any. Early unionization efforts often involved a great deal of violence on both sides. Eventually, the massive dislocations caused by the growth of the factory system and the imbalance in the workplace led to the successful formation of unions that could negotiate for better compensation and working conditions.

There is no question that labor unions primarily came about because of the failure of businesses to care about their workers as human beings. Workers were frequently seen as cogs in an industrial machine, and few industrial businesses paid much attention to their well-being.

Labor unions grew very powerful as the industrial factory system grew in the nineteenth and the first half of the twentieth century. The industrial part of the economy became largely unionized by the middle of the twentieth century. Private-sector union membership peaked at 36 percent in 1945 but has since declined to only 6.9 percent.[2] Public employee unions were mostly illegal (the argument being that government is a monopoly lacking market competition to check union power) until President Kennedy in 1962 issued an executive order permitting collective bargaining in federal bureaucracies. Since then, public employee unions have grown tremendously and now represent about 36 percent of all public workers.[3] Compelling arguments have been made that public employee unions are raising the cost of government tremendously and that they threaten the long-term solvency of many local, state, and federal governments.[4]

Whole Foods Market employs over sixty-seven thousand people, and none are unionized, despite the fact that we operate in a highly unionized segment of the economy. In a sense, unions compete with the company for the hearts and minds of team members. Our belief is that if a company does an outstanding job caring for its team members, creating value for them, and respecting them as key stakeholders, it can successfully avoid unionization. A conscious business knows that treating its people well is the right thing to do; it does not need to be coerced into doing so. Unions simply aren't necessary if a business operates with a stakeholder philosophy and if team members are seen as important stakeholders who should be well compensated, happy, and flourishing in the workplace.

Dealing with Unions Today

While we believe that the best approach is to avoid the need for unions in the first place, businesses that already have labor unions should strive to engage with them constructively rather than viewing them as adversaries. Companies should recognize the union as a stakeholder in the organization and seek win-win outcomes, as they should with all stakeholders. Southwest Airlines is a great example of a company that has had a predominantly positive and win-win relationship with its labor unions. The airline has shown that it is possible to work with unions to increase productivity and efficiency, while unions and their members flourish as well. When we asked former Southwest Airlines CEO Herb Kelleher how he had maintained such cordial relationships with the unions for decades, his response was simple but powerful: "I just treated them like human beings." Colleen Barrett, former president, added, "Everybody just wants to be treated with some respect." She told us that when there was a meeting between the union and management, all participants were mixed together rather than arrayed on opposite sides. An observer would have no idea who was part of management and who represented the union.[5]

The Madison Story

At Whole Foods Market, our experiences with labor unions have unfortunately been almost completely adversarial. We pride ourselves on our commitment and care toward our team members and how happy and satisfied the vast majority of them are. Years ago, unions maintained long-term picketers (none of whom were team members) for up to eighteen months in front of several stores to try to discourage customers from shopping with us. They also have funded many organized attacks against our company and have tried to smear our reputation and brand numerous times.

THE SECOND TENET: STAKEHOLDER INTEGRATION

In 2002, a narrow majority of team members at the Whole Foods Market store in Madison, Wisconsin, voted to unionize, in what we later discovered was a setup. Several union organizers gained employment at the store for the purpose of organizing it; most of them quit soon after the union was elected. The union organizers made many promises to our team members about what they would do for them if the store was successfully unionized: raise their pay, increase vacation time, increase their store discounts, improve their health coverage, liberalize the dress code, and so on. Unrealistic promises by unions are common when an organization campaign is under way, and the many restrictions that now exist due to strict National Labor Relations Board regulations make these promises almost impossible for companies to counter effectively. Ironically, companies are prohibited from making any promises concerning either compensation or working conditions once a union-organizing campaign has begun and the National Labor Relations Board has been notified.

The union-organizing campaign was a huge wake-up call for me personally. My reaction was "Wow—how is this possible?" Clearly, we were not doing a good-enough job of ensuring team member happiness. If we were, the union would not have been able to get a foothold. So I took it upon myself personally to find out where we had gone wrong and how we could improve. I traveled the country and visited every single store over the next twelve months, having one-on-one discussions and group meetings with team members. I was there to listen and learn, to understand how Whole Foods Market could become a better company and a better place to work, and what leadership could do to help our team members do their jobs better. It was a fascinating experience, and I learned a lot. For example, I learned that we needed to greatly improve our health insurance. As a result, the health plans were significantly transformed to the system in place today, along with several other improvements.

Because of how we chose to respond, the ultimate result of the union vote in Madison was to help make Whole Foods Market a better company. The union's competition for the hearts and minds of our team members helped us evolve in a positive way. Interestingly, the union wasn't able to deliver on any of its promises to the Madison team members. While we were making many improvements throughout the rest of the company, the union wouldn't let us implement any of those improvements at the Madison store. Our team members in the Madison store were quite aware of all the improvements taking place at other stores: health-care benefits were improved, paid time off was increased, and wages went up. But they couldn't receive those improvements, because the union wouldn't allow it until the contract was fully negotiated. Due to this union inflexibility, our team members in Madison soon realized they didn't want or need a union. Twelve months after voting it in, the team members circulated a petition, and the union was decertified. There was actually never a union contract signed for Madison or for any other Whole Foods Market store.

Media

The media should also be considered a stakeholder, and the company's relationship with it should be managed accordingly. It is important to understand what the media wants and how to constructively engage with it. This can lead to synergistic relationships that create value for both the media and the business.

The media tends to focus and report on the three Cs: controversy, conflict, and change. It sometimes spins things to make them seem controversial and looks for conflict where there isn't any. Members of the media are always interested in writing about change, both positive and negative.

The traditional media needs to evolve and become more conscious. This means rediscovering its higher purpose. For the news media, its higher purpose probably should be to seek and disseminate what is true. A good investigative journalist has a passion to unearth things and get the truth out. Many people have lost trust in the media because they think it is no longer honest with them, but is more interested in spinning a story or engaging in entertainment or sensationalism to attract a larger audience.

To a degree, the media has become philosophically corrupted by the postmodernist philosophy that there is no objective truth, only subjective interpretations that are dependent on context and viewpoint. From this perspective, all interpretations are seen as equally valid, and one's ideology becomes the dominant prism through which to view reality. People then twist things to make them fit their ideological biases, rather than evolving their beliefs and ideologies to fit the evidence and facts. If the media were to reengage in the pursuit of the objective truth, even though the reality of context and viewpoint will always exist, it could regain public trust and serve a more beneficial role in our society.

When it functions well, the media makes all societal institutions, including business, better because it fosters a higher level of openness, transparency, and accountability. Of course, the media frequently goes overboard, and many business leaders have felt the brunt of overzealous, inaccurate, and agenda-driven reporting. But overall, there is no question that having a free media delivers significant societal benefits.

Traditionally, members of mass media such as newspapers, television, and radio have operated as middlemen, interpreting events about the business to the outside world. Businesses had no easy ways to connect directly with many of their stakeholders except through the interpretations provided by the media or through expensive advertising. This made businesses both dependent on the media and vulnerable to the various interpretations, spin, and filters the media might use to explain events. Now, with social media such as Facebook, Twitter, YouTube, as well as through company websites, it's much easier for a business to engage directly with its stakeholders without needing the traditional media to act as a go-between. Social media created a revolution because it allowed businesses to have a more direct, ongoing connection with their key stakeholders, which is very empowering. At Whole Foods Market, we have a communications team that is focused on earned media (primarily, public relations), social media, in-store communication, and community involvement. We still interact with traditional media, of course, but increasingly we see social media as the most important way to engage constructively with our stakeholders. Many companies dedicate huge budgets to advertisements for a 100 percent controlled message. This delivers the message exactly as the company wants, but it lacks credibility of earned media or third-party reporters, writers, and bloggers telling a company's story—an approach that Whole Foods facilitates every day with great results.

Government

The government is an important stakeholder for all businesses and a major one for some. For example, companies in the health-care and utilities sectors understand that the government is everywhere and has to be considered a major stakeholder. For companies in the defense business, the government is the customer and clearly the most important stakeholder.

There is no doubt the government plays an important role in society; the main question is how significant that role should be. When does the government go from being helpful to being dictatorial and harmful to business? In some industries, such as in health care and education, the government is now so powerful and dominant that entrepreneurship and innovation are being curtailed. Beyond the question of whether the government's role is big or small, what truly matters is whether it is conscious or unconscious, value creating or value destroying.[6]

When it comes to business, the government's responsibility is to be an impartial umpire: to create a system of just property rights, to make sure that businesses follow the rules and apply them fairly to ensure a level playing field. Some regulations are good and necessary and make for a better society. But many are a nuisance and counterproductive. They can be enormously costly; according to the Small Business Administration (SBA), total regulatory costs in the United States amount to about $1.75 trillion annually, nearly twice as much as all individual income taxes collected in 2009.[7] The burden of regulations falls disproportionately on small businesses. The SBA study shows that the cost of regulations per team member for firms with fewer than twenty team members is now $10,585, which is 36 percent higher than the cost for larger firms.[8]

While some regulations create important safeguards for public health and the environment, far too many simply protect existing business interests and discourage entrepreneurship. Specifically, many government regulations in education, health care, and energy prevent entrepreneurship and innovation from revolutionizing and reenergizing these critical parts of our economy.

Currently, thousands of new regulations are added each year, and virtually none ever disappear. A simple reform that would make a monumental difference would be to require all federal regulations to have a sunset provision. That is, they should automatically expire after ten years unless an independent, mandatory cost-benefit analysis proves they have created significantly more societal benefit than harm.

In a competitive market, no matter how large a business becomes, it never acquires coercive power over customers, team members, or other stakeholders. All the business can do is offer each of its stakeholders a menu of choices; the stakeholders have the freedom to choose. But uniquely among societal institutions, the government has coercive power, which makes it exceptionally powerful and potentially threatening. The government alone can arrest people, imprison them, take away all their assets, even put them to death. When government is constructive, it can be a good and healthy thing. But when it is corrupt or becomes too powerful, government becomes quite dangerous.

In many democratic countries, the government has indeed been corrupted through the lobbying power of special interests. Some businesses, labor unions, and governments have made unhealthy alliances where the narrow interests of a few take precedence over the well-being of the many. These interests end up twisting the system to benefit themselves at the expense of the collective good, relying on the coercive power of government to protect and defend their entrenched position.

Government regulators often come from the very industries they are charged with regulating. These people know that when they leave the government, they can secure a lucrative contract working within the industry. In such situations, regulations are often crafted to benefit the industry (or certain companies in the industry) rather than to serve the public interest.[9]

Society has countless examples of special favors being granted to well-connected people. When people see this kind of corruption, they usually blame business for doing the corrupting. But the government is equally to blame. This kind of crony capitalism represents the worst danger to free-enterprise capitalism. The danger is especially great in emerging economies, but is a problem everywhere and is becoming a serious problem in the United States. Many people who condemn capitalism do so for this reason. But crony capitalism is not free-enterprise capitalism; it is a perversion of it.

The bottom line is that good government is absolutely essential. If government becomes too corrupt, it is impossible to have a free-enterprise system and healthy capitalism. We need the rule of law, but our regulations and taxes must be applied fairly to all. Regulations and taxes need to be set in such a way that the overall well-being of society comes first, with the guiding principle of seeking the common good while safeguarding individual freedom.

Responding Creatively and Constructively to Conflict

There is a common theme to our view of how to relate to competitors, activists, and unions. Any stakeholder can develop a deeply adversarial relationship with a business if conflicts are handled in unconstructive ways. Conflicts are only bad if we respond to them badly. If we never had any conflict, we would also not have as much change. If we respond to conflict creatively and constructively, it can be an important trigger for positive change. Ed Freeman points out that when there is conflict between stakeholders, it is a point of business opportunity.

The pioneering management thinker Mary Parker Follett wrote that there are three possible responses to conflict: domination by the stronger party, compromise so that both meet halfway but neither is really happy, or integration—rising above the situation to create a solution that works for all without compromising. Integration can allow both parties to be better off than even their best-case scenarios. That is what we must strive for, and that is what we will turn our attention to next.

CHAPTER 12

The Interdependence of Stakeholders

Bill George, the former CEO of Medtronic and now a professor of leadership at Harvard Business School, understands well the interdependent nature of a company's stakeholders. He illustrates the idea using a virtuous circle. It starts with the company's purpose and values, which serve to attract and inspire the right team members. This leads to innovation and superior customer service, which then leads to improved market share and higher revenues, profits, and eventually shareholder value. As he puts it, "This is a reinforcing, virtuous circle. If you turn it around and start with shareholder value, you can't 'get there from here.' The clock only runs one way. If you start with the proposition that we have to satisfy the security analysts and hot-money shareholders, you will eventually destroy the enterprise. You will harm innovation and superior customer service, harm employee motivation, and ultimately destroy whatever shareholder value you have built up. That's what happened at General Motors, The Home Depot, Sears, Kodak, Motorola, and a host of other formerly great companies."[1]

THE SECOND TENET: STAKEHOLDER INTEGRATION

Beyond Analytical Thinking

One of the most challenging but important ideas about management and leadership involves understanding the relationships between stakeholders. Conflict between the various stakeholders in a business is inevitable from time to time simply because each stakeholder always wants more. However, most people create analytical separations between the stakeholders and take it no further. They see the stakeholder groups as separate from each other and the business—each entity pursuing its own interests.

This type of analytical separation is a form of reductionism—it ignores the relationships stakeholders have with the business and with each other. No complex, evolving, and self-adapting organization can be adequately understood merely through analyzing its parts and ignoring the full system. The business is more than just the sum of the individual stakeholders. It is also the interrelationship, the interconnection, the shared purposes, and the shared values that the various stakeholders of the business cocreate and coevolve together. The mortar that connects the bricks is as important as the bricks. When we fully comprehend the larger business system in action, with all the interdependencies and opportunities for voluntary cooperation for mutual benefit that exist within it, it can be beautiful and even awe-inspiring.

Ed Freeman suggests that putting stakeholder interests together in a harmonious way is akin to playing music and creating art. Most of us were taught to think with the analytical part of our mind: we divide things up into parts and analyze them. Analytical intelligence is obviously valuable and has served us well in many ways, especially in science and technology. However, it has limitations when we are trying to understand stakeholders. The analytical mind tends to see stakeholders as separate entities motivated primarily by self-interest and therefore likely to have frequent conflicts that necessitate trade-offs when those self-interests diverge. We have difficulty seeing the big, complex picture; as the expression goes, we can't see the forest for the trees. To understand stakeholder relationships, an additional kind of intelligence is required: systems intelligence.

Our analytical, logical intelligence was a great advance for humankind and took tens of thousands of years to develop. Even today, we must each work hard to develop this thinking skill in ourselves. It is the basis for logic and reason, and it led to the Enlightenment and the advancement of science. However, a holistic systems intelligence, or what Ken Wilber calls "integral consciousness" and Don Beck and Chris Cowan call "second tier consciousness," reflects an advance in both our individual and our collective consciousness.[2] In the twenty-first century, as this type of thinking skill becomes more important, we need to encourage and teach people to develop it. Without the ability to think with holistic systems intelligence, most of what we're talking about in Conscious Capitalism will not make sense to many people. They will see the separation and conflicts between the stakeholders, but not the unity and harmony that comes from the ability to successfully integrate them.

When medical students study anatomy, they take a cadaver and dissect it. They study the liver, the heart, the blood vessels, the brain—each of its various components. They learn to identify and memorize the different parts. But they cannot see the living relationships between the parts of something when it's dead, although they can imagine how the parts work together in a living being; this is, after all, the purpose of studying a cadaver. They are trying to understand people by viewing their bodies as machines with separate parts. This is necessary but not sufficient. The human body is made up of a hundred trillion living cells all cooperating with one another. Different cells have different functions, some more specialized than others. They have intricate, interdependent relationships with each another, and it is critical that we understand those.

One of the reasons many believe our medical paradigm has gotten off track is precisely because it views the body as a machine consisting of various parts, like an automobile. We think of food as fuel to make us go, rather than as the fundamental source of nourishment that maintains our vitality, our health, and our lives. When we are sick, we look at the part of our body that has "malfunctioned" and take a pharmaceutical drug to fix the malfunction. If that doesn't work (as is often the case), we may try to supplement or replace the part through surgery—such as with stents, pacemakers, kidney transplants, and knee or hip replacements. Medicine has become a very expensive automobile repair shop delivering first aid, pharmaceutical drugs, medical devices, and surgeries that primarily address symptoms rather than the sources of diseases. Instead, it should primarily be based on studying optimum health and teaching people how to live healthy lives through better diets, healthy lifestyles, exercise, rest, positive attitudes, and so forth. The same mind-set applies to organizations as well.

Uncovering Hidden Synergies

Just as we can't really understand health or life just by dividing it up and analyzing the parts, we cannot understand Conscious Capitalism very well until we are able to think with a holistic systems mind, until we can understand the interdependent relationships businesses have with their stakeholders, and stakeholders have with each other.

The first obstacle is the trade-off mentality that is so much a part of the analytical mind-set. This is one of the most important ideas in this book: *If you look for trade-offs, you will always find them.* We guarantee this. Humans have a strong confirmation bias.[3] If we expect to see something, we are likely to start seeing it. Even if they are not there, our analytical mind can always conjure up potential trade-offs and potential conflicts, and we will begin to see them.

Fortunately, the same is also true when we look for synergies: if we look for them, we are quite likely to find them too. But many people simply cannot understand the nature of systems and interdependencies, because their consciousness has not yet developed the skills to do so. It's like trying to explain snow to a Pacific Islander; the person just doesn't have the necessary experience to comprehend it.

Of course, it is not easy to simultaneously accommodate the needs and concerns of all stakeholders. But it is fundamentally necessary. The way to enable it is to focus on value *creation* rather than on value division; we should not ask how best we can distribute the burdens and benefits across the stakeholders, but how we can create as much value as possible for all of them.[4] We need to think in terms of expanding the pie, rather than just slicing it up more equitably.

Stakeholder Cancer

Returning to the biology theme, we find that cancer is a useful metaphor for understanding what goes wrong with stakeholders in many businesses. The human body has about one hundred trillion cells, interacting cooperatively to stay alive, grow, and reproduce. Cancer is a breakdown of the harmonious interdependency between cells that is essential to good health. A cancerous tumor starts because some cells mutate and begin to divide and grow, ignoring the warning signals of the body's immune system that they're not supposed to be growing that way and that such growth is harmful to the larger biological system. A healthy immune system is able to turn off, destroy, and recycle the mutating and rebellious cells to restore the body to health. However, if the immune system has been weakened (by genetics, an unhealthy diet, tobacco, drugs, alcohol, toxins, stress, or negative mental attitudes), the cancer may successfully resist the body's protective mechanisms and continue growing. Unless the weakness of the immune system is reversed, the cancer will continue growing and spreading, eventually killing its host (and itself as well; cancer is ultimately suicidal).

Cancer is a metaphor for the lack of cooperation within a business and between a business and its stakeholders. If we don't see the interdependencies within the business, and if we're unable to create Win^6 relationships with all the major stakeholders, then one of the stakeholders could become overly dominant and potentially cancerous, threatening the well-being of the entire system. In any interdependent system, it is extremely damaging to continuously trade off the interests of one group for those of another. Businesses that do so will decline and eventually perish. Any stakeholder that seeks to maximize its own interests without concern for the other interdependent stakeholders within the larger system harms and threatens the whole. If a stakeholder group becomes too dominant and selfish, as with cancer, it can ultimately destroy the host organism and itself in the process. This can happen with any stakeholder group, but the three most common types of stakeholder cancers involve investors, senior management, and team members.

THE SECOND TENET: STAKEHOLDER INTEGRATION

The most common type of stakeholder cancer in business results from the widespread idea of maximizing shareholder value and profits. When the investor is seen as the only stakeholder that matters, and the interdependency and the intrinsic value of the other stakeholders are denied, the business is at high risk of creating and growing a cancer that may one day destroy it. This type of thinking is partly what led to the recent financial crisis. Many financial institutions were focused only on maximizing their short-term profits, with little concern for the possible harmful impacts on their other stakeholders and the larger society. Their management teams were not looking out for the common good of their larger business system. Eventually, their myopic short-term profit maximization strategy blew up, not only damaging their businesses (though some companies have thrived because of favorable treatment by the government), but almost dragging down the entire U.S. economy.

The second stakeholder cancer threat comes from senior management teams that seek to maximize their own compensation without creating commensurate value. In many cases, executives simply pay themselves too much, with little concern for internal equity or connection with overall performance. In some companies, executive compensation is so high that it has a major impact on profits. In many cases, this cancer is due to excessive short-term option grants. Driven by the lure of huge gains in the value of their stock options, executives often make decisions that sacrifice long-term competitiveness to maximize short-term profits. They disrupt the Win[6] relationships of stakeholders with the company by unilaterally changing the terms of exchange—raising prices to customers, cutting wages or benefits or total employment, or pressing suppliers for discounts that may be too large. This can increase profits, the stock price, and management compensation in the short-term, but at the expense of long-term success and profitability. Unhappy stakeholders soon disengage from the company and start to undermine its viability.

The third common cause of stakeholder cancer is team members. Team members are vital to the success of every enterprise. However, they can sometimes become selfish, damaging the whole business system of which they are part. Some organizations that are not strongly subject to market discipline develop a culture of entitlement. We also see this when some powerful labor unions pursue their own short-term interests and ignore the collective good of the other stakeholders. In the United States, overly powerful labor unions have undermined the long-term competiveness of the automobile, steel, and airline industries (in addition to management failures, of course).

A Declaration of Interdependence

The Declaration of Interdependence is a unique manifesto that was created at Whole Foods Market in 1985 after a conflict among the original founders.[5] The conflict had led to the departure of one of the founders, and the company became divided into camps. We hired an outside consultant, Chris Hitt (who later joined the company), to take us through a vision and values clarification process. This helped us identify and make explicit the values we had been operating under for the previous five years; in other words, we made our unconscious values more conscious. Hitt was the first to articulate the interdependent nature of our stakeholders, and he helped our company leaders and others to see it. The declaration was then created, with sixty team members (representing 10 percent of the total company in 1985) participating in the process. Together, we decided what we really cared about, and consciously defined the values under which we would operate the business. In 1985, the declaration became our constitution, the guiding document that allowed Whole Foods Market to grow and expand. It was updated in subsequent years. The ideas are now firmly ingrained in the DNA of the company.

Many of the values we talk about in Conscious Capitalism are already present in most businesses; the businesses just aren't fully conscious of them. By making people more conscious and aware of them, we can create a path to build a more conscious company. By giving people the language and the structure they need, we enable their energy to be harnessed in constructive ways.

Future Search: Creating the Future Together

Whole Foods conducted its first so-called Future Search in 1988 and we've done a Future Search every five years since then.[6] This powerful process usually

173

lasts about three days. At each gathering, we bring together between 100 and 125 people, including customers, team members, suppliers, investors, some board members, and all of our senior leadership. During each Future Search, we envision how we want the company to evolve and what the collective dream of all the stakeholders is. All the participants bring their own specific perspectives. By bringing the whole system together, we can make extraordinary progress in a short amount of time. If only the leadership were involved, we would have to guess what each of the stakeholders most value, and the guesses would sometimes be wrong. But with representatives from each stakeholder group in the room together, there is no need to guess.

Of course, those present only represent a cross section of the thoughts and desires of all of our stakeholders. We can only bring a dozen or so customers to the event, and they can't speak for all of our twenty million–plus customers. Likewise, we can only have a limited number of team members, suppliers, and investors attend. But they still have a specific and valuable perspective. They appreciate Whole Foods Market in their own distinctive ways; they see the company through different eyes and can vividly convey what they see to the whole group. They also can transcend that narrow identity and develop a true sense of ownership and identification with the whole organization.

It is fascinating to watch the interactions that occur when we bring the whole system together like this. We did our first Future Search about three years after we created our Declaration of Interdependence. The process was so powerful that we decided to repeat it every few years. Every five years is frequent enough to put forth a compelling guiding vision, and long enough to allow for its implementation and refinement. It has been inspiring for us to see our vision evolve over the twenty-four years we have been doing this. Looking back, we can see how much Whole Foods Market has successfully actualized the visions articulated in our Future Search meetings.

There may be no more important truth in our book than this: *What we collectively envision, we can create and bring into reality.* Together we create our future reality, so we should do so consciously, collaboratively, and responsibly. The Good, the True, the Beautiful, and the Heroic can be made manifest in our world through the power of our collective creative dreams.

THE INTERDEPENDENCE OF STAKEHOLDERS

Owners and Investors and Legal Control

Optimizing value for all the interdependent stakeholders does not mean a loss of legal control of the business for the investors. The owners and investors must legally control the business to prevent their exploitation by management and by the other stakeholders. This is because owners and investors are paid last. The customers are paid first in their relationships with the business—in that they come in, find products or services they desire, purchase those products or services, receive those products or services fairly quickly, and often pay after the product or service has been rendered to them. For example, they eat before they have to pay at a café. Team members render their services and are paid on a short-term, periodic basis. The suppliers are paid according to agreed-upon terms and time frames, and government taxes are remitted monthly and quarterly. Owners and investors are paid last, after everyone else has received goods, services, wages, or payment. They are entitled to whatever is left over, the residual profits. Because they are paid last, investors must have legal and fiduciary control of the business to prevent management or other stakeholders from shortchanging them. Investors usually demand these conditions as a requirement for investing their capital in a business.

Since stockholders own the corporation but are paid last, from the residual profits left over from the business, it is essential that they have the final say, through the board of directors, on who makes up company management. They need to have the ultimate power to fire management if they are unhappy with the performance of the company. Without that power, inevitably the stockholders will eventually be exploited by management or some other stakeholder of the business.

In the next part of the book, we'll look at the third tenet of Conscious Capitalism: conscious leadership.

PART THREE

THE THIRD TENET

Conscious Leadership

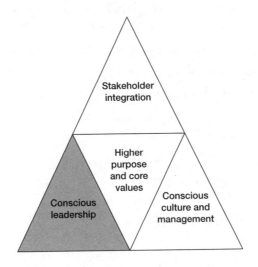

One of the most effective and powerful statements of purpose we have recently seen comes from the leadership development firm Pivot: "Better leaders = Better world."[1] Leadership matters a great deal, and the reason it matters is broader than organizational performance. The quality of our leaders affects the quality of our lives. Every good leader contributes in ways, big and small, toward making the world a better place—one day, one life, and one company at a time.

Conscious leadership is perhaps the most important element in Conscious Capitalism. Without conscious leadership, little else matters. The finest, most conscious corporation can be led badly astray and even destroyed if it hires or promotes the wrong kind of leaders.

From Military to Mercenary to Missionary Leaders

Our understanding of what constitutes great leadership has changed as our collective consciousness has grown. Leaders, like all people, are typically motivated by some combination of power, money, and purpose.

Historically, corporations were modeled on the military. The command-and-control leadership culture of the military became part of corporate culture as well. Companies attracted individuals who were primarily motivated by the opportunity to exercise a great deal of power. With the military as a model, business came to be seen as warfare, and the myth "The best warriors make the best leaders" became widely held. The language and metaphors of business borrowed heavily from the military: strategic and tactical decision making, and expressions such as *hit the deadline, engage the frontline, rally the troops, work with the staff*, and *capture market share.*[2]

With strong hired leaders at the helm, many large companies increasingly came to be seen as being run more for the benefit of managers than for shareholders. This led to the shareholder rights movement, one of the consequences of which was to start rewarding CEOs heavily for increasing the stock price. CEOs went from being quite modestly paid to receiving exorbitant salaries and large amounts of stock options. The rationale was to give managers strong incentives to become personally wealthy by increasing the stock price of the company. Thus, we went from military-style leadership to "mercenary leadership." Such leaders manage by the numbers, often viewing the business as an abstraction. They usually have no passion for any particular business, nor do they necessarily enjoy the exercise of power for its own sake. They are hired guns who seemingly possess the ability to spur companies to perform at a higher level and thus increase their market value. However, such leaders usually operate with short time horizons and tend to largely disregard the interests of stakeholders other than shareholders, because their own personal wealth is tied to the share price. Often, such leaders take actions that are harmful to the business in the long term. Their leadership approach is focused on eliciting compliance and is particularly ineffective at generating widespread team member engagement and enthusiasm.

Conscious companies are led by emotionally and spiritually mature leaders. Such conscious leaders are primarily motivated by service to the purpose of the business and its stakeholders, and not by the pursuit of power or personal enrichment. They develop and inspire, mentor and motivate, and lead by example. Rather than militaristic or mercenary, they are missionary leaders. They embody Mahatma Gandhi's dictum "We must be the change we wish to see in the world."

Conscious leaders are strong individuals who possess exceptional moral courage and are able to withstand constant scrutiny and criticism from those who view business in a more traditional, narrow manner. Above all, conscious leaders view themselves as trustees of the business, seeking to nurture and safeguard it for future generations, not to exploit it for the short-term gains of themselves or current stakeholders.

The Rise of Feminine Values

For millennia, human communities and most societal institutions have largely operated on the "masculine" traits of aggression, ambition, competition, and left-brain domination. The worlds of politics and business exemplified these traits and in fact demanded these of successful leaders.

However, we are now seeing a significant rise in the appreciation of the "feminine" values of caring, compassion, cooperation, and more right-brain qualities, heralding a harmonious blending of these human values in our work and life. Conscious businesses certainly embody both perspectives, whether they are led by men or women.

THE THIRD TENET: CONSCIOUS LEADERSHIP

Women around the world today have greater access to education, employment, and opportunities than they had before. Women already outnumber men in the workforce in the United States. The increase in women's access to higher education has been dramatic. A century ago, fewer than 20 percent of college students were women. Today, women account for almost 60 percent of college students at the undergraduate level and 70 percent at the graduate level in the United States. The numbers are similar in many other countries. On average, women also perform better academically. As a result, most white-collar professions will likely soon be dominated by women, including fields such as law, medicine, and education.

Further, the women who do rise to positions of power today are different from their earlier counterparts. In the male-dominated world a few decades ago, the only women who could rise to the top in countries or in companies were those who were tougher than the toughest men. Golda Meir in Israel, Indira Gandhi in India, and Margaret Thatcher in Great Britain demonstrated this. Thatcher was famously known as the Iron Lady, and Indira Gandhi was said to be the only man in her own cabinet. Women leaders today seem comfortable with their own femininity, recognizing and respecting the wisdom inherent in their caring and nurturing approach to leading organizations. Anne Mulcahy at Xerox; Indra Nooyi at PepsiCo, Inc.; Terri Kelly at W. L. Gore; and Sally Jewell at REI and their unique style of leadership demonstrate this shift.

Interestingly, as they age, many men also start exhibiting more of their own feminine qualities in their leadership style and relationships. This is partly related to hormonal changes, but also reflects life experience. Many women become more assertive, independent, and straightforward as they mature. Combined, these shifts point to the continued rise of feminine values in our culture, affecting all major societal institutions.

The business sector presents an interesting dichotomy. In the United States, women own over 40 percent of private businesses and start 70 percent of new businesses.[3] However, there are still very few women CEOs and directors at large publicly traded companies, which many women regard as hostile to families and feminine values. Women hold approximately 15 percent of board seats at *Fortune* 500 companies. As of this writing, there are eighteen women CEOs of *Fortune* 500 companies. That is only 3.6 percent, but it is up from just three women, or 0.6 percent, in 2000. Interestingly, Gallup's research on confidence in societal institutions shows that confidence in small businesses (where women are very well represented) is much higher, at around 65 percent, than confidence in big business (where women are under-represented), at around 19 percent.

These statistics evoke an interesting question: how would recent economic events have been different if so-called feminine values had been dominant in the past? Or as Christine Lagarde, managing director of the International Monetary Fund asked, "What if Lehman Brothers had been Lehman Sisters?"

Leadership and Management

Leadership and management are not synonymous. Leadership is mostly about change and transformation. Management is about efficiency and implementation. Leaders are the high-level architects, builders, and remodelers of the system, while managers ensure that the system works smoothly and take corrective actions when it doesn't. Leaders have an inherent systemic sensitivity that enables them to understand both how a group of people will behave as a system and how to change the system in order to change its behavior.

Mahatma Gandhi's approach to nonviolence was once challenged by a history professor, who cited his "knowledge of history" to argue that Gandhi's philosophy of nonviolence would never work. Gandhi replied, "Sir, your job is to teach history while mine is to create it."[4] Managers do not make history; conscious leaders do. They imagine and bring into existence that which did not exist before and which most thought could not be done.

We are not suggesting that companies always need more leadership and less management. They need both but in the right measure and in ways that are complementary. In other words, the leadership and management approaches need to be in harmony. As Harvard Business School professor John Kotter puts it, "Too much management without enough leadership leads to too much stability and inward focus. This eventually results in stagnation, decline and probably the death of the organization. Too much leadership without enough management is also dangerous; the company lacks organizational capacity, operational discipline and efficiency, and the business can become very risky."[5]

In this part of the book, we first discuss the qualities of conscious leaders and then provide some suggestions on how you can become a more conscious leader. Then in part 4, we will address conscious cultures and the kind of management philosophy needed to enable conscious businesses to function at their peak.

CHAPTER 13

The Qualities of Conscious Leaders

Conscious leaders abundantly display many of the qualities we most admire in exemplary human beings. They usually find great joy and beauty in their work, and in the opportunity to serve, lead, and help shape a better future. Since they are living their calling, they are authentic individuals who are eager to share their passion with others. They are very dedicated to their work, which recharges and energizes them instead of draining them.

Conscious leaders commonly have high analytical, emotional, spiritual, and systems intelligence. They also have an orientation toward servant leadership, high integrity, and a great capacity for love and care.

There is no one-size-fits-all model of leadership. Conscious leaders have much in common with each other, but much more that is unique to each individual. They are keenly self-aware and recognize their own deepest motivations and convictions. They don't try to be someone they are not. As Bill George, former CEO of Medtronic, puts it, "Great leadership is authentic leadership. Authenticity is not a characteristic; it is who you are. It means knowing who you are and what your purpose is. Your True North is what you believe at the deepest level, what truly defines you—your beliefs, your values, your passions, and the principles you live by."[1]

Types of Intelligence

In recent years, thanks largely to the work of Harvard professors and developmental psychologists Robert Kegan and Howard Gardner, we have come to understand human capabilities and potential in a much richer way. Kegan and Gardner's independent research shows that human beings are equipped with many kinds of intelligence in different proportions.[2] Most conscious leaders have high analytical intelligence (the kind measured by IQ tests). This is virtually a prerequisite for being a successful leader today in large, complex organizations. But we now recognize that having a high IQ without also having high emotional intelligence (EQ), spiritual intelligence (SQ), and systems intelligence (SYQ) is inadequate and can be harmful to an organization. Bad decisions will be made based on short-term considerations that lack a system wide perspective of what is good for all of the interdependent stakeholders over the long-term. The business will be suboptimized with this type of narrow high IQ leadership. Relationships, stakeholder management, and a keen appreciation for values and purpose are essential for effective leadership in the complex world of the twenty-first century, and analytical intelligence by itself does not equip leaders to handle these.

A crucial difference between the different types of intelligences is that a person's IQ does not easily change very much after adulthood begins, while emotional, spiritual, and systems intelligences can be developed and enhanced all our lives.

Emotional Intelligence

EQ combines intrapersonal (understanding oneself) and interpersonal (understanding others) intelligence. Self-awareness, the core of what it means to be more conscious, is the first pillar of emotional intelligence. Empathy—

the ability to feel and understand what others are feeling—is the second pillar. High EQ is increasingly important in all organizations because of the growing complexity of society and the multiplicity of stakeholders that must be understood and communicated with effectively.[3]

Whole Foods Market has found that it is far more important for our leaders to have high EQ than a high IQ. Our stores are organized into self-managing teams that focus intently on delivering high levels of customer service. We can't afford to have analytically brilliant people if they are also arrogant, insensitive, or tactless. Our company culture therefore tends to look for high EQ in leadership promotions. Chapter 14 will discuss in more detail how to cultivate higher EQ.

Spiritual Intelligence

Conscious leaders frequently have high SQ, which has been well defined in a wonderful book by Danah Zohar and Ian Marshall titled *Spiritual Capital*: "Spiritual intelligence is the intelligence with which we access our deepest meanings, values, purposes, and higher motivations. It is . . . our moral intelligence, giving us an innate ability to distinguish right from wrong. It is the intelligence with which we exercise goodness, truth, beauty, and compassion in our lives."[4] SQ is what helps us to discover our own personal higher purposes in our work and our lives. Conscious leaders with high SQ have a remarkable ability to help align their organizations with their organizations' higher purposes. They also have uncanny discernment to sense when things are beginning to go off track. A good example of high-SQ leadership was provided by Howard Schultz, the entrepreneur behind Starbucks' tremendous success. In 2008, Starbucks went through a very difficult time as its business declined. It had to close six hundred underperforming stores, eliminate twelve thousand jobs (out of two hundred thousand that had been created), and take a $340 million asset write-off for the closed stores. Schultz believed that Starbucks had moved away from its higher purpose and had gotten off track by just chasing after growth and higher financial returns. This happened over several years after he had stepped down as the CEO. As Schultz explains, he decided to return to Starbucks as the CEO to reconnect the company to its core purpose: "From the very beginning we always believed that the only way we could exceed the expectations of our customers was to exceed the expectations of our people. So given the external pressures, the cataclysmic financial crisis, it was time to return to the intimacy of communicating directly with our people, galvanizing our organization against a core purpose, and asking our people to understand what was at stake."[5]

After Schultz returned and recommitted Starbucks to its core purpose and its sense of authenticity, the company experienced an amazing turnaround. Same-store sales accelerated from negative 6 percent in fiscal 2009 to positive 8 percent in 2011, net profits more than tripled, and the value of the stock increased from about $7 to more than $50 over three years.

Systems Intelligence

Another important type of intelligence conscious leaders tend to have in abundance is SYQ, introduced in the preceding chapter. Conscious leaders are natural systems thinkers. They can see the bigger picture and understand how the different components of the system interconnect and behave over time. They can anticipate the immediate as well as long-term consequences of actions. Given their intuitive understanding of systems, conscious leaders are excellent organizational architects. They understand the roots of problems and how the problems relate to organizational design, and they devise fundamental solutions instead of applying symptomatic quick fixes.

Conscious leaders are also systems *feelers*; they feel the interconnectedness and oneness of the system within their being.[6] As a result, they can prevent many problems from occurring in the first place. This capacity is well illustrated by a story from Bian Que, a Chinese physician from 2,300 years ago. It is about three brothers, all doctors. The oldest was known for performing dramatic procedures on patients whose diseases had reached an advanced stage, and he was widely celebrated for his heroic efforts to save his patients. The middle brother was highly skilled at catching and curing diseases when they exhibited early symptoms; he was considered good for treating minor ailments and was only admired locally. The third brother had the ability to detect the earliest trace of a disease and cure it before the patient felt any symptoms at all. He was little appreciated and virtually unknown, but he saved many more lives than his more famous brothers.[7]

Many leaders in business and in politics lurch from crisis to crisis, repeatedly allowing situations to deteriorate until they reach a crisis point. They then take drastic actions to solve the problem, which often don't work. Like the third brother, the best leaders are those who prevent most problems from arising in the first place; their genius may go unrecognized and even unrewarded, but they are the most effective leaders, with keenly developed systems minds and sensibilities.

The next chapter will discuss how leaders can cultivate their SYQ.

Servant Leadership

The great humanitarian and Nobel Peace Prize winner Albert Schweitzer said, "I don't know what your destiny will be, but one thing I do know: the only ones among you who will be really happy are those who have sought and found how to serve." Conscious leaders, with their strong analytical, emotional, spiritual, and systems intelligences, are acutely aware of the importance of service in helping their organizations realize their highest potential. They also know that helping others leads to more personal happiness.

Such leaders have learned the secret of the "helpers' high:" we feel good when we make other people happy. It creates value for the giver and the recipient, as well as for the larger community. Servant leaders cultivate the noble virtue of generosity. They embrace transpersonal values—such as goodness, justice, truth, love, the alleviation of suffering, the salvation or enlightenment of others—that lift them to higher levels of consciousness.[8]

The story of Buckminster Fuller provides a great illustration of the power of servant leadership. At age thirty-two, Fuller was living in low-income public housing in Chicago. His daughter had recently died from polio and spinal meningitis. Fuller was drinking heavily, chronically depressed, and seriously considering committing suicide. One night, while standing on a bridge and trying to decide whether to jump to his death, he asked himself questions about the meaning of life. What would make life worth living? In a sudden flash of spiritual insight, the answer came to him. He would begin "an experiment, to determine how much a single individual could contribute to changing the world and benefiting all humankind."[9] The answer, it turns out, is "quite a lot." Over the next fifty-five years until his death, he patented over two thousand inventions, wrote twenty-five books, and went down in history as one of the greatest thinkers, inventors, and servant leaders who ever lived. The Buckminster Fuller game of doing as much good as possible to benefit the world is a game we can all play. Servant leaders show us how to do exactly this.[10]

Integrity: The Synthesis of the Virtues

Perhaps the most important virtue of conscious leaders is integrity. Honesty is often used as a synonym for integrity, but integrity is a more comprehensive virtue because, while it is partly about honesty, it goes beyond just telling the truth. Integrity has the same root as the word *integer*, which means "wholeness." It includes authenticity, fairness, trustworthiness, and moral courage; it involves doing what we believe is true to our values and the right thing to do whatever the circumstances, even when it may involve substantial personal cost.

We need not be a hero or saint to have high integrity. Integrity is neither particularly common nor exceptionally rare in life. Everyone can and should aspire to integrity in life—to unify his or her values and virtues and express them within the context of the larger community, including where a person works. People who fail to achieve integrity can be accurately described using terms such as hypocrites, opportunists, yes-men (or yes-women), and ethical cowards.[11]

Famous historical leaders with high integrity include Socrates, Abraham Lincoln, Gandhi, Martin Luther King Jr., Nelson Mandela, Aleksandr Solzhenitsyn, Margaret Thatcher, and Liu Xiaobo. These exceptional leaders greatly inspire us to seek to attain higher levels of integrity, especially in their expression of moral courage.

Capacity for Love and Care

Conscious leaders have a great capacity for love and care. They recognize how important it is to drive fear out of their organizations. When leaders combine their intellectual abilities with their ability to care for things beyond themselves, they have real power. Martin Luther King Jr. understood this well: "Power properly understood is nothing but the ability to achieve purpose. It is the strength required to bring about social, political, and economic change. There is nothing wrong with power if power is used correctly . . . Power at its best is love implementing the demands of justice, and justice at its best is power correcting everything that stands against love."[12]

Fear is the opposite of love. An organization suffused with fear is inherently less capable of real creativity and innovation. Fearful people are hypervigilant, defensive, and purely self-interested. We will discuss love and care further in chapter 15.

What Conscious Leaders Do

Conscious leaders seek to make a positive impact on the world through their organization. They deeply embed a sense of shared purpose, enabling people to derive meaning from their work. They help people grow and evolve as individuals and as leaders in their own right, and they make tough moral choices with clarity and consistency.

THE THIRD TENET: CONSCIOUS LEADERSHIP

Make a Positive Difference

Success has many definitions, including narrow ones such as "the attainment of wealth, favor, or eminence." But conscious leaders understand that the definition of success changes as we progress in our journey of rising consciousness. Today, people increasingly define success in ways that include making a lasting, positive impact on the world.

Conscious leaders have a passion for making the world better in some significant way. They shoulder responsibility not to maintain the status quo, but to make a positive difference. They want to alleviate human suffering and help others flourish. Of course, they can only do this by mobilizing others to strive toward the same ends. Effective leaders seldom have to *force* people to do things; they inspire and motivate others to commit to change voluntarily.

Embed a Shared Purpose

The best conscious leaders are merchants of hope and entrepreneurs of meaning. They continually engage their colleagues around questions of identity and purpose. They build organizations whose higher purpose becomes engrained into the DNA. This is most effectively done through story telling. As Gardner's research shows, people are able to effect real change only when their emotions are engaged. Stories are the most powerful way of engaging with people at an emotional level; they can cause people to think, feel, and behave differently. Gardner has found that effective leaders tell three types of stories: "Who I am," "Who we are," and "Where we're going."[13]

Help People Grow and Evolve

The human journey should be one of continuous growth and personal development. In addition to their personal life, people's work provides a great opportunity for growth. Some people find their greatest joy and calling in work that is not remunerative, in the work they do at home or in voluntary organizations.

THE QUALITIES OF CONSCIOUS LEADERS

Conscious leaders treat all people with respect, regardless of their rank or role. The late, legendary Indian business leader JRD Tata, longtime head of the highly conscious Tata Group, demonstrated this quality repeatedly. Some team members on strike were once demonstrating outside his office, waving flags and chanting slogans. Tata looked out and saw them as human beings first, not just as protesting laborers. He told the HR manager, "Look, they have the right to demonstrate, but they should not stand like that under the hot sun. Why don't you give them a cold drink and ask them to stand in the shade?"[14]

Conscious leaders appreciate the unique talents and gifts of each individual and play to a person's strengths, thus putting the individual in a position to succeed and contribute to the organization. Debashis Chatterjee, director of the Indian Institute of Management Kozhikode, puts it well: "We all have our own capabilities and talents, but if we demand from a person what is not his natural quality, if we ask a horse to fly or a bird to run, we will do a disservice both to the horse and to the bird . . . Business grows because people grow the business, and people grow in the business."[15]

Make Tough Moral Choices

Leaders are often confronted with dilemmas in which they have to choose between courses of action that may each be right from certain perspectives. Harvard professor of business ethics Joseph Badaracco points out that many moral issues are easy, because they involve a choice between something that is clearly right and something that is obviously wrong. The real test of leadership comes when "the choice is between right and right . . . Right versus right is much harder because you're pulled in different directions by things that are genuine responsibilities."[16] In such cases, conscious leaders act in accordance with the company's purpose and its core values to make choices that result in the most long-term value for all of the stakeholders. Rather than sacrifice a higher value for a lower value, they seek strategies that can simultaneously fulfill multiple values.

For example, a tough moral choice we face at Whole Foods is our simultaneous commitment to sell a full selection of animal foods because over 95 percent of the stores' customers eat these foods, and our commitment to improve the health and longevity of our customers, as well as our desire to improve animal welfare. Research shows that the consumption of animal foods beyond about 10 percent of total calories correlates closely with increases in obesity, heart disease, stroke, and cancer.[17] We want to simultaneously satisfy, delight, and nourish our customers while also helping them to be as healthy as possible. These are two of our most important core values. How can we satisfy both of these worthwhile core values, which can be in tension with each other? We try to do this in two ways. First, we educate our customers about the importance of eating primarily minimally processed and unrefined plant foods; these are the healthiest foods we can eat and should ideally constitute 90 percent or more of our total calories. Second, we continually work to upgrade the quality and welfare of the animal foods that we do sell. For example, all of our stores now carry 100 percent grass-fed beef and lamb, which is lower in saturated and total fats. We also offer chicken, eggs, pork, and turkey from pasture-raised animals. In addition, we help guide our shoppers to choose seafood that is low in mercury and high in omega-3 essential fatty acids (such as wild-caught sustainable salmon). We believe that our dual strategy of educating customers about the value of eating primarily minimally processed and unrefined plant foods, combined with improving the healthiness of the animal foods that we do sell, is a win-win approach.

The Danger of Charismatic Leadership

Leaders don't need to be particularly charismatic to be effective. Human willpower and charisma can be extraordinarily powerful, but they can be destructive as well. When power and virtue do not coexist in a leader, terrible things can result. We have seen this throughout history, especially in the twentieth century with leaders like Hitler, Stalin, and Mao.

Conscious leaders harness the "better angels of our nature" toward shared ideals. They have great determination, but it does not come from a place of ego or self-gratification. Rather than seeking to impose their individual will on the organization, they seek to sense and serve its collective spirit.

Conscious leaders are often quiet and down-to-earth, leading by example rather than through charm or the force of their personality. They focus on building great organizations that endure over time. Charismatic leaders, by contrast, tend to create organizations that are heavily dependent on them; as soon as they leave, things begin to fall apart. One of the most famous charismatic leader of all times was Alexander the Great, who conquered the world in eleven years. However, his empire fell apart soon after his death. That is why some leadership experts suggest that the real test of a leader's effectiveness should be judged by how well his or her successor does.[18]

Of course, some conscious leaders are also very charismatic; it is just not a necessary condition of leadership. Herb Kelleher, the longtime leader of Southwest Airlines, is one of the most charismatic business leaders of the past half century, but also one of the most authentic. Other less charismatic leaders have followed Kelleher, however, and the company has sustained its unique culture and record of success. Kelleher built a great organization with rock-solid values and an abiding sense of purpose. We expect that the company will continue to endure for many more decades with its values and essence intact.

All leaders, but especially highly charismatic ones, are susceptible to the trap of narcissism. The best way to fight this tendency is to have trusted advisers such as coaches, colleagues, and friends who have an independent perspective and can give leaders the straight truth they need to hear.

Why Leadership Matters

Leadership matters. It matters today more than ever. But the old way has run its course. Leadership in the third millennium must be based on the power of purpose, love, caring, and compassion. Conscious leadership is fully human leadership; it integrates the masculine and feminine, the heart and the mind, the spirit and the soul. It integrates Western systems and efficiency with Eastern wisdom and effectiveness.

For millennia, most men (and they were mostly men) who became leaders were driven to attain these roles because of their thirst for power or lust for riches. They used fear, oppression, and brutality to achieve their goals. But their successes were inevitably short-lived, because the leaders' actions continually sowed the seeds of the next upheaval, the next rebellion, the emergence of the next ruthless leader.

When businesses are led by individuals who are driven by service to people and the firm's higher purpose—who lead through developing and inspiring others—it leads, in author Fred Kofman's resonant words, to "peace and happiness in the individual, respect and solidarity in the community, and mission accomplishment in the organization."[19]

In the next chapter, we present some specific ideas on how an individual can evolve toward becoming a more conscious leader.

CHAPTER 14

Becoming a Conscious Leader

A business cannot truly evolve, learn, and grow if its leaders—particularly the CEO—are not learning and growing as well. Companies can become blocked from essential organizational evolution if their founder is psychologically and spiritually stuck. Some companies can only grow and evolve once the founder leaves. For example, the Ford Motor Company achieved great heights and had a huge impact on the world under Henry Ford's leadership. But eventually, his obstinate refusal to adapt his thinking to changed market circumstances started to really hurt the company. More than once in the history of Whole Foods Market, the company was unable to collectively evolve until I myself was able to evolve—in other words, I was holding the company back. My personal growth enabled the company also to evolve.

Since leadership can often prevent the company from reaching its highest potential, one of the best motivations for wanting to learn and grow is that it will be beneficial not just in our own lives, but also in the lives of all those with whom we interact, including the company and all the people it touches.

THE THIRD TENET: CONSCIOUS LEADERSHIP

To become a conscious leader, you have to aspire to be one. Without high intentionality, it just doesn't happen. Personal growth is rarely an easy thing; it takes great effort and usually involves some pain, as we make mistakes and learn from them.

Follow Your Heart and Find Your Purpose

Life is short and death is certain. No one is getting out of here alive. How, then, should we live our lives? For us, the answer is clear: commit ourselves to following our hearts and doing what we most love and what is most meaningful to us in life.

To discover your own higher life purposes, ask yourself what you really care about the most. What are your passions, your deepest yearnings? If you could do absolutely anything in the world, what would you do? Your inner heart knows the answers to these questions. It is whispering to you right now even as you read these words. Quiet your mind, listen attentively to your inner heart, and follow its guidance. This communication from your inner heart may come as gentle words or perhaps as a knowing intuition, but there is a quiet certainty to its truth. Our inner heart will always be our best guide in life if we can develop enough self-awareness to be able to hear it and the courage to follow it.

There are two important aspects to hearing and following our hearts. First, we need to enhance our self-awareness so we know when we are truly following our hearts and when we've lost our way. When we are truly following our hearts (and not just our egos, which is what most of us do most of the time), we are tapped into our true passions in life. We are doing what we most love, and we find our lives full of increased energy, creativity, joy, and purpose. We simply feel more alive when we are moving within the flow of life.

How do we know when we've stopped following our heart? When the opposite happens: we experience decreased energy, lack of creativity, no real sense of purpose, and unhappiness. It means that we have stepped out of the flow of our lives and are either just drifting along or actively working against our heart's guidance. When this happens, the solution is simple: choose again. Reconnect with your heart. As long as we are alive, it is never too late. We are free in each moment to choose the path of our heart, which never stops quietly whispering to us, urging us to follow it.

The second key to successfully following our hearts is to learn how to deal with fear. Fear prevents people from reaching their fullest potential in life. It comes in many flavors—fear of looking ridiculous, fear of failure, fear of rejection, fear that we simply aren't good enough, and sometimes even fear of our own potential greatness. Unfortunately, no one else can overcome our fear for us; we must learn to master it on our own.

The most important insight about fear is that it seldom exists in the present moment. It is almost always about the future, something we are afraid is going to happen. When we direct our attention fully into the present moment, fear greatly lessens or disappears. The second important insight about fear is that it is almost always a creation of our minds; it rarely exists in the physical world. We can dissolve fear in our minds by bringing self-awareness to it and consciously choosing not to give any additional energy to the fearful thoughts. Rather, we should use the energy that fear creates to focus the mind more intently on the present moment—where fear doesn't exist. We must learn how to do this if we really want to be free from fear and stay connected to our hearts and to our higher purposes. Contemplative practices that teach us how to quiet our minds and focus our attention can also help us overcome fear.

Many people have found this quote from Frank Herbert's wonderful science fiction novel *Dune* useful when dealing with fear:

I must not fear.
Fear is the mind-killer.
Fear is the little-death that brings total obliteration.
I will face my fear.
I will permit it to pass over me and through me.
And when it has gone past I will turn the inner eye to see its path.
Where the fear has gone there will be nothing.
Only I will remain.[1]

Role Models

A time-tested way to grow is to find role models—people whom we most admire and want to emulate. We're naturally attracted to people who embody the qualities, ideals, and character virtues we most want to realize within ourselves. Those qualities and virtues are usually already within us, but are not yet fully developed.

It is very healthy to look up to admirable people. They could be friends, parents, siblings, or teachers. They could be people from history, such as Abraham Lincoln, Martin Luther King Jr., or Gandhi. We can admire and try to emulate living people whom we've never met, such as Nelson Mandela or Muhammad Yunus. If we follow a particular religious faith, our inspiration might come from Moses, Jesus, St. Francis, Mohammed, Patanjali, Krishna, or Buddha. We can even look to fictional characters who vividly express admirable virtues, such as Atticus Finch in Harper Lee's *To Kill a Mockingbird* or Albus Dumbledore in J. K. Rowling's series of Harry Potter novels.

We should make a conscious decision and effort to begin practicing the virtues of people we admire. Ask yourself questions like, "What would Warren Buffett do in this situation?" or "How would my father have handled this?" By asking such questions, we push ourselves to grow, because the answers would probably be, "They would have done something prudent, but caring; they would have done something with integrity; they would have chosen to do the difficult but right thing." We can make the same choices.

Coaches and Mentors

A good coach or a mentor can be transformational. In my business career at Whole Foods Market, my father was my mentor from the time I cofounded the company at age twenty-five until I was about forty. In college, I had studied the humanities—philosophy, religion, history, and literature—and didn't take any business courses at all. So when we started the company, I had virtually no business experience or knowledge. I was very fortunate because my father knew a great deal about business. He had first been an accounting professor at

Rice University, after which he went into business and became a successful CEO of a public company. His mentorship, combined with the many hundreds of books I read on business, gave me the foundation I needed to make fewer mistakes and to learn quickly from the ones I did make. I don't think I would have been successful in business had I not had him as my coach and mentor. In fact, I'm pretty sure I would have wrecked Whole Foods Market in my youth.

There also may come a time when we have to let our mentor go. In my own life, this happened when I turned forty. Whole Foods Market had been a public company for a couple of years and we were very successful. My father was thirty-two years my senior. He had retired, and much of his wealth was then tied up in Whole Foods Market stock. He became increasingly conservative, because he understandably didn't want to lose what he had. He wanted me to lead the company differently than I thought was appropriate. He wanted the company to grow slowly, without taking risks, while I wanted it to grow much more rapidly.

For me, the big moment came when I realized I didn't want or need him to be my coach or mentor any longer. Our business disagreements were beginning to interfere with our close relationship as father and son. We were arguing frequently, especially at board meetings. After anguishing about our deteriorating relationship for several months, I finally decided to ask him to step down from the Whole Foods Market board. This was extremely difficult for me because I loved him very much, and I didn't want to hurt him or harm our relationship. I went to his office and said, "Dad, I'm forty years old. The business mentorship is over. For better or for worse, I'm moving on now on my own. I would still like you to be in my life and be supportive, but I have to make the major decisions about Whole Foods Market now, and I can't and won't always follow your advice." I told him he could stay on as an unpaid consultant to the company, and I would continue to ask his advice on important business decisions, but he needed to resign from the board of directors. I thanked him for all he had done for me and told him how much I loved him. This was a huge leap forward in my own personal growth, because I also let go of the emotional dependency I had on him. That helped me accelerate my own growth in new directions.

My father was hurt initially. But within a year, he told me I had made the right decision, and we were as close as ever.

THE THIRD TENET: CONSCIOUS LEADERSHIP

Cultivating the Higher Virtues

People develop their character by cultivating higher virtues and positive emotions. The most important virtues to help people learn and grow are universal and timeless: love, courage, integrity, generosity, gratitude, compassion, forgiveness, and temperance, to name a few. All these qualities define a good person and make for a good life. These life-affirming virtues seldom appear in our lives automatically; we usually have to consciously work to cultivate them within ourselves.

Ultimately, the aspiration to embody these virtues is what helps raise us to a higher level. It is essential that we strive to embody the higher virtues and practice living them every day. This isn't easy; it requires determination, consistency, persistence, and willpower. As Ralph Waldo Emerson said, "Sow a thought and you reap an action; sow an act and you reap a habit; sow a habit and you reap a character; sow a character and you reap a destiny."

Cultivating character through the intentional use of will is no longer a particularly fashionable idea, especially with many intellectuals who are apt to poke fun at the self-help books that advocate this. Immensely popular in the nineteenth-century Victorian age, conscious self-improvement fell out of intellectual favor in the latter half of the twentieth century with the development of many psychological theories that diminished the importance of self-responsibility. This is very unfortunate because cultivating our characters consciously through the practice of the higher virtues is still one of the most valuable strategies for personal growth available to us. A selective study of self-help books could prove to be catalytic for many people.[2]

Developing Your Emotional Intelligence

A time-tested way to learn and grow, as Socrates said, is to "know thyself." Self-awareness is also one of the key qualities that Daniel Goleman identified in his impactful book *Emotional Intelligence*. Our emotions, to a certain extent, are windows into our soul. There is an entire universe within us waiting to be discovered. We can learn so much about ourselves by being aware of our emotions and understanding why we're experiencing them. Over time, as our self-awareness grows, we can begin to observe ourselves as we experience our emotions. It's useful to ask, "Why does this make me angry?" "Why am I excited about that?" "Why am I envious of that person?" "Why do I feel joyful about this?" "Why am I experiencing love?" Each of our emotions is a window into who we are and what we care about.

If we lack awareness of our own feelings, values, aspirations, and ideals, we go through life following impulses and desires without being conscious of why we're doing what we are doing. Growing our self-awareness is a continuous process that lasts a lifetime.

Emotions arise from the various interpretations that we make about situations and events. But we often don't realize that we are largely free to interpret situations and events in different ways. For example, the emotion *anger* is based on the interpretation that we have been wronged in some way and that some type of punishment is appropriate for whoever has wronged us. However, if we change our interpretation about what has made us angry, we are likely to find that our anger diminishes as well. We may not be able to fully control our emotions, but we are certainly able to be more conscious of them, take responsibility for them, learn from them, and transcend them when appropriate, moving our consciousness to a higher level.[3]

As we become more aware of our emotions, we begin to realize that many of them, such as envy, resentment, greed, bitterness, malice, anger, and hatred, are life stultifying. They do not further our well-being. They are all natural human emotions, but getting caught up in them seldom makes our lives better. On the other hand, emotions such as love, generosity, gratitude, compassion, and forgiveness are expansive and life enhancing. They enrich our lives. We need to consciously cultivate life-enhancing emotions and learn to neutralize life-stultifying emotions when we become aware of their presence. This is the essence of personal mastery and emotional intelligence.

To be a conscious leader, we especially need to cultivate empathy—the ability to feel what another feels.[4] We need to grow beyond our own self-centeredness. Young children are naturally very egocentric, but as we grow emotionally, we develop the ability to empathize and sympathize with others. We begin to care about more than just ourselves, first with our love for family and friends, and then moving from there to our larger community. Beyond that, virtually every human being alive is someone we could care about, empathize with, understand, even love. And even beyond that, we can love animals and potentially all of life, and all existence. The potential for expansive love is virtually limitless, but it all starts with empathy.

Does this capacity for love start with loving ourselves? It's a tricky question. It usually does, but in recent years, too much emphasis has been placed on self-esteem and loving oneself. We do want to love ourselves, but not just ourselves. Far too many people stop there, and as a result, we now have become a fairly narcissistic society in the United States.[5] We worship celebrities, and millions of people want to be famous for the sake of fame alone and not for the skills or accomplishments that might naturally lead to fame. This is not emotionally intelligent. In fact, it reflects a very low level of overall development. We are not arguing against self-love, but it is just the first step. As we develop our capacity to love and care, we must expand it to include ever-larger and more-inclusive circles.

Developing Your Systems Intelligence

We need to effectively understand the larger business system of which we are a part, and for that we need a well-developed systems intelligence (SYQ), as mentioned earlier in the book. SYQ is not an intelligence that our society has traditionally recognized, admired, encouraged, or rewarded. And yet, in the twenty-first century, as our organizations become more complex and as the world itself is becoming increasingly interdependent, it's hard to overstate how valuable this type of intelligence is.

How can we develop our SYQ? First, we have to recognize that SYQ is different from analytical intelligence (IQ) but also complementary to it. Our analytical intelligence shows up in our ability to compare things and to break them down into parts so we can analyze them. It is also the basis for logic. It's clearly a very useful tool and one that our educational systems have developed reasonably well, at least at the highest levels, but as mentioned before, other types of intelligences are also critical.

One way to develop our SYQ is to study disciplines that clearly embody systems principles, such as ecology, which is the science of living organisms and the relationships between them and the environment. SYQ, above all, can see relationships; it sees how things connect—not separating them out, but seeing the relationships that bind them together.

A good way to develop our SYQ in the business context is to practice thinking in terms of the stakeholder system. The stakeholders of a business all exist in relationship with the business and with each other. The conscious leader knows that every strategic business decision must be made after considering how it will affect and create value for each of the major stakeholders. Will the decision harm one or more of the major stakeholders in some way? Are there any trade-offs? Would alternative strategies avoid creating detrimental trade-offs? Can we devise other strategies that create more total value for the entire interdependent business system?

The exercises that develop EQ and SQ can also help develop our SYQ. Slowing our mind down is essential; the speedy, skittish mind breaks things down, while the less speedy but attentive mind is more capable of being in the here and now, noticing things and the relationships between them, and seeing the larger system.

As always, intentionality plays an important part. We must *aspire* to develop our SYQ, to see the relationships between things. We must give our mind permission and encouragement to develop in that direction and believe that it's worth developing.

Evolving to Higher Levels of Consciousness in Stages

Conscious leaders are not static, because human beings are not static. We are dynamic and evolving. A number of theorists and researchers have produced strong evidence that human beings tend to evolve upward to higher levels of consciousness and complexity. One of the most important contributions of developmental psychology has been to show that this growth in consciousness generally proceeds through distinct stages or waves of development. Here are a few of the most important ones:

- Jean Piaget's work demonstrated how our cognitive intelligence develops through distinct, universal, and cross-cultural stages as children.[6] The highest level of cognitive or analytical intelligence described in his work was what he called formal operational, or the ability to think logically.

- Abraham Maslow's research on the hierarchy of needs shows that we tend to evolve upward to higher need levels, from physical needs at the bottom of the hierarchy to self-actualization and beyond.[7] Conscious businesses help to meet the needs of their stakeholders at all the levels, including self-actualization.

- The research of Clare Graves and his students Don Beck and Christopher Cowan demonstrates how both individuals and cultures tend to evolve upward in terms of a hierarchy of values-based worldviews.[8] Their theory postulates eight distinct stages or waves of values development. These stages can be applied to individuals and to cultures as a whole. Their work is especially important in distinguishing between traditional, modernist, postmodernist, and second-tier or integral levels of consciousness. We believe that the vision and values of Conscious Capitalism expressed in this book are consistent with their articulation of second-tier memes in *Spiral Dynamics*, as well as Ken Wilber's work on integral consciousness.

- Lawrence Kohlberg and Carol Gilligan's research suggests that over time, people's ethics tend to go through several ethical levels or stages, from "obedience to avoid punishment" at the first stage to "universal justice and love" at the highest stage.[9]

- Jane Loevinger, building on Erik Erikson's work, shows that our egos develop in distinct stages over time.[10] She theorizes that the ego can develop through nine levels, from infancy up to a fully integrated level. Conscious leaders tend to operate at Loevinger's highest levels.

People have great difficulty fully comprehending or appreciating stages of development that are higher or more complex than their current level. The higher levels just don't make much sense from the perspective of a lower level and therefore are usually ignored, dismissed, or disparaged. Our self-esteem is easily threatened by the possibility that our current personal level of development isn't really the highest pinnacle of human development. As a result, each developmental stage tends to develop its own unique form of orthodoxy, or *stage absolutism*, that keeps people stuck at a certain level.

Conscious leaders avoid becoming stuck in any kind of rigid ideological orthodoxy. Rather, they strive to evolve their consciousness upward in a variety of ways. Our personal evolution in consciousness is not only beneficial to ourselves, but also contributes greatly to the evolution of consciousness in other people and our organizations.

Life Is About Learning and Growing

We humans have the potential to learn and grow all of our lives. It is sad when we stop learning and growing, because as soon as we do so, we begin to die—biologically, psychologically, and spiritually.

In life, we are continually faced with the choice between playing it safe and growing. It is easy to get stuck in a rut, to live unchallenging lives of dull routines, or as Thoreau put it, "lives of quiet desperation." Millions of people do just that. But this need never happen if we continually learn and grow. That is the richest type of life, because it leads to more love, better friendships, and higher purposes. Conscious leaders make the intentional decision to continue to learn and grow throughout their lives, challenging themselves to be and do more.

To learn and grow, one must take chances and be willing to make mistakes. Unfortunately, many people are so defensive that they are fundamentally incapable of admitting their mistakes and are thus incapable of growing. They defend their decisions at all costs and attack anyone who tries to point out their mistakes or failures. But mistakes are actually great opportunities for learning and growth. The idea is not to celebrate our mistakes, but to learn from them as quickly as possible and move on. If we don't learn from our mistakes, we will keep repeating them, and it often becomes harder to deal with their consequences.

One of the most powerful ways to grow as a person and as a leader is through our relationships, especially with the people with whom we are most intimately connected, including our spouse or significant other, parents, children, friends, and coworkers. Potentially, everyone we interact with is our teacher. They can help us to change and improve—if only our minds and hearts will open wide enough. Recall our earlier discussion about how engaging with critics such as activists can lead to significant positive changes in our worldview and business practices.

Try this exercise: treat every person you encounter as fully enlightened. Everything they say and do, no matter how strange or harsh or even cruel it may seem, is intended to help us become a better person. Every interaction we have with people will now be seen as a new opportunity for learning and growth. Everyone becomes our teacher trying to help us and we will accelerate our personal growth in unexpected ways. This is a fun, but challenging exercise and can be done at any time. We simply need to consciously practice it. An interesting thing happens when we view people as enlightened: many start living up to that vision. They actually become kinder and gentler. As we treat them that way, they become attuned to it. In a way, we're giving them permission to be their own higher enlightened selves.[11]

Another useful exercise in our quest to be more self-aware is to keep a journal of feelings, thoughts, and dreams, or just whatever comes to mind. It can be quite revealing to look at a journal years later and see what we were thinking and feeling then. It also serves as a historical record of where we once were, so that we can look back and see our own personal growth. But more importantly, the practice can help leaders become more conscious in real time so that they can learn and adapt. We also recommend keeping a gratitude journal and adding to it at the end of each day. This helps you focus on the good things that have happened during the day. It allows you to become more relaxed and peaceful before falling asleep. It helps you gain a better perspective on life and your relationships with others.

A Crisis Is a Wonderful Growth Opportunity

When problems press all around us and we start feeling overwhelmed, the strategies that may have worked well in the past usually don't work any longer. Perhaps we made some foolish mistakes, and we have to experience the natural consequences of our actions. Or we're being called from within to grow to a higher plane. The set of life skills we currently have may be inadequate to solve the problem and to move past the particular situation we face.

I experienced this in 2007, when the Federal Trade Commission was trying to block Whole Foods Market's proposed merger with Wild Oats Markets. During its investigation, the commission downloaded most of my e-mails from my computer, learned a great deal about me that wasn't any of their business, and then leaked to the media that I had been posting under a screen name on the Yahoo! financial bulletin boards focused on Whole Foods Market and Wild Oats.

I had been doing these postings as a form of anonymous conversation and entertainment for about eight years and didn't see anything wrong with it (although I had lost a "bet" on the bulletin board and had to stop posting almost a year before the media leak). Everyone who posted on these financial bulletin boards used screen names, and no one knew who anyone else was. I greatly enjoyed debating with the other participants on these boards about Whole Foods Market, Wild Oats, and other food retailers in a way that I could not have if everyone knew who I was. No one participating took this activity seriously. It was just a form of play and entertainment. Unfortunately, a huge media scandal arose. It focused on a few of my comments that were critical of Wild Oats, and several other comments that were strongly supportive of Whole Foods Market (and which were also taken out of context by the media). The next thing I knew, I was being officially investigated by the Securities and Exchange Commission (SEC) and by the Whole Foods Market board of directors.

The whole thing was so bizarre to me, because I was just having fun when I did those postings. I didn't see how anyone was being harmed, and in fact no one was. Yet, it was made into a huge deal. My reputation was smeared in the media, and I was called a horrible person. Many outraged people publicly demanded I be fired. All the life skills I had previously mastered were simply inadequate for this situation. I just had to live day after day with the situation, while spending much of my time talking to lawyers.

Because of the ongoing investigations by the board and SEC, I also was unable to defend myself publicly. I wasn't permitted to write anything, talk to the media, record a video, go on television, or do anything else to present my side of the story to the world. Day after day after day, I had to listen silently to the incredibly distorted attacks on me in the media, while these intensely serious investigations were under way with dozens of lawyers poring over every word and punctuation mark of every posting, looking for whatever "secret meanings" I surely must have intended to communicate to the world.

A couple of things helped me get through this crisis. One was that I just stayed with the process. I tried to expand my consciousness wider and not be too defensive. When people are under intense stress, we tend to contract, to find someplace that feels familiar and safe. However, the best strategy most of the time is the opposite, which is to expand, to open our hearts and minds further, to make ourselves paradoxically even more vulnerable. I did that, even though it was extremely difficult and often hurt very badly.

I also engaged in several spiritual practices. I meditated much more frequently than before and for longer periods. I did "holotropic breathwork," an amazing process I had done many times previously. This psychological-spiritual technique helped me get back in touch with many of my deepest feelings and highest aspirations in life.[12] I just surrendered to it completely. I came to a place in my heart where whatever happened, it would be okay with me. I decided that I was going to stick this through, not be defensive, and not quit. I would continue to try to achieve the dreams and goals that were part of my own personal higher purposes. I would continue to follow my own heart, no matter where it led me.

Once I made that definitive decision to follow my highest life purposes, things began to clear up for me relatively quickly. The SEC ended its probe (it never had a full investigation), concluding that I hadn't done anything illegal. The Whole Foods Market board also ended its third-party investigation and concluded the same thing. Looking back on it today, I can now see that I grew tremendously as a person, not because of what had happened, but because of the way I was able to respond to it.

The most painful, horrible things that happen to us can also be our greatest opportunities to grow. It's a shame to waste any leadership crisis, because it's a great opportunity for us to become more conscious and to grow as people and leaders. When life is going along smoothly, there is a tendency to stagnate and become complacent. The great challenges we face help push us to the next level. We don't suggest the crisis will be enjoyable; it will no doubt be difficult and unpleasant. Nevertheless, a crisis is a tremendous opportunity to learn and grow. It shouldn't be wasted.

One of the most important lessons I learned from this episode was that I am now a public figure. Somewhere along the way, I had become semifamous. While I don't think of myself as a celebrity by any means, I am somebody who is frequently written about in the media. I realized that with everything I did from that point onward, I would have to ask myself this question: "How would I feel if what I'm doing right now is written up on the front page of the *Wall Street Journal* or the *New York Times* or if it is on television? Would I still do it?" That's a very useful exercise for leaders to engage in, because we shouldn't do anything we might be embarrassed by or ashamed of. That was my biggest lesson.

I don't think I did anything wrong by posting on the Yahoo! financial bulletin boards, but it was highly embarrassing to the company, and it gave people the opportunity to distort my motives and actions. It therefore was a mistake in judgment on my part. As a result, I'm not writing on any more bulletin boards under any screen names so long as I am co-CEO of Whole Foods Market. If I do write anything on the Internet, it's under my own name. I'm also very conscious that people can and probably will send to others anything I write, so I'm more circumspect in what I say and do and write. That doesn't mean I never do anything that other people might disapprove of. I still express my personal opinions publicly when it is appropriate to do so. This is sometimes controversial, but I weigh the consequences and determine whether I can live with it and not be embarrassed or ashamed.

THE THIRD TENET: CONSCIOUS LEADERSHIP

The Importance of Physical Health

To be fully effective as a conscious leader, in addition to being emotionally and spiritually healthy, we need to be as physically healthy as possible. It is essential for reaching our fullest potential as a leader and human being. If we are healthy, we have greater vitality, usually have more joy, and resist stress and disease better. Being the CEO of a large company, for example, is a very stressful job. There's a lot of pressure coming from a lot of directions, and you need to be physically very healthy to deal with it effectively.

We need to pay attention, first and foremost, to diet. Food forms the basis for our health and vitality. Americans in general do not eat a wholesome diet; 68 percent of us are overweight, and almost 34 percent are obese.[13] The United States has very high incidences of heart disease, cancer, diabetes, and autoimmune diseases, all of which are largely preventable diseases primarily caused by lifestyle choices. It's imperative to eat a wholesome diet, which we sum up with our four principles of healthy eating:

1. *Whole foods:* Eat only whole foods closest to their most natural state— free of artificial additives, sweeteners, colorings, and preservatives.

2. *Plant-strong:* Eat primarily plant foods such as raw and cooked vegetables, fruits, whole grains, legumes, and nuts and seeds, with no more than about 10 percent of calories coming from animal foods.

3. *Nutrient-dense:* Choose foods that are rich in micronutrients—vitamins, minerals, antioxidants, and phytochemicals—relative to their total caloric content. These are primarily vegetables and fruits.

4. *Healthy fats:* Eat healthy fats naturally derived from whole (i.e., minimally processed and refined) plant foods (fats are in virtually all plant foods). Nuts, seeds, and avocados are especially rich sources, and while very healthy foods, they should be eaten in small quantities. Minimize or avoid fats from vegetable oils (which aren't whole foods, are very high in calories, and have virtually no micronutrients) and restrict animal foods to no more than 10 percent of total calories.

Amazing things have happened at Whole Foods Market for our sickest team members after adopting this type of diet. Diabetes and heart disease have been reversed; people normalized their weight fairly quickly, often losing over one hundred pounds; and immune systems strengthened to better resist all diseases.[14] Our bodies are capable of healing themselves fairly rapidly once we stop poisoning them and provide them with the healthy foods that they need to flourish.

Second, make sure you exercise regularly. Under the stress of work, it's easy to neglect this, but it is crucial to make time for it. If you travel a lot, take a yoga mat and block with you to do yoga in your hotel room. It's also easy enough just to go outside and take a walk. Walk around the hotel parking lot if you have to. Many hotels also have an exercise room. The point is, there's always time to do what's truly important, and when we say we don't have time to exercise, what we're really saying is that we just don't value it or our health very much.

Third, be conscious of the toxins you put into your body. Obviously, everybody knows smoking is terribly destructive to our health. Even though many businesspeople who smoke rationalize it as a way to help them relax and manage their stress, it is an addicting toxic poison that systematically undermines our health.

Alcohol is another drug that is often abused because it is perceived as relaxing and has stress-relieving effects. It should be either completely avoided or consumed only in small quantities, and generally in convivial group settings, where it will have the most positive effects.

Caffeine is the most commonly abused drug throughout the world because of the virtually universal use of coffee, tea, cola, and so-called energy drinks. An estimated 90 percent of all adults in the United States use caffeine on a daily basis due to its addictive nature.[15] Caffeine only gives us the illusion of greater energy because it simply borrows from our reserves, resulting in an eventual energy crash as the caffeine wears off. The heavy use of caffeine slowly burns us out over time. It's a stimulant that over-amps our adrenal glands, gradually ages us, and drains our vitality.[16] Caffeine is not a healthy drug, and it should be indulged in only on occasion instead of daily. Both coffee and tea can safely be enjoyed in decaffeinated forms.

Of course, illegal drugs of all kinds should be avoided. We recommend judicious use of all pharmaceutical drugs as well. Americans take way too many pharmaceutical drugs in a futile effort to maintain their health and vitality. These are not nutritive substances, and all have some toxic effects on our bodies.[17]

Fourth, it is difficult to overestimate the importance of sleep, relaxation, and the use of stress management techniques for our health. Unfortunately, many adult Americans do not sleep well, because of stress and the regular use of alcohol, caffeine, and nicotine. Avoiding these drugs and substituting relaxation techniques such as meditation or listening to beautiful music will greatly help us manage stress better and improve our ability to sleep longer and deeper.

Contemplative Practices

Contemplative practices such as meditation, yoga, Tai Chi, breathing exercises, chanting, affirmations, visualizations, and prayer are all very valuable in helping an individual develop into a more conscious leader. They require setting time aside to be by ourselves, which is critical for self-awareness, as well as for helping us to center ourselves, become aware of our feelings, and slow down the mind.

Most of the great religions have cultivated classical meditative traditions in one form or another. The most important thing we can do is practice regularly. We can't just have a theoretical understanding of meditation—it's the practice that makes the difference. Almost any type of meditation will work, provided we do it regularly. A type of Buddhist meditation called *insight meditation* can be done in our normal working lives.[18] It doesn't require us to be alone, do breathing exercises, chant, or concentrate on a mantra. It is a discipline for being fully present and aware in each moment, instead of becoming lost in our own mental chatter. We're often not fully present, because even if we're half-listening to somebody, we might also be giving attention to our internal mind chatter. One of the best gifts we can give someone is to be fully present for him or her; people sense when we're really attentive.

Of course, it's challenging; as we go out into our daily workday, we become easily caught up in things and forget to stay conscious in the moment. In a sense, it's as if we're going back to sleep again. But the great thing is that as soon as we become aware that we've slipped, we can immediately come back to the present moment. It's something we can practice every single day. It's also complementary, because if we do other contemplative practices by ourselves, it is easier to carry on insight meditation in our daily life.

Timeless Wisdom

There is wisdom everywhere if we are open to it. In the modern world, we have a tendency to largely ignore the wisdom of the past, thinking that it's no longer relevant in our advanced technological society. But in fact, much of the philosophical wisdom of ancient traditions is timeless. People also have a tendency to reject wisdom that comes from traditions outside their own, while they may readily embrace products and food from other cultures. We should be willing to embrace wisdom of all kinds, and can find great value studying any of the great philosophical and spiritual traditions.

We are extraordinarily fortunate today to have the world's collective knowledge and wisdom from ancient times to the modern day at our fingertips, available to access anytime, anyplace, and virtually for free. We don't have to be restricted to only the mentors around us today, though some of them have much to offer. We can "hang out" with Buddha in the morning, Peter Drucker in the afternoon, and Jane Austen in the evening. It is well worth our while to engage with the wisest, most enlightened beings that humankind has produced. They will stoke our own aspirations to evolve higher, and we can learn many valuable things from them that will enrich our lives.

Unfortunately, many of us mostly read, watch, and listen to junk. Just as we should eat only the healthiest food and avoid junk food, we should also be feeding our minds with the most healthy thoughts and ideas from all time and all history—not junk ideas that have little real substance. An occasional indulgence, whether in junk food, junk television, or junk ideas, is not that harmful, but unfortunately, many of us are addicts who consume way too much of it; we fill our bodies, minds, and souls with trash and eventually suffer the consequences of these choices.

THE THIRD TENET: CONSCIOUS LEADERSHIP

Personal Growth Is a Choice

Ultimately, our greatest challenge as leaders is to manage and lead ourselves: to make wise choices, to learn and grow and evolve as human beings. Today's world offers us nearly limitless choices, says Peter Koestenbaum: "We've reached such explosive levels of freedom that, for the first time in history, we have to manage our own mutation. It's up to us to decide what it means to be a successful human being. That's the philosophical task of the age."[19]

It is also our greatest opportunity for service, and the rewards to our organizations, our families, and ourselves personally are virtually limitless. First we must become more conscious, act in ways that help make the world a better place, and then share our wisdom with the world. That is the hero's journey.

We close this chapter with a thoughtful quote from Steve McIntosh:

In the realm of consciousness and culture, evolution is a two way
street. Its persuasive influences move us not only to pursue our own
ascension, to improve ourselves, but also to try to make things better
here on earth during our brief sojourn in this world. That is, not only
are we called to rise to higher stages, but we are also called to bring the
wisdom of these higher stages down to the levels that need assistance.
Our world is full of trouble and suffering, and those who have attained
elevated states of consciousness have a sacred duty to use this light to
make a difference.[20]

PART FOUR

THE
FOURTH TENET

Conscious Culture and Management

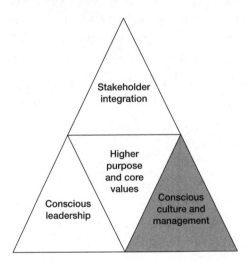

C ulture is a powerful but invisible force, and we must deal with it very consciously. As Edgar Schein, considered the father of organizational culture research, told the Academy of Management Conference in Montreal in 2010, "Culture is the biggest coercive persuader in society; if you do not conform to cultural norms, you could get locked up in jail or put into a mental hospital." According to Whole

Foods Market co-CEO Walter Robb, "The culture of a company is the place where people are front and center, where the richness and complexity of human beings resides, where your humanity shines through. As such it is the most powerful part of a business. When it is consciously affirmed, nurtured, and developed over time, it becomes both a true differentiator and the ultimate competitive weapon."

Conscious businesses have distinctive cultures that help them adhere to their higher purpose and maintain a harmony of interests across stakeholders. Conscious cultures are self-sustaining, self-healing, and evolutionary. They are resilient (though not impervious) to changes in leadership or external context.

An organization's culture and its approach to management must be in harmony. A company that has a militaristic, discipline-based culture functions best with a command-and-control approach to management. Conscious cultures are quite different and require a managerial approach that is based on decentralization, empowerment, and collaboration.

In this section, we first discuss some of the key cultural elements of conscious businesses. We then describe the kind of managerial approaches that are most effective in allowing such businesses to reach their full potential.

CHAPTER 15

Conscious Cultures

A company's culture can be a severe constraint on its success or a source of strength and sustained competitive advantage. As with so much else in life and business, it takes conscious intent and effort to create and maintain a vibrant, positive culture. As James Heskett of Harvard Business School says, "A strong culture can help or hurt performance. Culture can account for up to half of the difference in operating profit between two organizations in the same business. Shaping a culture is one of a leader's most important jobs; it can be ignored, but only for so long and at one's peril."[1]

Peter Drucker, one of the pioneering conscious-management thinkers (along with Mary Parker Follett and Douglas McGregor), is credited with the expression "culture eats strategy for breakfast." Drucker was not suggesting that strategy does not matter; it always has and always will. But a great strategy without a compelling purpose is like a beautiful highway that doesn't lead anywhere that people want to go. Likewise, the best-conceived, purpose-motivated strategy can come to naught if the organization's culture is incompatible with it or is infused with fear, distrust, and hostility.

THE FOURTH TENET: CONSCIOUS CULTURE AND MANAGEMENT

Walter Robb, co-CEO of Whole Foods, describes the company's culture:

At the heart of WFM are our core values which represent true stakes in the ground—deeply held beliefs which we use to guide our decisions. All around the values is our culture, which represents the actual practice of those values over time. This culture is a living thing that weaves in and throughout our company operations, breathes life into the company execution, and leaves team members feeling at a minimum connected, and from there full, affirmed, hopeful, and even joyous in the workplace. Culture is no less than "how we do things around here." Less tangible than other physical assets on a company balance sheet, it is nonetheless the most valuable asset a company has—for it stitches people together in common beliefs, values, and purpose and represents the basis for authenticity of experience for both team members and customers.[2]

How does a company with a conscious culture differ from one that is seen as a "great place to work"? Clearly, there is significant overlap between the two. But a great place to work may simply be one where employees are pampered, while other stakeholders may be given short shrift. In our view, a conscious culture goes beyond a great place to work because it imbues the work with a deeper sense of meaning. Embedded within the DNA of a conscious culture are the things that set a conscious business apart: its sense of purpose and an orientation toward caring for all stakeholders. A conscious culture facilitates the continued growth and evolution of the individual as well as the business.

Qualities of Conscious Cultures: TACTILE

Conscious cultures include seven characteristics, which can be remembered using the mnemonic TACTILE. As that term suggests, conscious cultures are so strong that they have a tangible, almost physical presence; it is impossible, for example, to walk into The Container Store or Whole Foods Market or to board a Southwest Airlines flight and not feel the positive energy emanating from team members and customers. Let's examine the seven characteristics:

Trust: Conscious businesses have high levels of internal and external trust. Within the company, there is a high level of trust, both vertically (between the leadership and frontline team members) and horizontally (within the leadership team as well as within and across teams at all levels). Externally, there is a high degree of trust between the company and its customers, suppliers, other business partners, the communities within which it operates, investors, and governments.

Accountability: Conscious cultures combine high levels of trust and caring with a strong emphasis on accountability. Team members are accountable to each other and to customers. People stick to their commitments and hold each other responsible for performance, efficiency, and deliverables. Suppliers are accountable to the company, and vice versa. Accountability goes hand-in-hand with high levels of decentralization and empowerment, both of which are the norm in conscious businesses.

Caring: The human need to care and be cared for is an extremely powerful motivation—often equal to and sometimes even exceeding the need to pursue one's self-interest. Conscious cultures are marked by genuine, heartfelt love and care for all stakeholders. Caring begets caring, and the company's stakeholders in turn exhibit genuine caring toward the company. People in conscious cultures behave in ways that are thoughtful, authentic, considerate, and compassionate.

Transparency: There are few secrets in a conscious culture because there is little to hide. Financial books are usually open (even in private companies), salary information is more readily available, and strategic plans are widely discussed and disseminated. The reality is that we live in an increasingly transparent world in which most information of genuine significance soon becomes known. Conscious firms embrace this reality and benefit from it.

Integrity: A conscious culture is marked by strict adherence to truth telling and fair dealing. Conscious firms readily forgive lapses in judgment, but do not tolerate lapses in integrity. The commitment to integrity goes far beyond mere adherence to laws. Conscious firms typically set global standards that exceed the requirements placed on them by local governments. They are guided by what they believe is ethically right, not merely by what is legally required or socially acceptable.

Loyalty: Conscious businesses exist in a system of high loyalty. All the stakeholders are loyal to each other and to the company. This is a natural consequence of the relationship mind-set that permeates such businesses. It means that these businesses do not have a "What have you done for me lately?" mind-set. Stakeholders are more patient and understanding with each other when short-term blips or other unusual situations occur. Of course, since these cultures also have high accountability, loyalty does not descend into blind fealty to those who consistently fail to live up to expectations.

Egalitarianism: Conscious companies do not have a class system that separates leaders from team members at large. Everyone is treated with respect and dignity. The salary differential between the top and the front lines is smaller than typically found at traditional companies. Senior executives generally do not enjoy special privileges and perks that are not available to others. To a large extent, all team members have input into how the company is managed and led. There is usually an open-door policy so that team members can communicate with the leadership team in an informal way.

In the rest of this chapter, we will focus on two key elements of conscious cultures: trust and caring.

Trust

Trust is an essential human attribute and virtue. Trusting others and being trustworthy oneself are central to what it means to be fully human. When we are born, we are completely helpless and at the mercy of others. If we have a healthy childhood with a great deal of strong parental love and care, then we have the foundation to more easily give and receive trust.

Unfortunately, there is a crisis of trust in society today. Many of the major institutions on which we depend, including governments of all types, the health-care system, the financial system, and our schools, seem to be failing us. There is high distrust toward business, especially toward large companies and their leaders. Within companies, there is often a lack of trust among team members, and between team members and customers, suppliers, investors, and managers. All of this matters greatly because trust is essential to building social capital, defined as the "shared norms or values that promote social cooperation."[3] Social capital is vital for the development of organizations as well as for society as a whole.

Trust is the essential lubricant of a smoothly functioning conscious organization. High-trust businesses are usually energetic, optimistic, can-do organizations that can overcome great odds. Trust within the company radiates out to all stakeholders. Team members of high-trust organizations are far more engaged and effective in their work. High-trust organizations benefit from greater synergy among stakeholders, enabling people collectively to achieve far more than they could as individuals. With its enhanced reputation, a high-trust company can attract more committed and compatible team members, customers, suppliers, and investors—starting a virtuous cycle that builds over time to create a truly great company that generates value and well-being for all.

A culture lacking in trust fosters a defensive, suspicious, insular, and fearful mind-set, depleting organizational energy and hampering creativity. A low level of trust increases friction and operating costs, particularly the direct financial burden of higher monitoring and legal costs. Without trust, companies become sluggish, unresponsive, and indifferent toward customer needs. A lack of trust thus sows the seeds for the eventual decline of the organization.

What can companies do to build trust? They certainly cannot buy it. A major corporation recently hired a consulting firm to design a $500 million marketing campaign to build trust! Such efforts are doomed to fail. There is no quick marketing or financial fix to a problem with deep cultural roots. Trust can only be earned slowly, as a result of actions and not just words.

While building trust is a slow and difficult process, destroying it is quick and easy. It doesn't take much: blatantly self-serving actions by senior leaders, people consistently getting away with toxic behavior, inconsistent and unfair treatment by managers, and distorting or withholding essential information all rapidly erode trust.

The following sections describe some ways in which conscious companies build a culture of high trust.

Being Truly Purpose-Motivated

High-trust organizations are always high-purpose organizations. Over time, however, many organizations lose sight of their reason for existing. Today, many societal institutions have lost sight of their purpose. They are motivated instead by narrow individual and institutional self-interests. Governments all too frequently serve the interests of politicians and public employee unions rather than of citizens. Schools too often serve the educational bureaucracy and teachers' unions instead of improving the education of their students. In the same way, many health-care systems operate to maximize the profits of pharmaceutical companies, hospitals, doctors, and insurance companies rather than the health and well-being of patients. The financial system is too often motivated by profiting from short-term arbitrage opportunities rather than directing societal savings into the most worthwhile investments. Finally, many corporations seem to exist primarily to maximize the compensation of their executives and secondarily to create shareholder value, rather than to optimize sustained value creation for all stakeholders.

Higher purpose and shared core values unify the organization and create a higher degree of shared ethical commitment. With this sense of organizational unity come higher levels of trust.

Fostering Conscious Leadership

Trust and hypocritical, inauthentic leadership can never coexist. An organization's purpose is meaningless if the leadership doesn't manifest it and serve it. Fidelity to the purpose and core values builds trust, while any deviation undermines it. Conscious leaders operate with a sincerely felt sense of trusteeship. They consider the impacts of their actions far into the future, not just on the next quarter's bottom line. They feel a great sense of responsibility toward the organization with which they have been entrusted, considering it a sacred duty to leave it healthier and stronger than they found it.

Recognizing That Trust Is Reciprocal

Trust is a two-way street. In order to be trusted, we need to show trust. Leaders must trust people to use their best judgment, instead of trying to control them with too many directives and rules. Research shows that the performance of team members is strongly correlated with the degree to which they are trusted by their supervisors. Overly close supervision erodes trust on both sides. Recognizing that trust is reciprocal, many companies have discontinued trust-destroying practices such as monitoring and spying on their team members' online activities. Being spied upon makes team members hostile and more disengaged—if they are simply trusted to do the right thing, people usually respond very positively.

A good example of the power of trust-based management comes from Dallas-based marketing agency MEplusYOU. As founder and CEO Doug Levy says, "Almost all companies have an out-of-office policy that states the configuration of days employees can take off for different things. We recently changed our out-of-office policy to not include any specifications, rather to just allow each team member to take off whenever they want. The policy says 'we trust you.' Our people love the trust, and they honor it. In fact, we've had to prod people to take *more* time off!"[4]

Transparency

To enhance trust, we must embrace transparency. Transparency is not an end in itself; it is important because it builds more trust in the organization. When we keep something hidden, the motivation is almost always a lack of trust; we are afraid the information would cause more harm than good if it were known. While some discretion is necessary to protect important organizational information from being leaked to competitors or others who mean harm, secrecy is often taken too far. The high-trust organization is willing to risk having some valuable information fall into the wrong hands, because the benefits of transparency and trust are far greater.

Transparency exists on a continuum. The cultures of organizations that have virtually no transparency usually have a great deal of fear. Some companies adopt a compliance mind-set, with limited transparency. They provide information only on a need-to-know basis. By contrast, conscious businesses only withhold information that would be harmful if made public. Companies cannot disclose everything, but people must trust their reasons for not disclosing. Complete transparency is neither necessary nor desirable. In fact, it can be exploitative if it reveals private information about team members. Each business must determine the appropriate balance.

We tell the truth to the people whom we trust. Conscious cultures are marked by an absence of artifice and by a genuine commitment to authenticity. What leaders and managers say, what team members do, and what customers experience must all be aligned with the company's guiding philosophy and defining purpose. Internal and external communications are honest and straightforward, devoid of the spin control that is now so common in the business and political worlds. Advertising tends to be factual rather than hyperbolic; when you have a genuinely good story to tell, there is no need to embellish it. Companies that say one thing, but behave differently breed cynicism among stakeholders. Like the barnacles that attach themselves to a ship's underside over time, this cynicism is very difficult for companies to remove.

An important benefit of creating a culture of transparency is that any unintentional unfairness can be immediately detected and quickly corrected. This is important because trust quickly unravels when there is a perception of unfairness. Human beings have a strong need to be respected, heard, and treated fairly. Research has shown that most people would rather have a fair and transparent process for making decisions, even if it leads to an unfavorable outcome for them personally, than an unfair process that may result in a positive outcome for them.[5]

It is essential that the ethic of fairness apply to all key organizational processes, such as hiring, promotion, compensation, discipline, and termination. Favoritism and nepotism undermine organizational trust and must not be tolerated. People are prone to envy, and any perceived unfairness exacerbates this tendency, giving it the energy of justification.

Love and Caring

We don't usually associate love and care with organizations. Instead, people tend to think of love and care as something we only share with our families, friends, or community organizations. This cultural bias comes from the common belief that love and care interfere with effectiveness in the real world. People see the marketplace as a jungle of competition; they fear that businesses that emphasize love and care cannot possibly be competitive and win. In fact, the opposite is true. Love and care are not weak virtues; they are the strongest of all human traits. Companies that operate on fear are the ones headed for extinction.

Marc Gafni, director of the Center for World Spirituality, is eloquent on the issue of business and caring: "The world of business is becoming one of the great cathedrals of spirit. Businesses are becoming places in which meaning can be created, in which mutuality begins to happen. Business is the force in the world that is fulfilling every major value of the great spiritual traditions: intimacy, trust, a shared vision, cooperation, collaboration, friendship, and ultimately love. After all, what is love at its core? It is the movement of evolution to higher and higher levels of mutuality, recognition, union and embrace."[6]

We must move past the cultural myths such as "Only the paranoid survive" and "Nice guys finish last," and allow our organizations and our leaders to be more fully human. They need to be able to express the highest and best virtues that humans embody—and love and care are right at the top of that list. As Jane Dutton of the University of Michigan says, "Humans are born to care. Our institutions magnify or depress our capacity to care."[7]

Most corporate cultures don't value love and caring enough, because their leaders have not fully integrated these virtues into their own lives. We need role models who are fully integrated human beings, loving as well as strong, and who show that there need not be any contradiction between the two. Leaders like Abraham Lincoln, Gandhi, Martin Luther King Jr.,

Nelson Mandela, and Mother Teresa are considered strong as well as truly loving and compassionate. Few prominent business leaders can be described in the same way (Herb Kelleher of Southwest Airlines comes to mind). Business leaders should aspire to enter into the pantheon of strong and effective leaders who are also caring, loving, and compassionate.

A very healthy development in business today is that women are increasingly stepping into leadership roles. Women, on average, seem to be more at ease in expressing love, care, and compassion. No doubt, women will continue to make significant gains in years to come, and this will have a marked impact on the cultures of large corporations. Even the men ascending to leadership positions are increasingly those who are more in harmony with the virtues of love, care, and compassion.

Banishing Fear

Sadly, too many leaders continue to believe that fear is a better motivator than love. Fear is the opposite of love. When we are completely grounded in love and care, fear is not present. Most organizations have both love and fear, but one or the other usually predominates. Conscious businesses seek to eliminate fear; the emotion prevents people from fully self-actualizing and prevents organizations from realizing their full potential. Fear is especially deadly for creativity. To be really creative, people need to be in a flow state, and fear doesn't permit that to happen.[8]

A company built on fear and stress is like a house infested with termites; it may look fine from the outside but it is being eaten away from the inside until one day, it just collapses. When a culture is full of fear, work becomes a painful ordeal to be endured. Unfortunately, this is far too common. People who don't suffer from the Monday morning blues have become a rarity.

Of course, love and care must be combined with excellence and strength. Otherwise, the business can become weak and ineffectual. Judging and condemning cause people to contract and become fearful. Organizations that consistently produce high performance gently but firmly synthesize excellence with love and care. Instead of judging and condemning, they help people recognize their mistakes and learn and grow from them.

Howard Behar, former president of Starbucks, speaks of the strength shown through caring: "Caring is not a sign of weakness but rather a sign of strength, and it can't be faked—within an organization, with the people we serve, or in the local or global community. Without trust and caring we'll never know what could have been possible. Without freedom from fear, we can't dream and we can't reach our potential."[9]

Creating More Love and Care

Organizations can manifest more love and care by doing two key things: hiring and promoting people with their capacity for love and care in mind, and allowing love and care to be more openly expressed.

Organizations must be very careful in whom they promote. They won't have the type of leaders they most need—caring, compassionate, and loving—if they don't promote them. The criteria for promotion must go beyond technical competence to include a high degree of emotional intelligence and a capacity for love and care. Leaders need to be fully integrated human beings who transcend the typical dualities; they are strong and loving, masculine and feminine, and have high standards of excellence and a high degree of emotional intelligence.

We need to give permission for love and care to be expressed in the work setting as qualities that are not taboo but encouraged and celebrated. In some ways, most organizations have gone in the opposite direction because of the great fear about sexual harassment. This has had a chilling impact on men's and women's ability to have any type of physical contact or express appreciation to each other. Organizations need to work through this apparent contradiction and find the appropriate balance.

Making Tough Decisions with Love and Care

Organizations face tough choices when they must take actions that cause significant pain and dislocation for some of their stakeholders. Even in these situations, love and care can be successfully expressed. One such tough choice many organizations face is the need to downsize or reduce total employment. Another common transition for many organizations is the need to outsource jobs previously done in-house. A third difficult transition occurs when someone who isn't performing well must be removed from a leadership position. How can these difficult situations be handled in conscious, loving, and caring ways?

Downsizing

It is very much in all the stakeholders' interests to have a business continue to flourish. It is not an act of love or care to let an organization fail if it could be made successful. Unfortunately, sometimes an organization must contract to avoid failure and to be successful in a competitive marketplace.

The ideal scenario is to let attrition address the need for downsizing. If a company is patient, attrition can often solve the problem of overstaffing within a year or two. If leadership feels it can't wait that long, it can implement a combination of some downsizing and a hiring freeze until, combined with normal attrition, total employment comes down to a level that is sustainable.

When Whole Foods Market hit a major rough spot due to the economic dislocation that occurred in late 2008, we were forced to downsize our global support team. The few team members we had to let go at our headquarters equated to less than 0.1 percent of the workforce (forty-eight people out of nearly fifty thousand team members at the time). Same-store sales had begun to decline for the first time in our history, and it was necessary to slow down our rate of new store development to conserve our capital. We also needed to reduce our total employment to bring expenses in line with our sales. We believed that the company had to downsize if we were going to continue to create long-term value on behalf of all of our stakeholders. But how could we handle this situation in a loving and caring way?

The first strategy an organization should use when it is forced to downsize is to be as honest and transparent as possible about what is going on with the entire organization. The message could be something like this:

> As many of you know, the company has been struggling for the past
> several months. Our sales have been very weak, and both our profits
> and our cash flow have dropped a great deal. We believe this downturn

in our sales is primarily due to the impact of the very poor economy we are all experiencing. In order for our company to continue to be viable, we are going to have to reduce our total employment to y from x by this date z. We have to get there one way or another. We know we can achieve some of the reduction from normal team member attrition, and we can also relocate some team members to other vacant positions within the company. We also will implement a temporary hiring freeze to protect as many current jobs as possible. In addition, it might be possible for some teams to vote to take voluntary reductions in weekly hours to protect jobs on their teams, but it will be up to each team member to vote on whether he or she prefers this option. However, by this date z, we need total employment down to y, and if we're not there, we're going to have to do some other type of downsizing by involuntarily reducing the total number of jobs. We are very, very sorry this has become necessary. We welcome any and all serious suggestions and alternatives you'd like us to consider.

The conscious business has this type of discussion in a fully transparent way, with integrity and honesty, and invites team members to make suggestions for how to solve the problem. It is not a management problem or a team member problem; it's a company problem. Team members often have insights and suggestions that can help solve the problem. For example, a team could collectively decide that all team members will reduce their hours, so as not to lose anyone from their team. It is much better if the team members vote and decide collectively that this is the action they wish to take. Trying to force everyone to reduce hours could cause resentment. If they don't respect the leadership, team members may say, "Company leaders are just afraid to make difficult choices. As a result of their poor leadership decisions in the past, the company is now in trouble, and they are taking their mistakes out on us. Because they're unwilling to let some of the weaker team members go, all of us will now suffer. That isn't fair."

A second effective downsizing strategy is to offer strong incentives to team members to leave voluntarily. In every organization, there are always team members who are planning on quitting in the near future for a variety of reasons. If a company can offer these team members several months of pay in a lump sum, many may willingly accelerate their departure from the company. The compensation offer can continue to be raised until the organization has enough volunteers to achieve its downsizing goal. A good analogy for this is how some airlines deal with overbooked flights. They ask for volunteers to drop off the flight to catch a later flight in exchange for a future travel voucher worth a few hundred dollars. They keep raising the value of the travel voucher until they have induced enough volunteers to rebook to a later flight.

Obviously, downsizing hurts the morale of the organization. Any time leaders bring fear into the organization, even if it is handled in a professional and caring way, people start worrying that they will be next to be let go. Anxiety mounts as they wait for the other shoe to drop, and their focus and level of engagement suffer. Instead of downsizing in stages, it is much better to do it just one time and to make it clear that there will not be any more cuts. It is therefore necessary to cut significantly enough to provide a margin of error; if the organization finds it has gone too far, it can always hire people back. Once the reductions have been made and promises are given that no more reductions will occur, people will begin to relax and let go of fear; the morale of the organization will begin to heal.

Finally, downsizing can be viewed by leadership as an opportunity for the organization to consciously make its overall team better and more capable. Within every organization, there are always a few people who don't fit quite as well or contribute as much, so this can be an opportunity—if it's done in a conscious way—to improve the overall quality of the team members in the organization.

Downsizing should definitely not be a routine occurrence. It has happened only twice in Whole Foods Market's thirty-two-year history. If we eliminate people's jobs, we believe we have a responsibility to help them try to find jobs elsewhere. We devoted quite a bit of money and time to this effort the two times we found it necessary to downsize. Most of the people we let go volunteered to do so. We had motivated them to leave with generous severance packages. To the greatest degree possible, we also tried to transfer people within the company where there were open positions, especially if they were willing and able to relocate to another city. For those who were not, we hired relocation firms to help place them in positions outside the company.

Outsourcing

If a business needs to outsource jobs to another company or country to maintain overall competitiveness, many of the same strategies discussed above can be useful. It is essential to demonstrate as much authentic concern and care as possible to the team members losing their jobs because of the outsourcing. Conscious businesses do it in such a way that they protect the overall morale of their organization. The nature of the problem, as well as various possible solutions, should be discussed with the entire team, and ideas solicited. If a company decides to go forward with an outsourcing strategy, it should announce these plans in advance so that people become used to the idea. Next, the company should try to relocate and retrain as many people as possible within the organization to minimize the immediate loss of jobs and allow normal attrition to gradually reduce the total number of team members. In some cases, the company is able to place people in the outsourced company that is taking over the work. Third, leadership can ask for volunteers to leave in exchange for generous severance packages. Finally, the company can provide valuable outside job relocation support and counseling. Doing outsourcing in a conscious way cannot remove all the pain, but it does lessen the sting, while helping the business be sustainable and successful in the long run in a competitive environment.

Recycling Unsuccessful Leaders

An unpleasant situation arises when it becomes necessary to remove someone from a leadership position. This occurs when the company has promoted someone into a leadership position that is beyond the individual's level of competence. An unsuccessful promotion is really the responsibility of the person who made the decision. Rather than lose a valuable and committed team member from the company, it is better to help the member learn and grow from the experience and then provide him or her with new leadership opportunities.

At Whole Foods Market, one solution we employ when leaders are unsuccessful is not to fire them from the organization, but simply to remove them from the job they are currently doing. We then provide them with a "bridge," a three- to six-month period at full pay during which time they try to find another job within the organization. With the bridge, these team members usually have time to successfully make a transition somewhere else in the company.

Whole Foods Market has long "recycled" leaders in this way. It is not seen as a permanent failure, but as a valuable learning experience. The recycled team member is encouraged to continue learning and growing and to seek other leadership opportunities in the future. Some of our best and most senior leaders at Whole Foods Market have been through recycling experiences at some point in their careers with the company and grew so much as a result that they became far more capable leaders.

Using Appreciations

One simple thing we do at Whole Foods Market has proven to be transformative in helping create a workplace of love and care: all our meetings end with voluntary *appreciations*. We set aside time at the end to allow anyone in attendance to appreciate anyone else participating in the meeting—for something they've done recently together, some favor or hospitality, or even just qualities about somebody they like or admire. Usually a person appreciates several people, not just one.

Sometimes, people are in a bad mood and don't intend to offer any appreciations. But after receiving caring appreciations from other people, their consciousness shifts, their heart opens up, and they feel a strong desire to appreciate others. It's human nature to want to reciprocate love when someone is extending love to us. This creates an upward spiral of appreciations, building on each other. It's a great way to create a context to help work out difficulties, and the impact of the appreciations extends beyond the actual meetings and into daily work life.

Appreciations are powerful because they offset the tendency for people to move into negative states of consciousness during meetings. People often move into a judgmental space, where they silently begin to find fault in what others are saying. By ending meetings with appreciations, we can shift people out of their space of judgment and back into one of love.

Interestingly, the person who often gains the most from an appreciation is not the person being appreciated but the one doing the appreciating. Once we shift into the mode of authentic appreciation of others, our consciousness shifts towards love and care. Expressing appreciation is a form of kindness that has powerful effects on everyone involved. Wayne Dyer, renowned author and speaker in the field of self-development, writes that "research has shown that a simple act of kindness directed toward another improves the functioning of the immune system and stimulates the production of serotonin in both the recipient of the kindness and the person extending the kindness. Even more amazing is that persons *observing* the act of kindness have similar beneficial results. Imagine this! Kindness extended, received, or observed beneficially impacts the physical health and feelings of everyone involved!"[10]

In a workplace that already has a great deal of love and trust, appreciations simply reinforce that love and trust and help them grow fuller. This practice has spread throughout all of Whole Foods Market; even our board of directors' meetings end with appreciations. It has certainly made for more harmonious meetings and led to a greater sense of camaraderie and trust. This is a simple technique that increases the level of trust, friendship, love, and care in an organization. We highly recommend that leaders experiment with this practice in their own organizations.

A couple of years ago, we saw a billboard for CareerBuilder.com at a bus shelter in New York City. The sign read, "If your company cared, it would be in the caring business." This is a sad but largely true statement; too many companies do not care and are not designed to care about anything other than their own prosperity. But society is steadily moving toward a better world in which a more accurate statement would be, "If your company doesn't care, it will not be in business for long." Companies need to care, not only about customers and investors, but also about team members and their families, suppliers, communities, and the environment.

In the introduction, we wrote about the Memorial Day flood in 1981, when Whole Foods' customers, investors, neighbors, suppliers, and team members rallied around us to save the company. We had asked ourselves when we started the business, "Can we create a company based on love?" Whole Foods Market would not exist today were it not for the power of love.

CHAPTER 16

Conscious Management

The four tenets of Conscious Capitalism comprise an organic whole; they are interconnected and interdependent. All the elements need to be in harmony and support each other. It is important, then, that the approach to management in a conscious business be consistent with the other tenets of Conscious Capitalism. In particular, the emotional and spiritual elements that define a conscious culture call for a particular kind of management approach so they can be fully expressed and reinforced.

The cultural elements of trust, authenticity, transparency, love, and care create the conditions in which humans can act as sources of creative energy, passion, and inspiration. Conscious management seeks to focus these creative energies in the most effective way possible by creating a virtuous cycle of reinforcing organizational practices. Decentralization, combined with empowerment, fosters innovation. Through collaboration, these innovations are shared, improved upon, and diffused throughout the organization, multiplying their effect and helping the company grow, evolve, and prosper.

As discussed earlier, conscious businesses are largely self-organizing, self-motivating, and self-healing organizations. The most evolved ones are largely self-managing as well. Of course, this does not happen automatically; it requires a kind of "intelligent design" to create an operating system that is in harmony with the culture of a conscious organization and the fundamentals of human nature.

The Role of Management in a Conscious Business

In a conscious culture, traditional approaches to management can backfire very badly. As Brian Robertson, the creator of the Holocracy management system, says, "Healthy behaviors in a pathological environment become pathological behaviors in a healthy environment."[1] The traditional definition of management includes activities and functions like organizing, planning, controlling, and directing resources to achieve organizational goals. Such an approach assumes that managers manage, while others do the actual work. This may make sense in certain contexts, such as in hierarchical organizations in which the vast majority of workers are engaged in routine tasks that offer little or no scope for individual creativity. The conventional view is that workers in such settings need to be controlled and motivated by managers using extrinsic motivators, otherwise known as carrots and sticks. However, this mind-set has increasingly become an anachronism because that kind of work is becoming less common.

In his excellent book *Drive: The Surprising Truth About What Motivates Us*, Dan Pink points to extensive research suggesting that what works better in the vast majority of contexts today is intrinsic motivation, loosely translated as the joy of work for its own sake.[2] As discussed earlier, Pink has distilled the three key drivers of intrinsic motivation: autonomy (the desire to direct our own lives), mastery (the desire to continually improve at something that matters), and purpose (the desire to do things in service of something larger than ourselves).

The role of management in a conscious business is therefore limited but crucial: managers must create, sustain, and strengthen the conditions whereby team members operate primarily from intrinsic motivation. This means, first, hiring the right people, namely, those whose personal passions align with the corporate purpose. Second, it means putting people in the right roles to take full advantage of their strengths, and giving them great freedom to operate. Third, it means creating opportunities for people to flourish and grow while helping the organization fulfill its purpose in an effective and efficient way.

A landmark contribution to management thinking was made by Douglas McGregor in his 1960 book *The Human Side of Enterprise*. The book questioned the implicit and explicit assumptions people hold about the most effective ways to manage people. McGregor categorized these assumptions into his now classic Theory X and Theory Y views of management. Theory X represents "the traditional view of direction and control," while Theory Y is about "the integration of individual and organizational goals."[3] Like Theory Y, conscious management recognizes the link between meaningful work and happiness. It builds on the significant evolution of both people and the nature of work in the last fifty years.

We will focus here on four key elements of conscious management: decentralization, empowerment, innovation, and collaboration.

Decentralization

There has long been discussion within management theory regarding the appropriate balance between decentralization and centralization. Of course, every organization is partly centralized and partly decentralized. There is no right mix that is universally appropriate; it depends on factors such as the scope for scale economies, the need for greater control and precision in situations of higher risk, and whether the business is involved in manufacturing or the delivery of services.

A smoothly functioning, centralized organization in which every team member has a well-defined job can be compared to a symphony orchestra. Individual players can excel but only to the degree they faithfully adhere to the master design, that is, the symphony. But increasingly in the world of business today, individual creativity and innovation must be combined with a shared sense of harmony and purposeful creation. A decentralized and empowered organization does not perform a symphony; it engages in a kind of improvisational jazz.[4] The organization's shared values and higher purpose provide the guard rails that ensure that the result is still beautiful music and not a cacophony.

Widely Dispersed Collective Intelligence

One of the reasons free-enterprise capitalism works better than any other economic system that's ever been created—particularly better than governmental bureaucracies or command-and-control structures—is that it recognizes that the collective knowledge and intelligence in a society and in organizations are widely diffused. This was Friedrich Hayek's brilliant insight in the mid-twentieth century.[5] The most dynamic and successful companies, as well as the most vibrant economies, are those that readily permit the expression of the decentralized knowledge and intelligence that resides in them. In stagnant companies and countries, planners and bureaucrats say, in effect, "We don't care what you think or want to do or want to create. We know what's best and will do it our way." This greatly diminishes the possibilities for real innovation.

High-performance organizations use approaches to management that tap into their collective intelligence. To foster greater creativity and innovation, they decentralize decision making and power. They recognize that unless there are overwhelming economies of scale to be gained by doing things centrally, it is better to decentralize and encourage widespread experimentation. In other words, they believe that companies and their stakeholders are best served by "letting a thousand flowers bloom."[6]

Decentralization empowers the team members who interact with customers and have a good understanding of their needs. It also facilitates widespread experimentation at every level of the organization. For example, Whole Foods Market currently has 329 stores divided into twelve distinct geographic regions. Each store is divided into ten or so self-managing work teams. The stores and regions are tied to the whole company through its shared purpose, core values, and certain centralized functions at the global support office. But at the operating level, the company is highly decentralized, allowing individual stores and teams great autonomy to experiment and see what works and doesn't work. With so much entrepreneurial experimentation going on throughout the entire organization at all times, new ideas are constantly generated.

We believe in decentralizing to the greatest extent possible, provided it fosters more innovation and does not compromise the core values and integrity of the organization. The key principle we follow is to locate decision making at the lowest possible level unless there is truly compelling evidence the organization would be better off making decisions at a higher level. In other words, there is a strong bias to decentralize. At Whole Foods Market, the global support office makes global decisions, regional teams make the regional decisions, stores make the store decisions, teams within stores make decisions that are appropriate to the teams, and team members within each team make the decisions that are appropriate to them.

Balancing Decentralization and Centralization

Of course, companies must override the decentralization bias when it makes business sense to do so, but they must take care to do it in a way that does not compromise the sense of individual autonomy critical to maintaining a high level of intrinsic motivation in the organization. For example, because it makes little sense at Whole Foods Market for the regions to have their own private-label products, that part of the business is controlled centrally. This allows us to take advantage of our purchasing economies of scale and offer our customers more attractive and affordable private-label products. Regions and stores are free to experiment with new branded products that are not private-label products, and they do so all the time. This is especially true in their support of local foods, which allows a constant supply of new and innovative products to bubble up from local sources, with the most successful ones eventually spreading across the company.

Two potential problems with decentralization are that we may sometimes reinvent the wheel with ideas that are already known but are not yet part of the organizational culture, and that many of the experiments will not be successful. When we allow a lot of experiments, we necessarily have a lot of failures. As a result, decentralized businesses must tolerate a certain amount of inherent "waste" or inefficiency in the system.

To the engineering or bureaucratic mind, which tends to believe that there is always one best way to do anything, these potential problems are frustrating and unacceptable. But in a healthy organizational system, these problems are only temporary because the conscious organization quickly learns and stops doing the wasteful things. Successes eventually far outweigh the failures, and continual innovation and progress result.

Decentralization can sometimes lead to a lack of enterprise focus—a tendency to only think about your own part of the company. W. L. Gore & Associates CEO Terri Kelly has developed ways to overcome the challenge. "We have these very powerful divisions of Gore," she says. "Medical, fabrics— and they're in their own little world . . . If you're not careful, they will only worry about their division, their business, their team, and so you've got to put these counterbalancing mechanisms that force the leadership to actually wear an enterprise hat, and make enterprise decisions."[7]

Empowerment

Decentralization without empowerment is a waste of time. Empowerment means giving people the authority to make decisions that affect how they do their work. Without empowerment, there is little innovation or creativity, just people engaging in conformist or ritualistic behaviors. Once we decentralize, it is essential that people be freed to use their best judgment and experiment with new ideas. Every team member of a conscious business acts as a microcosm of the whole business, authorized to act on its behalf for the benefit of the whole. The company trusts the members to act intelligently and thoughtfully in service of the firm's overarching purpose and its stakeholders. As Howard Behar, the former president of Starbucks, puts it, "The person who sweeps the floor should choose the broom . . . We need to get rid of rules—real and imagined—and encourage independent thinking."[8] Especially in a service business, it is critical to empower people to do what it takes to satisfy customers. It is terrible when companies let rules get in the way of satisfying customers. Indifferent team members can easily hide behind such rules.

Empowerment encourages creativity and innovation and accelerates the evolution of the organization. Fully empowered organizations have tremendous competitive advantages because they tap into sources of energy and commitment within team members that their competitors cannot access.

Many organizations talk about empowerment, but most are afraid of it because they fear losing control. Most people want to maintain control at all times. But control and creativity are often antithetical to one another. The biggest roadblock to workplace empowerment is the leadership philosophy of command and control, which is based on a lack of trust in team members. It usually involves detailed rules and bureaucratic structures to enforce those rules. These structures inhibit innovation and creativity because team members become fearful of breaking the rules and being punished. People get promoted in such organizations not by being innovative, but by following the rules and playing it safe. Command and control elicits compliance from the workforce, but seldom unleashes passion or creativity toward fulfilling the purpose of the organization.

Nordstrom has long believed in empowering frontline team members to use their best judgment in serving customers. For many years, the text of its one-page employee handbook read, in its entirety:[9]

WELCOME TO NORDSTROM

We're glad to have you with our Company. Our number one goal is to provide outstanding customer service. Set both your personal and professional goals high. We have great confidence in your ability to achieve them.

Nordstrom Rules: Rule #1: Use good judgment in all situations. There will be no additional rules.

Please feel free to ask your department manager, store manager, or division general manager any question at any time.

THE FOURTH TENET: CONSCIOUS CULTURE AND MANAGEMENT

Accountability

Empowerment without accountability leads to broken promises, unhappy customers, and weakened performance. Bill George discovered this when he became CEO of Medtronic:

> I look at culture as two things: values plus norms. When I joined the company, Medtronic had a very good values-centered culture, but not a performance culture. Deadlines were routinely missed, R&D programs that should have taken two years took four. People didn't fulfill their commitments; they rationalized. There was no sense of accountability. This was not healthy or sustainable. We had to set some normative standards that were much more challenging, and that was hard for people to come to grips with. I talked about empowerment with accountability. There is no other kind. There were people dying every day if we didn't deliver.
>
> When we held people to account, some had to go away and some were demoted to lower-level jobs because they couldn't keep up. We said we work together as a team, but we all have to pull our weight to be on that team. I would tell people, "I'm gowning up to see procedures; are you?" They would say, "Oh, I don't have time for that." I said, "Well, you'd better find time. You don't have time not to do it. This is the business." Everybody has to be engaged. That's how you build the culture.[10]

Shared Fate

At Whole Foods Market, we teach the importance of shared fate. It means that the better the company does, the better the customers do, the better the team members do, and the better the investors do.

At many companies, team members develop an entitlement mentality. They want to benefit from boom times but wish to be shielded from the tough times. This is not the case at conscious companies. A good example of this comes from Intrepid Travel, a twenty-three-year-old Australian company

242

that delivers "real life experiences" to a hundred thousand visitors to ninety countries a year. Intrepid offers adventure travel for ordinary people with "innocent curiosity." As the founders Geoff Manchester and Darrel Wade say, "In these uncertain days it is all the more important that we get out and explore our wonderful world. It is through travel we break down prejudice, build understanding and create a better and more caring world." Intrepid guarantees departures for all trips, even if there is only one traveler, unlike normal industry practice. Many of its team members are former customers.[11]

Intrepid is subject to the travel industry's usual vulnerabilities to external shocks, such as 9/11, followed by the bird flu epidemic, SARS, the terrorist bombings in Bali, and most recently the global financial crisis of 2008. Surviving these downturns has enhanced Intrepid's resiliency, creating a strong cohesive culture in which all stakeholders feel a sense of shared fate. For example, during the SARS crisis, 70 percent of the staff took a voluntary 10 percent pay cut.

In 2008, the company experienced the global financial crisis and lost a contract that accounted for 15 percent of its business. To survive, it was compelled to reduce overhead costs. Voluntary pay cuts were not enough this time, and the company had no option but to let nine people go. It did so in a conscious way, giving them six weeks' notice and assistance with outplacement, and was able to place seven of the nine within that period. When the business recovered after four months, two of the nine former team members were invited back in different roles, and the salaries of those who had taken a voluntary pay cut were made whole with interest.

DOING THE RIGHT THING IN HARTFORD

On the afternoon of December 13, 2007, as a major snowstorm raged outside, the cash registers at the Bishops Corner Whole Foods Market store in West Hartford, Connecticut, suddenly stopped working. The store had recently been converted from a Wild Oats store after an acquisition, and the technology systems were still not fully integrated. As the lines of customers waiting to pay grew longer, Ted Donoghue, the assistant store team leader running the store that day, consulted with his team members and made a quick decision: they would not charge customers until the problem was resolved. Customers needed to get home safely, and that meant checking out as quickly as possible. Store team leader Kimberly Hall said later, "It was clearly a snafu on our end, and it didn't seem right [to make customers wait]." As customers came to the front of the line, cashiers told them there was a problem with the registers. They bagged their groceries, wished them happy holidays, and asked them to drive carefully because of the storm. It took about thirty minutes to get the registers working again, during which time the store gave away about $4,000 in groceries.

Donoghue did not have to check with either global or regional leadership or even his store team leader for permission to do what he did, and there was no second-guessing the decision afterward by anyone. As Hall said, "They just totally trust us to do what is right for our customers."*

This seemed to be the end of the story. But a few days later, a customer who had been in the store that day called a reporter at the *Hartford Courant* to tell him what had happened, describing it as "the perfect Christmas story." The customer had not been charged for $70 worth of groceries. She was so surprised and grateful that she decided to donate $70 to a food bank. She said, "I thank Whole Foods heartily for what I think is truly the essence of Christmas spirit." The reporter closed his story with the following: "Imagine the kind of world we would live in if all corporations were run like Whole Foods."† This story was posted on the newspaper's Web site and, within a few days, became one of the most e-mailed stories of the day—which is how the executive leadership team in Austin, Texas, found out about it.

This kind of thing happens frequently at Whole Foods Market. We know that consistently trying to serve all our major stakeholders pays off in

---

* George Gombossy, "Whole Foods Shows You Can Get Something for Nothing," *The Hartford Courant*, December 21, 2007.
† Ibid.

countless ways, big and small. Our people know that if they use their best judgment and try to do the right thing, they will never be second-guessed. The Hartford story was seen by numerous people all over the country and created great goodwill for the company—something no amount of paid advertising can buy and certainly worth far more than the $4,000 it cost. But the assistant store team leader did not do it for that reason; nor did he put out a press release to let the world know what Whole Foods Market had done. He was just trying to serve our customers and used his best judgment to do so.

Innovation

The greatest long-term, sustainable competitive advantage a business has is the ability to out-innovate its competitors in ways that enhance efficiency or create greater value for customers. Of course, no innovation bestows permanent advantage; patents expire or new innovations make them obsolete (in fact, many businesses—like retail—don't even have patents), and everything a company does can be studied and copied. But organizations that innovate continuously and rapidly and diffuse those innovations quickly throughout their system have significant long-term competitive advantages. By the time their competitors catch up in one area, such companies have leapfrogged ahead in several other ways.

Whole Foods Market's strongest competitive advantage is that we are an innovative, creative company in an industry that is not particularly innovative. The food retailing business largely adheres to a strategy based on efficiency and cost-cutting. Walmart is the best example of this, as the long-time leader in supply-chain efficiencies, distribution scale, and lowering the overall cost of operations. It is very difficult for heavily unionized supermarket chains such as Kroger, Safeway, and Supervalu to compete successfully with that type of efficiency. At Whole Foods Market, while we continuously strive to improve our productivity and efficiency, our competitive strategy for over thirty years has been to differentiate ourselves from our competitors through innovation.

At most companies, the responsibility and opportunity for innovation is concentrated in just a few designated innovators such as an R&D team. Everybody else is supposed to just carry out orders. In a command-and-control structure, the message to most team members is, "We don't pay you to think; we just pay you to put these boxes on the shelves or check these customers out." Often, such companies hire expensive outside consultants to serve as designated innovators.

Any organization that depends on a few geniuses at the top and outside consultants, regardless of how brilliant they are, is at a competitive disadvantage to businesses that more fully utilize all of their intellectual capital and decentralized knowledge. As discussed earlier in this chapter, organizations that tap into the creative genius of all their people will dominate in the twenty-first century. Imagine the impact if every single person working for a company were able to be a creator and an innovator. Team members should be enabled, empowered, and challenged to unleash their entrepreneurial energy and their creativity to help improve their team, store, and company. This is Whole Foods Market's secret, in a nutshell: we have found a way, by empowering our team members, to create a workplace based on love and care and that is also fun, where people aren't afraid and collaboration is the norm. This releases far, far more creativity and innovation, enabling our company to improve and evolve rapidly.

Conscious companies strike a dynamic balance between the spirit of entrepreneurship and the spirit of stability and control (which we call bureaucracy). As it becomes successful and grows, every company must create some bureaucracy to bring necessary controls, order, and stability to the organization. The problem is that the bureaucracy often begins to dampen the company's entrepreneurial spirit. Bureaucrats, whether working for government or corporations, are seldom innovative. They tend to create rigid systems and rules that are deadly for creativity and innovation.

At Whole Foods Market we have tried hard to maintain our entrepreneurial spirit even as we have grown into a large company with over $11 billion in sales and more than sixty-seven thousand team members. We continually struggle to make sure that our bureaucracy does not overwhelm the entrepreneurial spirit that defines our company. We have developed several strategies for this. For example, our culture recognizes, celebrates, and rewards entrepreneurial behavior. We encourage internal entrepreneurs, recognize them, give them opportunities to implement their ideas, reward them for successes, and never punish them for their failures.

Collaboration

Done right, decentralization and empowerment typically result in a great deal of innovation and creativity. But innovation without a culture of collaboration is of limited value; a good idea that is generated in one part of the company but that nobody else knows about or can use usually does not have a large impact. A culture of collaboration enables successful ideas and innovations to be shared and spread rapidly throughout the organization. Almost every company has pockets of excellence that usually remain just that—isolated pockets. But with the technologies that are available today, good ideas can spread throughout an organization almost instantly and be improved upon. A collaborative culture is thus also a culture of continuous learning and improvement. The best ideas don't die on the vine; they are recognized, studied, emulated, diffused, and enhanced throughout the organization.

A good example of this is the rapid spread of taprooms and bars within Whole Foods Market's stores. While a few of our stores sold beer and wine from various prepared-foods venues within the store, none had a dedicated space for a bar that primarily sold beer and wine. At first thought, having a bar in a supermarket doesn't seem like a terribly good idea; people tend to think of bars as a part of a restaurant or a stand-alone location in a local neighborhood. However, our Northern California region decided to experiment with a bar in a new store that opened in Santa Rosa in 2010. They located the bar right in the middle of the beer and wine department and created a partly enclosed area called the Tap Room. The bar offered sixteen artisan beers on tap, as well as any beer or wine sold in the store. Our customers loved it. The new venue was hugely successful from the day it opened, with very strong sales and high profit margins. It turned out that our customers identify Whole Foods Market (as they do Starbucks) as a "third place" (home and work being the first two) where they enjoy hanging out. A taproom reinforces the third-place feeling of our stores and strengthens their appeal to our customers.

This successful entrepreneurial idea was quickly studied, copied, and improved on throughout Whole Foods Market. Digital photography and the Web enabled pictures, schematics, and financial results to be shared throughout the company virtually overnight. Within just a few months, other regions were opening their own Tap Rooms, innovating and improving on the original one. In less than two years, more than seventy-five Tap Rooms and various other dedicated bars had opened throughout the company—all without any global directives to do so.

Conscious Businesses as Learning Organizations

When decentralization, empowerment, and collaboration are all integrated into a management system that also takes advantage of scale opportunities, the result is an innovative, agile, caring, and powerfully competitive business. Decentralization combined with empowerment leads to experimentation and innovation; these attributes, coupled with collaboration, create a learning organization. When all of these work together, both individuals and organizations are able to learn and grow. Continual growth is not only accepted, but also expected and strongly supported. That is a pretty powerful formula for individual happiness and business success. Eric Hoffer's well-known statement highlights the importance of continuous growth and learning: "In times of change, learners inherit the earth, while the learned find themselves beautifully equipped to deal with a world that no longer exists."

A biological metaphor for this is a complex living system that continuously adapts and evolves. Contrast this with a mechanistic model of business based on the factory system. Machines must be designed down to the last detail. Somebody can tinker with and improve the design, but the machines themselves cannot evolve. They are dependent on outside experts, such as programmers and mechanics. A conscious business is a type of self-organizing, living system that learns, grows, evolves, self-organizes, and even self-actualizes on its own. The right degree of decentralization, empowerment, collaboration, love, and care in the workplace enables organizations to adapt, innovate, and evolve faster and enjoy a strong, sustainable competitive advantage.

Toward Self-Management

Pioneering management thinker Gary Hamel describes the new imperatives for management in today's world: "Instead of asking how employees can better serve the organizations they work for, we need to ask, 'How do we build organizations that deserve the extraordinary gifts that employees could bring to work?' To put it bluntly, the most important task for any manager today is to create a work environment that inspires exceptional contribution and that merits an outpouring of passion, imagination and initiative."[12]

Conscious managers exercise a minimal amount of control. Their role is not to control other people; it is to create the conditions that allow for more self-management.

CHAPTER 17

Becoming a Conscious Business

We have written this book to inspire the creation of more conscious businesses because we genuinely believe that this will lead to a better world for all of us. In our view, all new businesses should be created with the tenets of Conscious Capitalism firmly embedded in their DNA from the outset. We also want to see established firms become excited about this life-affirming philosophy and embark on the challenging but joyful journey of becoming conscious businesses themselves. To revisit the metaphor we used earlier, we want to help create a world of fewer business caterpillars and more butterflies, each unique and beautiful and value creating in its own way. In this chapter, we offer some practical suggestions on how such a transformation can occur.

Starting a Conscious Business

A conscious business is still a business and faces the same formidable challenges any new business does. Starting a business is never easy. The first challenge most businesses face is inadequate capital. Second, every new business must offer its potential customers a compelling value proposition. Third, it has to develop the structures, processes, strategies, and business models necessary for it to operate and to create value for its stakeholders. The difference is that the conscious business approaches these challenges with a different mind-set.

Building a meaningful business starts with a compelling vision or dream. Visionary entrepreneurs rarely think in terms of trying to fill a known need. The greatest advancements come from entrepreneurs who think outside the box, who dream about how the world could be, and create a business to realize that dream. Entrepreneurs are dreamers, but the really successful ones are also pragmatic, resilient, and uncommonly tenacious. They have the self-confidence and courage to resist the legion of naysayers who are ever present to say, "This will never work."

It is not enough just to have a dream. Entrepreneurs need to be able to motivate others to share in their dream. That only happens if the dream is truly compelling and if it embodies a purpose that resonates with other people. There's a kind of inception that occurs as the entrepreneurial dream is implanted in other peoples' minds, particularly investors and potential team members.[1] The entrepreneur's dream then becomes a shared dream that grows and becomes richer and eventually transforms into a concrete and purposeful business.

The company's purpose should be stated as simply as possible so that everyone can quickly grasp it. If you can't explain your business purpose in one sentence, you probably don't have a good understanding of it yourself, and you have little hope of getting others to understand it.

From the outset, it is essential to think in terms of creating value for the company's future stakeholders. Start with customers. How will the business create value for them and improve their quality of life? Next, think about suppliers and other partners, identifying those who have similar value systems and resonate strongly with the company's purpose. From the outset the company should focus on forging long-term relationships of mutual trust and interdependence with them.

To build a great conscious company, leaders need to intentionally shape their culture from the beginning—a culture that reflects, supports, and leverages the full humanity of all its stakeholders. Unfortunately, few startups pay much attention to their culture. They just let it evolve as a consequence of their purpose, the values of the leadership team, and serendipity.

A good example of a business designed with conscious principles from its founding is Google. From the beginning, Google had a clear and compelling purpose and a conscious stakeholder philosophy. The founders created a great place to work; team members are smart, empowered, innovative, very well looked after, and highly customer focused. They were clear about the kinds of investors they wanted to attract, clearly laying out their business philosophy in their prospectus. Google had a wonderful philanthropic strategy for its community stakeholders, and it implemented the strategy before its initial public offering, setting aside 1 percent of the company's stock for the Google Foundation, and pledging to contribute 1 percent of profits to the foundation annually.

Biz Stone, cofounder of Twitter, emphasizes that businesses should think about their broader societal impact from the outset: "Entrepreneurs are realizing that they don't need to wait until they have big piles of money to start helping others in need. In fact, the earlier you align your company with social causes, the better."[2] He offers the following tips for entrepreneurs: "Be emotionally invested in your work; define success as equal parts loving work, having a positive impact, and making money; and empathize with people—take time to walk in the shoes of others."[3]

Transforming to a Conscious Business

For people as well as organizations, it is always best to change when there is no imminent crisis, when you can take the time to do it right. However, that is also the most difficult time to convince people to accept the need for significant change. Leaders need to create a sense of urgency to shake a culture out of its inertia and complacency and galvanize team members into action.

These are some of the requirements for becoming a conscious business:

Authentic Commitment by Leadership

Becoming a truly conscious business requires a fundamental philosophical realignment. The tenets of Conscious Capitalism must resonate *intellectually*, *emotionally*, and *spiritually* with the leadership team. If they do not experience a visceral, almost physical reaction to the idea when they are first exposed to it, it is probably not the right time or the right leadership team, and the change process is most likely doomed to failure.

PEDIGREE: BECOMING "THE DOG-LOVING COMPANY"

It is generally easier for entrepreneurs to create a new conscious business than it is for an existing business to make the transition. The bigger and older the organization, the harder it is to make this transition, because established cultures always resist substantive change. But it can be done, as the story of Pedigree's transformation shows.

Despite spending more $178 million on advertising and promotion in 2004 and being the leading global dog food brand, Pedigree (wholly owned by Mars, Incorporated) found itself in an existential tailspin. Loss of market share, a squeeze on margins, strained retailer relations, lackluster customer loyalty, and undifferentiated product offerings meant difficult times and possible extinction ahead.*

After considerable soul searching, the company realized that all it really did was "put wet food in tins and dry food in bags to make a profit." This uninspiring look in the mirror led to the questions "What is our purpose?" and "Why do we do what we do?"

Working with TBWA/Chiat/Day in 2005, the company embraced the idea of becoming "the dog-loving company." It articulated its newly discovered purpose "We're for dogs" in a manifesto, appropriately titled *Dogma*:

*Tim Calkins and Ann Deming, "Pedigree Growth Strategy (A) & (B)," Case KEL497-8 (Evanston, Ill.: Kellogg School of Management, 2010); Reg Bryson, presentation at Conscious Capitalism launch event, Sydney, Australia, April 30, 2012.

We're for dogs.
Some people are for the whales,
Some are for the trees ...
We're for dogs.
The big ones and the little ones,
The guardians and the comedians,
The pure breeds and the mutts.
We're for walks, runs, and romps,
Digging, scratching, sniffing and fetching.
We're for dog parks, dog doors and dog days.
If there were an international holiday for dogs
On which all dogs were universally recognized
For the quality of their contribution to our lives,
We'd be for that too.
Because we're for dogs.
Dogs rule.

This manifesto became the centerpiece of a bold new advertising campaign. The company shifted from product advertising to philosophy-based advertising, spending less but having a much greater impact. Importantly, Pedigree carried the idea all the way through the business, putting dogs and dog welfare front and center for every business activity. On every team member's business card is a picture of his or her dog. This helps forge a connection with other dog lovers, including dog-food buyers at retailers. The decor of the offices was changed to celebrate dogs. The offices became very dog-friendly, and team members were invited to bring their dogs to work, any day or every day. When a team member acquires a new puppy, it is treated like the birth of a child. The company even set up a foundation to support dog adoption.

The new approach took root slowly, but within a couple of years, the company was reaping tremendous benefits, in terms of both strong brand health and stellar financial results. Team member morale and engagement soared. The company had its best year ever in 2009, as dog lovers loved the company's obvious love for dogs all the way to the bank!

The new and noble purpose has revitalized the core business and enabled the organization to expand into a number of related areas, such as dog dentistry, dog health, and dog stores. The lack of purpose and consequent lack of prospects are a distant if scary memory for the company. Competing dog food brands are greatly challenged to compete with the emotional and philosophical high ground that Pedigree now occupies.

Some business leaders are attracted to the message of Conscious Capitalism primarily because of the superior long-term financial results achieved by conscious businesses. If this is the only thing about Conscious Capitalism that resonates with them, they are unlikely to be able to successfully implement this philosophy and realize its rich potential.

It is possible for a determined leader to make a conscious approach work in a business division or another unit of a company and through that spark change on a larger scale. But this is rare. Generally speaking, a bottom-up approach does not work for this kind of transformation. A grassroots campaign may convince senior management of the need for change or demonstrate its potential in a limited sphere. But unless the senior leadership team genuinely desires to have a more conscious business for the right reasons, it just won't happen.

The commitment by the leadership team to being more conscious needs to be authentic as well as sustained. The members of the team must embody the change and become conscious leaders, because everyone in the organization will look to them to see if they really mean it. Any inconsistencies or perceived hypocrisy will undermine, if not entirely derail, the transformation.

Remember, *the four pillars of Conscious Capitalism are tenets, not tactics.*[4] Each tenet must be understood and lived in an authentic way to come alive. All four go together and are mutually reinforcing.

A company's board of directors does not have to be fully aligned with Conscious Capitalism at the outset of the transformation. In the long run, of course, the board needs to be "on board." It needs to appoint a conscious CEO and give the leadership team sufficient time and steady support as the company works to realize the transformation. Over time, the board must become fully attuned to this way of thinking about business and work to ensure that the mind-set gradually becomes part of the company's DNA.

Once the senior leadership team is fully committed to transforming to a conscious business, we recommend bringing in outside consultants to provide the support and the context the organization needs. As a first step, the company could undertake a "Conscious Business Audit" to see where the firm stands on the four pillars of Conscious Capitalism.[5] Such an audit can provide actionable insights on the areas that the company needs to focus on to become a truly conscious business.

Purpose Search

After the audit is concluded, the business needs to consider its higher purpose. Does the company have a clearly articulated and genuinely felt purpose? Is the purpose relevant in today's world, and is it something the world really needs? Is it inspiring to all stakeholders? We recommend a purpose search, which, as described in chapter 4, is designed to help companies discover or rediscover their higher purpose.[6]

Developing a Stakeholder Mind-Set

Next, the leadership team needs to learn how to think differently about, and communicate effectively with, its stakeholders. Businesses must develop higher levels of stakeholder empathy and stakeholder intelligence, including the ability to better understand and anticipate stakeholder needs even before the stakeholders become aware of them. It also means understanding that the motives behind actions are as important as the actions themselves. For example, in a profit-centered business, customer happiness is merely a means to the end goal of maximizing profits. In a conscious business, customer happiness is an end in itself and is pursued with greater commitment, passion, and empathy than a profit-centered business can provide. Likewise with team members, suppliers, and all the other stakeholders: the mind-set must shift from one of extracting and leveraging to one of value creation and service. In other words, authentic love and care must permeate how the organization relates to all its stakeholders.

Changing the Culture

Every organization has a culture, and every culture has an immune system that resists radical change. Therefore, the greatest challenge in becoming a conscious business is often changing the culture. If leadership has articulated a compelling purpose and made an authentic commitment to stakeholders, but the company's culture is indifferent or hostile toward those principles, the transformation effort is probably doomed.

The conscious business audit mentioned earlier includes an assessment of the degree to which the firm's culture embodies the qualities captured in the mnemonic TACTILE that we used earlier: trust, accountability, caring, transparency, integrity, loyalty, and egalitarianism. It is also essential that the company become aware of aspects of the existing culture that are particularly toxic or antithetical to a conscious way of being. The Barrett Values Centre (www.valuescentre.com) has developed a simple but powerful methodology for assessing cultural values that incorporates seven levels of consciousness. The tool is particularly well aligned with Conscious Capitalism.

All the processes, structures, and strategies of the company need to be examined to assess their fit with a conscious approach to business. Those that do not align need to be altered. This is never easy. Any established business has a cultural integrity that resists these kinds of changes. Businesses that are very stuck in their patterns may require, metaphorically speaking, more radical surgery. It might be necessary to remove the most hostile people, particularly those in senior leadership roles. Otherwise, the transformation effort may not be successful.

REINVENTING HCL

One of the most dramatic transformations of a major corporation in recent years took place at HCL Technologies in India. HCL is a leading provider of information technology consulting services and solutions to many of the world's largest companies. The change agent was Vineet Nayar, a CEO with many radical ideas about leadership and management. Nayar took over a company that appeared to be healthy. But conscious leaders see reality as it truly exists, not as they would wish it to be. Nayar saw what others did not see and what they would not acknowledge—that HCL was headed for trouble.[*]

To convince his colleagues of the need for change, Nayar recognized that he had to create a state of deep dissatisfaction with the status quo. As he frames it, all change involves getting from point A (where a company is today) to point B (where it wants to go). For the change journey to be successful, the key players need to feel profoundly unhappy with point A and truly excited about point B, which should be a positive, even romantic vision of the future.

Most companies engaged in transformation initiatives focus only on point B and spend little time examining the current reality. But it is impossible to chart a meaningful course toward a destination when you don't know the starting point. Nayar accomplished this through a process he dubbed "Mirror, Mirror on the Wall." He had his leadership team take a hard, unblinking look at where the company was, not just in terms of revenue growth but also in terms of other important factors such as employee engagement and customer advocacy. What the team saw was not pretty. While the company was profitable and growing in sales, it was losing market share. Its customers were satisfied but not delighted. It was not regarded as a special place to work. Like most of its competitors, it operated with a traditional approach to management in a knowledge business whose team members are virtually

---

[*] Vineet Nayar, *Employees First, Customers Second: Turning Conventional Management Upside Down* (Boston: Harvard Business Press, 2010); see also Gary Hamel, *The Future of Management* (Boston: Harvard Business School Press, 2007).

all highly trained professionals. The magnitude of the challenges facing the company soon became clear to the leadership team.

Nayar grouped the company's employees into three categories based on their attitude toward the transformation project: transformers (about 20 percent), fence sitters (60 percent), and lost souls (20 percent). He believed that if he could empower and excite the transformers, the fence sitters would soon join them, and the lost souls would gradually be rendered irrelevant.

After generating widespread acceptance of the need for change and enthusiasm about a compelling vision for the future, Nayar started by implementing one simple but radical idea: *reverse accountability*. In a business like HCL, most team members are professionals responsible for producing high-impact, creative work for clients. They create most of the value in the business. Nayar refers to these team members as being part of the "value zone." At most companies, such team members spend a lot of time in unproductive meetings and on paperwork. As Nayar put it, "Management does not live in the value zone or anywhere near it. Management at times gets in the way of creating value. We waste the precious time and energy [of those in the value zone] by requiring them to make endless presentations to us about irrelevant things and write reports about what they had or had not done."[†] The solution: instead of holding team members in the value zone accountable to managers, he made managers accountable to them. Managers have to ensure that those team members had everything they needed to be able to function at their peak, without having to waste time in non-value-adding activities.

Organizations, like people, can be self-learning and self-healing entities. The transformation does not always require dramatic, sustained, painstaking, micromanaged efforts. It may be achievable with a few simple but profound changes. Such catalytic ideas can set in motion a series

[†] Nayar, *Employees First, Customers Second*.

of changes. Reverse accountability was one such idea at HCL. Others followed in rapid succession:

Radical transparency: HCL created a system whereby any team member can ask any question of the leadership team at any time. All the questions and responses are posted on an intranet site. This creates a high degree of awareness of the challenges and opportunities that the company faces, and helps foster transparency and trust.

Open 360 feedback: Anyone is free to give feedback on anyone else in the company. This allows the company to gauge the degree to which an individual's sphere of influence and value creation extends beyond his or her direct connections, helping identify good candidates for promotion to broader roles.

Reinventing the role of the CEO: Nayar opened an intranet section called "My Problems," where he poses his strategic challenges for any team member to read and respond to. This gives him access to a huge amount of fresh thinking about such questions, and it also encourages more people to think more broadly and strategically about the business.

Each relatively simple change set in motion a series of other changes. The transformation started in 2005, when HCL's revenues were $762 million. By any measure, it has been very successful and the business results have been spectacular. By 2011, revenues had climbed to $3.53 billion, despite a difficult global economy.[§]

[§] HCL Technologies, Annual Report (US GAAP), 2005–2006; and *Wikipedia*, s.v. "HCL Technologies," last modified June 24, 2012, http://en.wikipedia.org/wiki/HCL_Technologies.

A Journey Worth Taking

Building a conscious business is a challenging but wonderfully rewarding and meaningful undertaking, whether such a business is created from scratch or is the outcome of a transformation. We recognize that many leaders have become weary of change. It seems there is a new set of buzzwords to deal with every few years—from total quality management to the reengineering of business processes to Six Sigma and numerous others. But Conscious Capitalism is no flavor-of-the-month fad. The ideas we have articulated result in a more robust business model than the profit-maximization model it competes against, because they acknowledge and tap into more powerful motivations than self-interest alone. Unlike many other types of changes, the move toward becoming a conscious business feels natural, because it is aligned with the natural human qualities of all stakeholders. Failing to do so threatens the future relevance and viability of any business.

CHAPTER 18

The Power
and Beauty of
Conscious Capitalism

Business plays a central role in our lives. We are affected more by businesses than by any other social institution. Most of us earn our livelihood and provide for our families by working for companies, and all of us purchase the goods and services companies produce with extraordinary efficiency and ingenuity. The quality of our lives, our health, our overall well-being, and even our happiness depend greatly on the ways in which businesses operate.

We have tried to stress throughout the book that business is not inherently flawed and sinful or in need of redemption. Business is fundamentally about people working together cooperatively to create value for other people. It is the greatest creator of value in the world. This is what makes business ethical and what makes it beautiful. It is fundamentally good. It becomes even better when it is more fully conscious of its inherent higher purposes and extraordinary potential for value creation.

Human beings are evolving rapidly, as we have discussed throughout the book. To reiterate, we are becoming more intelligent in multiple ways, better informed, more closely connected, and more driven by higher-level aspirations and values. Most of us, men and women alike, are becoming better at integrating the masculine and feminine sides of our personae. We are becoming more conscious: we are evolving ethically, we are taking responsibility for more of the consequences of our actions, and we better understand interdependencies and the nuances of larger systems.

In this rapidly changing world, businesses must learn to operate "with the grain" of change rather than against it. They must *lead* in the journey of human evolution rather than trail behind or be victimized by it. Business leaders must learn to heed the call for transformation and growth coming from within themselves, from their stakeholders, from society, and from evolution itself.

The powerful positive impacts of conscious businesses on the world are not just consequences of their acting more virtuously. It is also because they act more wisely. Their wisdom enables them to harness for the greater good the motivational power of higher purpose and the extraordinary levels of team member commitment that result when intense personal passions align with resolute corporate purposes. Their higher consciousness enables them to see the interdependencies across all stakeholders and to realize synergies from situations that otherwise seem rife with trade-offs. They create enduring and endearing cultures that enable the businesses to continue operating in a conscious way even after their founders have passed from the stage. Their leaders consciously build organizations that are self-organizing, self-motivating, self-managing, and self-evolving.

The Great Transition

We are in the midst of a historic transition where it is becoming clear that the old paradigms no longer work well and people's minds are open to new possibilities. The great challenges and exciting opportunities of our era demand visionary thought and bold action. In Tom Stoppard's play *Arcadia*, the mathematician

Valentine says: "The future is disorder. A door like this has cracked open five or six times since we got up on our hind legs. It's the best possible time to be alive, when almost everything you thought you knew is wrong." We need to critically reassess all of our mental models, assumptions, and theories for their continued accuracy and relevance. It is scary but also exhilarating to see so many new possibilities. We have an invaluable opportunity today to effect fundamental changes that will set our course for the future, because the resistance to change in society at this moment appears to be lower than it has been in a long time.

Resistance to change may be lower, but it still exists. Experience shows that dominant paradigms die hard. When a new paradigm, even a clearly compelling one, is put forward, it encounters resistance from those with entrenched worldviews and much invested in the status quo. As the logical and empirical support for the new paradigm mounts, its opponents begin to attack it, often viciously. The next phase is usually an uneasy coexistence between the two paradigms. Eventually, the weight of accumulated evidence creates a tipping point in favor of the new paradigm. People then start to say, "What's the big deal? Why are we even talking about this? It is so obvious." This transition is just beginning, and a coherent new philosophy of capitalism is only now beginning to take shape. It will take time and concerted effort by many before this new philosophy becomes widely accepted and routinely practiced.

The transition is gathering some momentum. Many current leaders and established companies are responding to the philosophy of Conscious Capitalism and are taking tentative steps in this direction. But we believe that the millennial generation (those born between approximately 1980 and 2000) that is coming of age right now will be the primary creators of change.[1] From their ranks will emerge the entrepreneurs who will create the future conscious businesses and conscious nonprofits that will radically accelerate our collective social and economic evolution. According to Jeanne Meister and Karie Willyerd, "Millennials view work as a key part of life, not a separate activity that needs to be 'balanced' by it . . . They want work to afford them the opportunity to make new friends, learn new skills, and connect to a larger purpose. That sense of purpose is a key factor in their job satisfaction; according to our research, they're the most socially conscious generation since the 1960s."[2]

CONSCIOUS CAPITALISM

A Shared Dream

Our dream for the Conscious Capitalism movement is simple: *One day, virtually every business will operate with a sense of higher purpose, integrate the interests of all stakeholders, develop and elevate conscious leaders, and build a culture of trust, accountability, and caring.* Today this is the exception. Our goal is to make it the norm as quickly as possible. Of course, we are not so arrogant as to presume that the way we have defined Conscious Capitalism is the final word. What we have offered is a dynamic definition, one that will continue to evolve as our consciousness grows and the collective wisdom of business leaders and thinkers enriches our understanding.

Thomas Paine, one of the founding fathers of the United States, published a famous pamphlet titled "Common Sense" in January 1776 that became an immediate sensation and is thought to have catalyzed the issuing of the Declaration of Independence six months later. Nearly universally read in the colonies, the pamphlet made a powerful case for the idea of republicanism and making a clean break from Great Britain. It opens with the following passage: "Perhaps the sentiments contained in the following pages, are not *yet* sufficiently fashionable to procure them general favor; a long habit of not thinking a thing *wrong*, gives it a superficial appearance of being *right*, and raises at first a formidable outcry in defense of custom. But the tumult soon subsides. Time makes more converts than reason."[3] We believe that much the same could be said of Conscious Capitalism vis-à-vis the traditional view of business.

We have no doubt that one day, Conscious Capitalism will become the dominant business paradigm for one simple reason: it is simply a better way to do business. It just works better, and over the long term, it will outcompete other business philosophies. As Kip Tindell, cofounder and CEO of The Container Store, says, "The universe conspires to help you. Everyone wants you to succeed." Since conscious companies win in the marketplace, their approaches will be copied over time. However, that could be a slow process, and many companies seeking to become conscious businesses may not fully understand what that entails. Some may just pay lip service to the idea or

266

embrace it only for its promised financial benefits. The Conscious Capitalism movement exists to help bring about this shift more rapidly and in a more conscious manner, so that companies understand what it truly takes to be an authentically conscious business. When most businesses operate in this way, humanity and our planet will flourish.

The Road Ahead

We see our work in the Conscious Capitalism movement as akin to building a road for aspiring conscious businesses to follow. The trail has been blazed by a few visionary pioneers who are continually experimenting; some have gone down side trails and discovered new things there. Our job is to broaden the trail, smooth it out, create a road map, and provide support along the way.

The good news is that, unlike twenty-five or thirty years ago, there are now many good examples of conscious businesses that have already blazed this trail, so a new conscious business has plenty of guidance as it moves along this path. It can go forward with more certainty and confidence because loved companies like Southwest Airlines, Google, Costco, UPS, POSCO, Tata, The Container Store, Amazon.com, Whole Foods Market, Nordstrom, Patagonia, Trader Joe's, Panera, and Bright Horizons have shown that this way of doing business leads to multifaceted success over time.

There is an old paved road out there already, an expressway that traditional businesses have been on for a long time. It is well worn and well marked and feels like a safe, comfortable place to be. But the old, traditional way is no longer the safer way or the right way; there are now many potholes on that path. More importantly, it does not lead to anywhere we want to go anymore. The conscious business path may not be as well trod, but it will lead to long-term success and long-term flourishing. Today, companies don't need a great leap of faith to get on this path, as many of the earlier pioneers needed. The journey is joyful but not easy. It calls for vision, purpose, courage, and determination.

An Agenda for Action

Everyone can play a role in spreading Conscious Capitalism. If you are already running a business or a significant unit within an existing business, you can start implementing this way of being right away. As soon as possible, bring together your whole system, and ask the fundamental questions: Why does this business exist? What value do we create? How can we create more value for all our major stakeholders? How can we transcend the trade-offs we currently tolerate? How can we create a workplace full of love, joy, and meaning? How can we show more love and care to our customers and suppliers? How should we change our hiring and promotion practices? These questions are only the starting point for beginning to create a more conscious business. Every aspect of the business needs to be closely examined in terms of the four tenets that we have discussed in this book.

We have no time to waste. As the expression goes, the best time to plant an oak tree was twenty years ago; the second-best time is right now. The lead agents of change need to be those who are engaged in business—not politicians, bureaucrats, or regulators. The status quo simply cannot continue; it is unsustainable in so many respects. The question is what will replace it. If we don't step forward to defend the fundamental essence of capitalism, its indispensability and its extraordinary upside as businesses become more conscious, we will soon find our lives dominated and diminished by dangerous and distorted forms such as crony capitalism or some form of state capitalism.

The Limitless Possibilities of Human Ingenuity

We humans are capable of extraordinary things. Think of all our astonishing accomplishments in just the last two hundred years, when our numbers grew exponentially and more of us were given the opportunity to realize our full creative potential. We have created physical structures that boggle the mind, undertaken feats of daring that are breathtaking in their audacity, shown leaps of imagination that are stunning to contemplate. We have tunneled through mountains, built edifices stretching thousands of feet into the heavens, sent and safely brought back humans from the moon. We have put up satellites and space stations, invented technologies that make magic look mundane, unlocked the awe-inspiring power of the atom. We think nothing of putting hundreds of people in aluminum tubes and hurtling them around the world at astounding speeds eight miles above the ground. We have created communication systems that weave us together into an unbroken tapestry of connections, from the remotest hamlet to the deepest jungle to the tallest mountains. None of these magnificent human achievements were divinely handed down. They were all conceived and brought into being by ordinary mortals, in an incredibly short amount of time.

Our great triumphs and extraordinary potential bring into sharp relief the sadness of our everyday frailties and the myriad ways in which most of us squander our gifts and our time. Where we could be joyously creating, most of us are content to complacently coast. Where we could experience the thrill of discovery, we settle for mindless routine. Where we could live each day suffused in love and fulfillment, we allow ourselves to be imprisoned by our own fear-based thoughts and actions.

Nowhere is this more evident or more vexing than in the world of business. We have taken this extraordinary social technology for cooperation and value creation and far too often rendered it dull and dispiriting. Our work, which should be a source of great achievement and authentic fulfillment, has become for most of us an ordeal to be endured. This can and must change.

The Choice Businesses Face

Unconscious businesses focus on creating as much financial wealth for their investors as possible. Everyone and everything else is a means to that end. And yet they increasingly fail to accomplish that which they so single-mindedly pursue. The cycle is predictable. Leaders proclaim repeatedly and proudly that their focus is profit maximization. This sends a loud and unmistakable message to everyone the organization touches: they too must focus on maximizing their own profits. Team members decide to give as little and take as much as possible. Suppliers try to squeeze and cut corners where they can so that they can maximize their own profits. Governments and local communities think about how they can extract as much out of the business as possible. Customers feel no hesitation in taking advantage of the company whenever they can. Everyone becomes a taker and not a giver to the system. This erodes and eventually destroys a company's ability to achieve its profit goals because the self-serving impulse becomes rampant throughout the system. It damages everyone's ability to create value for each other and, through that, value and fulfillment for themselves.

A conscious business aspires to create financial, intellectual, social, cultural, emotional, spiritual, physical, and ecological wealth for all its major stakeholders: team members, customers, investors, suppliers, and communities. Each stakeholder is both a means and an end, an instrument of value creation as well as its beneficiary. The well-being of each is intimately tied in with the well-being of all. Trade-offs are largely eliminated, and the business system flourishes and grows of its own accord. Everyone is a willing, enthusiastic, and grateful contributor to the undertaking, serene in the trust that their caring, loyalty, and diligence will be amply reciprocated in numerous ways.

The difference between these realities is large and consequential. The choice is ours.

Liberating Our Heroic Spirit

The great jurist Oliver Wendell Holmes Jr. said, "I would not give a fig for the simplicity on this side of complexity, but I would give my life for the simplicity on the other side of complexity." We can no longer be content with a simplistic approach to work, business, and capitalism—an approach that has become so deeply ingrained in our psyche and in society. It is not serving us well; in fact, it is eating away at the fabric of our communities and stultifying our souls. It necessitates too many unsavory trade-offs and results in too much unhappiness and suffering for too many people. We must do what it will take to move collectively to the other side of complexity in the world of business and capitalism, for that is where we will find peace and prosperity, joy and justice, love and caring, money and meaning.

The subtitle of this book is *Liberating the Heroic Spirit of Business*. We chose these words with great care and for very particular reasons. The sad reality is that for too long, business has been stuck in a defensive and reactive posture. Entrepreneurs and businesspeople are the heroes of our modern world, yet they have been caricatured as heartless and soulless mercenaries.

As Marc Gafni of the Center for World Spirituality says, "We must change the core narrative of business to make it an accurate reflection of the transformative impact of business, its true identity as the great healer . . . This is a huge and dramatic paradigm shift that can actually shift the very source code of our self-understanding."[4]

It has been well said that those of us alive today truly have the opportunity to live the most meaningful lives human beings have collectively ever led.[5] Our challenges have never been greater, but so too is our consciousness and deep understanding of those challenges. Our collective determination to address those challenges and our ability to do so have also never been greater. We have at our disposal all the tools and technologies we need to solve virtually every one of our challenges, and we have the capacity and creativity to invent anything that we need but do not yet have. If we can marshal the latent energy that lies largely dormant in each of us and channel it through creative organizational forms, we can and will eradicate poverty in this century, create a more peaceful planet, restore and replenish our environment and threatened species, eliminate most major diseases, and enable all humans to lead long, healthy, vibrant, productive, and meaningful lives. Our children and grandchildren will collectively flourish in ways that we can't even imagine today.

This is the power, promise, and beauty of Conscious Capitalism.

THE CONSCIOUS CAPITALISM CREDO

We believe that business is good because it creates value, it is ethical because it is based on voluntary exchange, it is noble because it can elevate our existence, and it is heroic because it lifts people out of poverty and creates prosperity. Free-enterprise capitalism is the most powerful system for social cooperation and human progress ever conceived. It is one of the most compelling ideas we humans have ever had. But we can aspire to something even greater.

Conscious Capitalism is a way of thinking about capitalism and business that better reflects where we are in the human journey, the state of our world today, and the innate potential of business to have a positive impact on the world. Conscious businesses are galvanized by higher purposes that serve, align, and integrate the interests of all their major stakeholders. Their higher state of consciousness enables them to see the interdependencies that exist among all their stakeholders, and this, in turn, allows them to discover and harvest synergies from situations that otherwise seem burdened with trade-offs. Conscious businesses have conscious leaders who are driven by dedication to the company's purpose, to all the people the business touches, and to the planet we all share. Conscious businesses have trusting, authentic, innovative, and caring cultures that make working within them a source of both personal growth and professional fulfillment. They endeavor to create financial, intellectual, social, cultural, emotional, spiritual, physical, and ecological wealth for all their stakeholders.

Conscious businesses can help evolve our world in such a way that billions of people can flourish, leading lives infused with passion, purpose, love, and creativity—a world of freedom, harmony, prosperity, and compassion.

To learn more, visit www.consciouscapitalism.org.

The Business Case
for Conscious Capitalism

Businesses need to look at their performance with a broad set of criteria. They should not be judged purely on financial results. As discussed early in the book, businesses can create but also potentially destroy many kinds of wealth: financial, intellectual, social, cultural, emotional, spiritual, physical, and environmental. The larger the company, the greater its impact on the world in all these dimensions. A business that generates financial wealth but destroys other forms of wealth (which can have greater impacts on people's well-being) adds far less value to the world than it is capable of. If it destroys enough of the other kinds of wealth, the business has a negative net impact on the world and could even be described as a parasite on society.

A key principle of systems thinking, identified throughout this book as an essential aspect of Conscious Capitalism, is that there are no such things as main effects and side effects. We take actions, and they have effects. All of the effects are potentially significant, and all must be accounted for. As in medicine, we tend to label some as "main" effects to emphasize them more, and some as "side" effects to downplay them (since they are almost always negative). Often, however, the so-called side effects can overwhelm the main effects in their cumulative impact. Some effects may manifest immediately; others may occur in the future. Each effect can in turn trigger other effects, which too must be understood.

In business as in other aspects of life, being conscious means taking responsibility for all the consequences of our actions, not just the ones that reflect well on us. The wonderful thing about thinking in a conscious way about business is that it enables business to make decisions in such a way that they have positive impacts in multiple dimensions for all stakeholders. This is far more fulfilling than simply striving to create financial wealth for shareholders.

The Logic of Superior Financial Performance

The financial dimension of corporate performance depends on a company's ability to grow its revenues and improve its efficiency. Conscious businesses are superior in both regards. They are better aligned with the tangible and intangible needs of their customers. Their spending priorities are clear: invest money·where it makes a difference (such as on team member happiness, a great customer experience, and high-quality products), and save money in non-value-adding areas (such as frequent sales promotions, high levels of team member turnover, and the administrative overhead associated with operating large bureaucracies).

Conscious businesses tend to grow much faster than their competitors. They do this by expanding the overall market (as Southwest Airlines has done throughout its history for the air travel market and Starbucks has through its ubiquitous coffee bars) as well as by taking market share away from their less conscious competitors. Of course, conscious businesses sometimes create entirely new markets where virtually none existed before, such as Amazon.com through online book retailing or Apple through its iPods, iTunes, and iPad innovations. Over time, we expect there to be fewer less conscious businesses, as they will be unable to compete with more-conscious businesses. This will increase the direct competition between conscious businesses, leading to more innovation and value creation, which will enhance the quality of life for all stakeholders.

In this appendix, we will provide direct and indirect evidence that conscious companies perform better financially in the long run. The direct evidence is based on looking at the performance of a representative set of publicly traded conscious businesses over the past fifteen years. The indirect evidence is based on some proxy variables—criteria for selecting firms that are consistent with, but not the same as, those that define a conscious business. Let's start with the direct evidence.

Direct Evidence of Superior Financial Performance

In *Firms of Endearment: How World-Class Companies Profit from Passion and Purpose*, Raj Sisodia and coauthors selected companies on the basis of their so-called humanistic profiles (their sense of purpose; how well they were loved by the customers, team members, suppliers, and communities; their cultures; and their leadership), not their financial performance.[1] The only financial criterion used was that the companies be "going concerns"; in other words, they were not under the imminent threat of bankruptcy. Starting with several hundred, the authors selected eighteen publicly traded companies and ten that were private. The degree to which these selected firms could be described as "conscious" varies, but it is clear that they're all pretty far along on that dimension.

In terms of financial performance, the authors' expectations were modest: that these companies would be average or slightly better. They based this belief on several factors. First, the companies did not state their goal as "maximizing shareholder returns." Second, most of these companies pay their team members well and provide generous benefits. At the time, for example, Costco paid its team members double what Walmart did and covered 98 percent of its team members' health-care costs, whereas Walmart covered a much smaller fraction (Walmart is starting to do more, but it is still not comparable to Costco). Third, these companies paid taxes at a much higher rate than that paid by most other companies. Fourth, the selected companies did not squeeze their suppliers to secure the lowest possible price, and their suppliers were innovative and profitable. Fifth, the "firms of endearment" invested a lot in their communities, and in reducing the company's impact on the environment. Finally, they provided great customer value and outstanding customer service.

Most of us have become conditioned to believe that business is a zero-sum game that requires numerous trade-offs. Therefore, if these "firms of endearment" were spending all this extra money on team members, suppliers, customers, and communities, it has to come from somewhere else—probably from investors. Sisodia and coauthors expected that since these are well-managed businesses with loyal team members and customers, investors would do as well with these companies as they would with other companies. In the authors' view, that would be more than acceptable, since these companies also create so many other kinds of value. However, they found that these companies not only do all those good things, but also deliver extraordinary returns to their investors, outperforming the market by a nine-to-one ratio over ten years (from 1996 to 2006). Clearly, this was not just about "nice" companies doing good things. A lot more value creation is going on with these companies than is at first evident.

The authors have updated the data to span a fifteen-year period from 1996 to 2011. As table A-1 shows, these same companies outperformed the S&P 500 index by a factor of 10.5 over that period.[2]

TABLE A-1

Investment performance of *Firms of Endearment* companies versus the S&P 500, 1996 to 2011

Return	Fifteen-year		Ten-year		Five-year	
	Cumulative	Annualized	Cumulative	Annualized	Cumulative	Annualized
FoE[a]	1,646.1%	21.0%	254.4%	13.5%	56.4%	9.4%
S&P 500[b]	157.0%	6.5%	30.7%	2.7%	15.6%	2.9%

Note: company returns are total returns with dividends reinvested and compounded.
a. Companies from *Firms of Endearment*, updated by authors.
b. Standard & Poor's index of five hundred U.S. companies.

APPENDIX A: THE BUSINESS CASE FOR CONSCIOUS CAPITALISM

Indirect Evidence of Superior Financial Performance

Companies with Superior Work Environments

A good proxy for a conscious business is a company that is regarded as a "great place to work." The Great Place to Work (GPTW) Institute has been conducting research on this since 1988. In a similar vein, Gallup has been conducting research on team member engagement for thirty years.

The GPTW Institute uses criteria such as trust, pride, and camaraderie to determine whether a company provides a work environment that creates a genuine sense of satisfaction and fulfillment among team members. Since 1997, it has partnered with *Fortune* magazine to produce an annual listing of America's "100 Best Companies to Work For." As figure A-1 indicates, these firms have dramatically outperformed the market between 1997 and 2011. On the 2012 list, conscious companies mentioned in this text ranked as follows: Google (number 1), Wegmans (4), REI (8), The Container Store (22), Whole

FIGURE A-1

Comparative annualized stock market returns versus *Fortune's* "100 Best Companies to Work For," 1997 to 2011

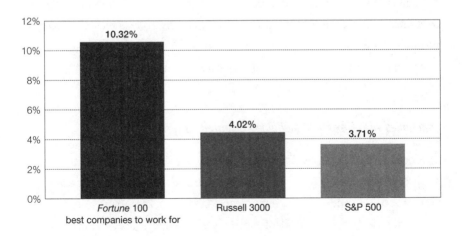

Foods Market (32), Nordstrom (61), and Starbucks (73).[3] Glassdoor compiles its own list of the fifty best places to work on the basis of employee input. In addition to some of the companies on *Fortune*'s list, the Glassdoor list includes Trader Joe's at number 9, Southwest Airlines at number 17, and Costco at number 23.[4]

As discussed earlier, Gallup has found that the average level of employee engagement at U.S. companies has ranged between 26 and 30 percent over the past decade. Gallup has also found that in high-performance businesses, the ratio of engaged to "not engaged" team members is 10 to 1. For average companies, the ratio is 1.8 to 1.[5]

Companies That Are Highly Ethical

Since 2007, an organization called Ethisphere has produced an annual list of the world's most ethical companies. Companies are assessed in seven areas: corporate citizenship and responsibility; corporate governance; innovation that contributes to public well-being; industry leadership; executive leadership and tone from the top; legal, regulatory, and reputation track record; and internal systems and ethics or compliance programs. In 2011, 110 companies were recognized.

Collectively, the selected companies have outperformed the S&P 500 every year since the inception of the program in 2007, by an average of 7.3 percent annually. The companies have been found to enjoy superior brand reputations, higher customer loyalty, and lower team member turnover.[6]

Companies with Flexible Stakeholder-Oriented Cultures

In 1992, Harvard Business School professors John Kotter and James Heskett published the landmark book *Corporate Culture and Performance*.[7] Kotter and Heskett studied the performance of 207 large U.S. companies in twenty-two industries over a period of eleven years. They found that companies with strong and flexible business cultures that addressed all stakeholders and empowered managers at all levels dramatically outperformed companies that did not by wide margins on three key indicators: revenue growth (682 versus 166 percent), stock price increase (901 versus 74 percent), and net income increase (756 versus 1 percent). The authors describe the companies' stakeholder-oriented cultures: "All their managers care strongly about people who have a stake in the business (customers, team members, stockholders, suppliers)."

Companies with Visionary Leaders

In a large-scale academic study, researchers studied 520 companies in seventeen countries to determine the financial impact of autocratic versus visionary leadership and emphasis on broad stakeholder value versus just economic value.[8] Autocratic leaders emphasized numbers and financial results, while visionary leaders focused on purpose and values. The researchers found that visionary leadership was strongly related to "extra effort," which was positively related to firm performance. Autocratic leadership had a strong negative impact on stakeholder value and no impact on financial performance. Over time, firms led by visionary leaders significantly outperformed those led by financially focused, autocratic leaders.

Counterintuitive Evidence

There is plenty of evidence that conscious businesses perform outstandingly well on every criterion that matters. What about companies that are resolutely profit driven? Surely, they should excel at the one overriding goal they set for themselves.

Jim Collins's *Good to Great* is the best-selling business book of all time.[9] Collins looked at the universe of publicly traded companies for the past eighty years or so and identified eleven companies that met the following financial criterion: they outperformed the market by at least three to one over at least a fourteen-year period. The book analyzes how and why these eleven companies went from average performance to this extended period of outperformance.

Two important questions to ask are, who are these companies, and do they truly deserve the moniker *great*? The list includes Circuit City, Fannie Mae, and Wells Fargo. Before it went bankrupt, Circuit City did some rather unconscious things, like firing experienced team members and replacing them with new hires whom it could pay less. Fannie Mae was in the middle of the recent financial crisis. Wells Fargo received $25 billion in bailout money from the U.S. government in 2008.

But more egregiously, the list of "great" companies includes Altria (formerly Philip Morris). What has been the net impact of Philip Morris, the world's largest tobacco company for much of the past century? Has its impact on the world been positive, neutral, or negative? It is glaringly obvious that if you net it all out, the impact is strongly negative. Six million people die each year directly from smoking-related illnesses, and one *billion* are expected to die this century from tobacco use. The average life expectancy of a smoker declines by fifteen years, and public health systems spend an estimated $650 billion a year directly on tobacco-related illnesses.[10] There is no hiding from these numbers. Most tobacco companies not only are focused on meeting existing demand, but also have continued to work to create new demand, decades after it was conclusively established that smoking is profoundly harmful to health.

Taking a broader view from a societal standpoint, is the world a better place because that company exists? Sure, some people have jobs, and investors have enjoyed good returns. But at what cost? If the company were forced to account for all the costs that it externalized to society, would its financial performance look as good? We think not.

It matters how the money is made. As Gregory David Roberts writes, "If we can't respect the way we earn it, money has no value. If we can't use it to make life better for our families and loved ones, money has no purpose."[11] A far richer definition of a great business is one that maximizes the *total* value it creates, not just financial wealth for investors but all the kinds of wealth listed earlier, for all its stakeholders. A great business enhances the overall health and well-being of society. It helps bring greater prosperity and fulfillment to all its stakeholders. Its very existence enriches the world. These are far better standards to apply in judging the greatness of a business.

TABLE A-2

Investment performance of *Firms of Endearment* companies versus S&P 500 and *Good to Great* companies, 1996 to 2011

Return	Fifteen-year		Ten-year		Five-year		Three-year	
	Cumula-tive	Annu-alized	Cumu-lative	Annu-alized	Cumu-lative	Annu-alized	Cumu-lative	Annu-alized
FoE[a]	1,646.1%	21.0%	254.4%	13.5%	56.4%	9.4%	77.4%	21.1%
GtG[b]	177.5%	7.0%	14.0%	1.3%	−35.6%	−8.4%	−23.2%	−8.4%
S&P 500[c]	157.0%	6.5%	30.7%	2.7%	15.6%	2.9%	10.3%	3.3%

Note: company returns are total returns with dividends reinvested and compounded.
a. Companies from *Firms of Endearment*, updated by authors.
b. Companies from *Good to Great*.
c. Standard & Poor's index of five hundred U.S. companies.

Importantly, all these considerations eventually show up in financial performance. The companies that were held up as financial exemplars in *Good to Great* have only slightly outpaced the market over the past fifteen years and have performed much worse than the conscious firms studied in *Firms of Endearment* (table A-2). Over the past ten-, five-, and three-year periods, *Good to Great* companies have significantly underperformed the market. Of course, the firms were cited as being great in different periods, but we believe that companies that are truly deserving of the label *great* should stand the test of time and continue to perform well.

Explaining Superior Performance

How do conscious businesses deliver superior financial results while creating many other forms of wealth and well-being for all of their stakeholders, including society? It boils down to these factors: these companies generate very high levels of sales because they excel at creating value for customers; they willingly operate with lower gross margins than they are capable of, yet they achieve higher net margins than their traditional counterparts. Over time, conscious businesses develop sterling reputations and grow faster. They attract more loyal customers, committed team members, higher-quality suppliers and generate greater community goodwill. All of this also helps these firms earn more and receive higher valuations relative to their earnings.

High Sales

The number one explanation of the superior performance of conscious businesses is their superior acceptance by customers. Conscious companies are loved by their customers, who are not just satisfied and loyal, but are also ardent fans and advocates. As a result, conscious companies generate very high sales. They routinely outperform their industry averages on metrics such as sales per square foot for retailers and revenue per team member for all businesses.

When a company generates more revenues on a comparable asset base than its competitors, it can afford to pay its team members better wages and still be cost competitive. It operates in a virtuous cycle: well-paid team members with true passion for their work and for serving customers help create a superior experience for customers. The company achieves greater economies of scale and is able to continuously improve its value proposition to customers. The combination of the two attracts even more customers over time, allowing the company to continue to pay its team members well and achieve further scale economies.

Essentially, conscious companies are much more productive than their traditional counterparts. But it is not the kind of productivity that is squeezed out of harried, pressured team members through threats and incentives. It is the kind that results when people are in a state of flow, producing excellence, creating innovations, and loving what they do. You can move mountains with that kind of energy.

Here are some examples of conscious retailers and their superior abilities to generate higher sales and better operating efficiencies:

- Grocery retailer Wegmans has sales per square foot that are 50 percent higher than the industry average and achieves operating margins estimated at 7.5 percent, about double those of its competitors.[12] Like most conscious businesses, Wegmans pays its team members well, provides generous health-care benefits even for part-time team members, and offers extensive training.

· Costco generates sales of nearly $140 million per warehouse and $1,000 per square foot. Its competitor Sam's Club generates $78 million and $586, respectively, and BJ's Wholesale Club does $54 million and $500. With its much higher sales per employees, Costco can afford to pay its people well, and the fact that it does so contributes in turn to its outstanding performance.[13]

· Furniture retailer Jordan's sells $950 per square foot of furniture a year, compared with $150 for the industry. It turns over its inventory thirteen times a year, also well above the norm.[14]

· Sales at Trader Joe's exceed $1,750 per square foot, more than *three times* the industry average. The company pays its people near the top of the industry, yet still has a total payroll cost percentage that is nearly the lowest in the industry.[15]

Margin Mirage

Most companies try to maximize their gross margin by looking for inexpensive suppliers and then using their own bargaining power to squeeze the suppliers to get ever-lower prices. The companies often end up with suppliers that struggle to stay profitable and cannot afford to invest in quality improvement or innovation. Conscious businesses, by contrast, are very selective about their suppliers. They seek to partner with innovative, quality-focused companies that also operate in a conscious manner. Suppliers are well paid and in turn pay their own suppliers and team members well.

Most companies also try hard to minimize their payroll costs, especially when it comes to what they pay their frontline team members, and are stingy with critical benefits such as health insurance. They try to use part-time team members as much as possible, usually keeping them under the hours-worked threshold where they would qualify for better benefits. They usually provide minimal training to their team members and accept high team member turnover as inevitable.

Conscious businesses pay their own frontline team members well, often significantly above the industry norm, and are generous with benefits. Since its direct costs are by choice *higher* than they could be, the gross margin of a conscious business is typically *lower* than it would be if it adopted a mind-set of maximization.

The next line items on the income statement relate to SG&A (sales, general and administration), and this is where the investments that conscious businesses make in people, quality inputs, and purposeful cultures really pay off. Traditional businesses squander their hard-won high gross margins by spending heavily on marketing, managerial overhead, legal fees, and high levels of executive compensation. They incur high recruiting and training costs due to high team member turnover. Their team members are frequently disengaged and unproductive. Their product quality is often poor, leading to low customer loyalty and high product returns.

Lower Marketing Costs

Conscious businesses typically spend less overall on advertising and marketing, and what they do spend is handled differently. This is because they have legions of satisfied and delighted customers who are loyal and passionate advocates for the company. Many conscious businesses spend as little as 10 to 25 percent of the industry average spending on marketing. This is a huge cost saving, since marketing costs have risen more rapidly than other areas of spending and now represent one of the largest expenditures for most companies.[16] For example, Whole Foods Market only spends about 20 percent of the industry average on marketing. Of this, 90 percent is spent at the store level rather than by our Global Support offices, and most of that amount relates to the company's community service activities. Conscious companies receive the benefit of the best kind of marketing there is—free marketing—not only from their customers but also from their team members, their suppliers, their communities, and the media. Google and Starbucks are other examples of companies that spend relatively little on marketing but have gained great success and adoration through their conscious approach to business.

Conscious companies benefit from the explosion of social media by acting in accordance with their purpose and using social media to serve customers rather than try to persuade them. While these companies may spend more in this area, their overall marketing costs can be lower because the firms don't need to do as much paid advertising, which is where the bulk of marketing budgets go. Nor do these companies need to discount their products or replace churning customers as much.[17]

Lower Team Member Turnover, Much Higher Engagement

A conscious business takes great care to hire people whose personal passions align well with the company purpose. The business typically operates with much lower levels of team member turnover, thus saving significantly on new team member hiring and training. For example, turnover at The Container Store, a perennial on Best Places to Work lists, is in the low single digits, in an industry where turnover often exceeds 100 percent every year. Team members at such companies are loyal, experienced, passionate, energetic, creative, engaged, and extraordinarily productive. Starbucks is another good example. When it provides health benefits to its part-time workers (spending more on health care than it does on coffee), the team members clearly win. Customers win from having more-engaged and caring team members, such as baristas who remember their names and the details of their orders.[18]

Lower Administrative Costs

A conscious business has lower administrative costs because it continuously strives to eliminate non-value-adding expenses, gathering ideas from its team members and suppliers about how to do so. It also looks to control essential expenses such as health-care costs, not through across-the-board cuts, but by devising creative ways to achieve win-win outcomes. For example, Whole Foods Market is combating rising health-care costs through a range of comprehensive team member wellness initiatives that go way beyond those found at a typical company. We are not only lowering costs, but also saving and transforming lives in the process.

Conscious companies typically operate with smaller bureaucracies and thus leaner management structures than do traditional businesses. They create systems in which the right people do the right jobs and are given a great deal of autonomy. Most team members are engaged in actively creating real value for customers rather than "managing" each other. These companies are designed to be largely self-organizing, self-motivating, and self-managing. Senior leaders at most conscious companies are paid modestly relative to their peers at other companies. As we discussed, Whole Foods Market has adopted a policy that no one can be paid more than 19 times the average salary of all full-time team members, even though the typical ratio at large publicly traded companies has ranged between 350—500 times in recent years. The only way for executives to earn more at such companies is to raise the average salary of all team members.

As a result of the high trust between all stakeholders, the legal costs of conscious companies are much lower than the norm. They truly understand their customers, produce outstanding products (due in no small part to the world-class suppliers that these companies work with), and do not engage in hard-sell tactics, so their product-return levels are also comparatively low.

A Better Way to Win

A business that effectively utilizes the synergies created from stakeholder interdependency, and encourages the expression of the creative energy that usually lies dormant in most people, is very difficult to compete with in the marketplace. Businesses often fail because they don't have a high enough degree of innovation, cooperation, or collaboration. Inevitably, a competitor comes along with a higher degree of teamwork, cooperation, collaboration, and interdependency, and eventually the less effective organization is unable to effectively compete. Just look at the great success of Trader Joe's, Whole Foods Market, Wegmans, Publix, and HEB: these more conscious food retailers are all growing and thriving, while food retailers still following the old traditional business paradigm are struggling.

In fact, conscious businesses are already starting to take over significant market share in many industries, not just in food retailing. Southwest Airlines used to be a small, inconsequential operator, but is now one of the most profitable and valuable airlines in the United States. Conscious capitalism will ultimately triumph because it is based on higher levels of innovation, collaboration, and cooperation. Eventually, the marketplace will weed out businesses that aren't sufficiently conscious.

Conscious Capitalism and Related Ideas

Dissatisfaction with the status quo in the world of business and capitalism has been brewing for quite some time. The Occupy movement of 2011 channeled some of this angst into protests that spread to a number of cities, but ultimately did not amount to much because it did not offer a coherent alternative vision.

In recent years, many business thinkers and some CEOs have started to speak of alternative or modified forms of capitalism. In this appendix, we discuss how Conscious Capitalism relates to some of these ideas on how capitalism needs to evolve.

Natural Capitalism

Natural capitalism is an important idea put forward in 1999 by Paul Hawken, Amory Lovins, and Hunter Lovins.[1] Its key thesis is that traditional or industrial capitalism is unsustainable and misleading because it does not account for some of its most critical inputs: natural resources, living systems, and human capital. Fundamentally, natural capitalism argues that businesses must fairly value and price these critical inputs, because if these numbers are omitted, then financial statements are an illusion, the world's resources will get rapidly depleted, and nature will not be able to replenish them. The authors estimated that nature provides services to business worth $33 trillion a year for "free." They recommend that we adopt new technologies that enhance the value of natural resources, eliminate waste from production systems, and make strenuous efforts to alleviate the environmental damage from economic activity (such as planting trees to offset carbon emissions). They argue that business must learn to work in harmony with nature rather than against it, and they show how this can be a profitable as well as sustainable approach.

Natural Capitalism has been an influential book that raised the consciousness of many business leaders, specifically around environmental sustainability. A well-known example is Ray Anderson, the late CEO of Interface Carpet, who started to describe himself and his fellow CEOs as "plunderers" of natural capital. He initiated a major transformation of his highly energy-intensive and resource-intensive business and found that it eventually led to far more innovation and success in the marketplace.

Conscious Capitalism includes the principles of natural capitalism that focus on environmental sustainability. It incorporates what we have learned and continue to learn about living in harmony with nature, not only doing minimal harm but actually healing our ecosystems as we do business. But it extends that thinking by also bringing business into closer harmony with human nature. Conscious Capitalism recognizes that our natural resources are ultimately finite and must be protected and conserved. But it also recognizes that our creativity and inner resources are infinite, provided we can learn how to activate and deploy them. As emphasized earlier, the most powerful form of renewable energy on the planet is a turned-on, fully alive, and awake human being.

We therefore see no contradiction between Conscious Capitalism and natural capitalism. Conscious Capitalism includes the valuable insights that natural capitalism offers about the environment and transcends them with a more comprehensive view of the entire business and economic system.

Triple Bottom Line

John Elkington, the founder of a British consulting company called Sustain-Ability, coined the phrase *triple bottom line* (TBL) in 1994.[2] The three bottom lines he wanted companies to pay attention to are people, planet, and profit. Elkington called for tracking financial, social, and environmental performance over time. Andrew Savitz wrote an excellent book on this approach: *The Triple Bottom Line: How Today's Best-Run Companies Are Achieving Economic, Social, and Environmental Success—and How You Can Too*.[3]

The idea caught on, and many companies now produce reports that provide detailed information on their triple bottom lines. It is certainly consistent with some of the most important principles of Conscious Capitalism, particularly in its emphasis on managing businesses on behalf of multiple stakeholders. We see the TBL movement as a fellow traveler in helping to evolve business and capitalism to a higher consciousness.

Whereas the corporate social responsibility (CSR) mind-set attempts to graft social responsibility and environmental sustainability onto the profit maximization model as add-ons, the TBL movement wants to make them equal partners in the business with the investors. While TBL is definitely an improvement over the CSR model, the TBL movement tends to focus heavily on social responsibility and environmental sustainability as the major areas for business to concentrate on besides achieving economic success. The movement neglects other Conscious Capitalism tenets that are equally important, such as both a wider and a more nuanced view of stakeholders. Moreover, the TBL movement lacks emphasis on having a vision about purpose, leadership, management, and culture. Conscious Capitalism is thus a more comprehensive way of thinking about business; the concept includes the TBL stakeholder approach, while going significantly beyond it with valuable insights into how to help evolve business to a higher level.

Shared-Value Capitalism

Put forth by Michael Porter and Mark Kramer in 2011, shared-value capitalism (SVC) refers to practices that make a company more competitive while enhancing the economic and social well-being of the communities in which it operates.[4] Porter and Kramer argue that companies should broaden the definition of value and more closely align value creation for shareholders with value for society. At a global level, societal needs such as housing, energy, sanitation, and health care are still unmet for a huge number of people. But most big companies largely focus on stimulating further demand among affluent customers. The past, narrow focus on shareholder value has led to a growing divergence between business and society.

Porter and Kramer suggest that companies can create shared value in three ways: by rethinking products so they are good for customers and create social benefits; by making the value chain more efficient and sustainable; and by enabling local cluster development. They conclude by asserting, "Not all profit is equal. Profits involving a social purpose represent a higher form of capitalism, one that creates a positive cycle of company and community prosperity."

SVC differs from traditional capitalism in that it places greater emphasis on value creation for society, going beyond shareholder wealth maximization. It explicitly recognizes that companies cannot long prosper in the midst of communities that are struggling.

Conscious Capitalism focuses on shared human *values*, in addition to shared economic value. SVC is a pragmatic way to better align business and societal interests, but it lacks the intangible but critical emotional and spiritual motivators that give Conscious Capitalism its extraordinary power. It feels more like a tactical readjustment rather than the kind of fundamental rethinking that we believe is required today. Moreover, the performance implications of SVC are unclear, whereas there is a great deal of evidence that conscious businesses outperform traditional businesses.

Creative Capitalism

In a widely noted speech at the 2008 World Economic Forum in Davos, Bill Gates put forward a vision for what he termed *creative capitalism*.[5] He suggested that businesses expand the reach of market forces so they can benefit more people at the lower end of the income spectrum. Companies should work with governments and nonprofits to meet the needs of the poorest people and should invest in innovation specifically aimed at the "base of the pyramid."[6]

Creative capitalism applies to products with high fixed costs and low variable costs, such as software and pharmaceuticals. Companies can use variable pricing to make such products affordable to poor people and still make a profit. Additionally, the companies benefit through public recognition and an enhanced reputation, which enables them to hire and retain additional talented team members. Rather than profit maximization, creative capitalism emphasizes impact maximization. It entails a high degree of cross-subsidy between more prosperous and less prosperous customers.

The limitation of creative capitalism, like CSR, is that it is largely an add-on to the traditional business model. It simply suggests that companies develop better go-to-market strategies for low-income markets. The concept only applies to a relatively small subset of industries with cost structures that allow for radically variable pricing. Great emphasis is placed on the reputational value of offering low income customers low prices on products with low variable costs. Conscious Capitalism places a strong emphasis on society and thus incorporates much of what creative capitalism is about, while going much further to transform the core of the business. The creativity in creative capitalism is limited to devising sliding-scale pricing strategies, whereas creativity and innovation on a broad scale are central to Conscious Capitalism.

B Corporations

In the last few years, a new corporate form has come into being: *B corporations*, or *benefit corporations*. B corporations adopt charters that explicitly address social and environmental problems. These companies are certified by a nonprofit organization called B Lab, which ensures that they are legally accountable for meeting defined social and environmental performance standards. An estimated 450 small to midsize companies have received this certification as of this writing, and seven states have passed legislation permitting companies to incorporate as benefit corporations. By mutual agreement, certified companies receive discounts when transacting with other certified companies.[7]

Although B corporations are compatible with the tenets of Conscious Capitalism, we do not see them as a revolutionary advance. Here is why: corporations as they are currently structured are ultimately controlled by their investors or owners. This means that the owners proportionately own the corporation according to the number of shares in the corporation they own. The owners of the business collectively determine the basic governance of the company and therefore determine, through their elected representatives on the board of directors, who the management of the company is. The owners therefore ultimately control the company. Such owner control makes sense because, of all the stakeholders in a business, the owners are the most vulnerable to exploitation by both management and the other stakeholders. This is contrary to what many people believe. Remember, owners are paid last—after all the other stakeholders have been paid for their exchanges with the business, and only if there is something left over. It is therefore essential that the owners of the business have the final say on management and the governance principles of the corporation.

B corporations appear to violate the important principle that owners should ultimately control the corporation. Management has far more control of B corporations, regardless of financial performance, provided they are fulfilling the social and environmental goals they set out for themselves. The system protects the management from owners, but who protects the owners from management? What prevents the owners from being exploited by management? Can the owners still fire the management and install new leadership? If they can, then B corporations are really not any different from ordinary corporations and therefore aren't really necessary except as some type of socially and environmentally responsible "affiliates club." If the owners have no control over management, then B corporations will surely be restricted to a relatively small niche category of businesses whose owners are willing to accept lower financial returns on behalf of other goals established by the management—goals that may not be aligned with the interests of the owners.

There is nothing wrong with any corporation's setting itself up as a B corporation if that is what the founders wish to do and if they can find investors who willingly agree to the terms of the B corporation and the apparent relinquishing of their legal rights as owners to the power of management. Benefit corporations are perfectly consistent with capitalism as a type of voluntary organization that creates value for its stakeholders in proportions different from those used by ordinary corporations. However, B corporations fall far short of being revolutionary, because they will likely be only a relatively small niche in the greater capitalistic universe.

B corporations are potentially less competitive than both owner-controlled corporations and nonprofit organizations. In terms of raising capital, owner-controlled corporations will have stronger competitive advantages than B corporations, as most investors are seeking to receive high long-term returns. While B corporations are not prevented from seeking high returns on capital, they have a marketing challenge of convincing potential investors that they wish to do this. Unlike donors to nonprofits, people who invest in B corporations enjoy no tax deductions for their investment. This means that nonprofit organizations will likely have a competitive advantage in receiving money from socially and environmentally driven people who value the tax deductions that accompany their philanthropy.

Benefit corporations do have a legitimate niche between ordinary owner-controlled corporations and nonprofit organizations. It is a valuable and useful niche. We hope it will grow over time, but it will probably not become mainstream, whereas we believe that Conscious Capitalism will eventually become the default way for companies to be.

Misconceptions About Conscious Capitalism

Some people view the idea of Conscious Capitalism as idealistic and impractical. In their view, the world of business is a brutal, rough-and-tumble, dog-eat-dog school of hard knocks, to mix a few metaphors. In this world, nice guys always finish last. To them, Conscious Capitalism is just a pipe dream, wishful thinking on the part of wooly-headed idealists.

In fact, this way of doing business not only creates a great deal of well-being and happiness for all the stakeholders, but it is also the secret to sustained high performance. Traditional businesses that must compete against a truly conscious business soon discover just how strong, resolute, and resilient these enterprises can be. Ask an executive of now-bankrupt American Airlines what it has been like to compete with Southwest Airlines in its own backyard for the last 40 years.

This appendix addresses some common misconceptions and criticisms about Conscious Capitalism and our responses.

Conscious Capitalism is just "putting lipstick" on a pig. Business is still all about profits.

The cynics out there insist that all of this is just happy talk—that business is, always was, and always will be about generating as much profit as possible. Nothing else comes even close.

We believe strongly that profits are essential for a company to better fulfill its purpose. Creating profits provides the capital our world needs to innovate and progress—no profits, no progress. If you're only making enough money to cover your costs, your impact is going to be minimal. Whole Foods Market has a much greater impact today than we did thirty, twenty, or ten years ago, because we've been highly profitable. This has enabled us to grow and to realize our higher purposes much more successfully. We've been able to reach and help millions of people instead of just a few thousand.

The problem is that most corporations pursue profits the way misguided human beings pursue happiness. As noted before, Viktor Frankl said, "Happiness cannot be pursued; it *ensues*."[1] People obsessed with finding their own happiness tend to be self-absorbed narcissists. Happiness is the by-product of things such as living a life of meaning and purpose, service to others, striving for excellence, growing as an individual, friendship, parenting, love, and generosity. Similarly, profits are best realized when they are not the primary goal of the business. They are the by-product of higher purposes, great products and service, customer delight, team member happiness, and social and environmental stewardship. Companies that elevate the pursuit of profit above everything else eventually will discover the folly of doing so.

Conscious Capitalism only works in good times.

Many people believe that caring, generosity, and a sense of shared destiny all rapidly evaporate when the heat is on. It is easy to treat people well when you're feeling flush; the question is, what will such companies do when the going gets tough? Truly conscious companies rise to the occasion and become even more compassionate when they experience difficult times. They emerge with their core values strengthened and their humanness intact.

The actions they undertake to survive the tough times actually bring the company closer together and strengthen its culture.

Here is an example. Windsor Marketing Group is a small Connecticut company that produces in-store signage for some of the largest retailers in the country. Founder and CEO Kevin Armata recalls a tough situation the company faced as the last recession took hold: "Our business declined by 30 percent. If we had laid off even 20 percent of our workforce (as all our competitors were doing), it probably would have resulted in seven or eight families losing their homes, and maybe six or seven divorces. We realized the company was in a better position to make it through the crisis than many of these families were, so I decided not to lay anyone off. We would get through it together."[2]

When the recession hit, the company had already initiated work on a large new factory. Rather than suspend work on the factory, Armata came up with an innovative solution. He asked the team members (who had a lot of spare time because business was so slow) if they had any construction experience. It turned out that a number of them had been masonry workers, carpenters, plumbers, and electricians earlier in their life, most only for a brief period. So the company put its people to work building the new factory whenever they had extra time on their hands.

Eventually, the company had a brand-new 160,000-square-foot factory building that had largely been built by its own team members. As the recession ended, the business came roaring back, growing 40 percent quarter over quarter. The level of engagement, commitment, and gratitude the team members feel toward the company is just immense. They built walls for the company; now, even more than before, they are willing to walk through walls for it.[3]

Conscious Capitalism is a luxury good; only companies in high-end markets can afford it.

Conscious Capitalism is not a luxury good that is only affordable to a select few. There are numerous companies that offer high levels of affordability to customers while practicing the tenets of Conscious Capitalism.

Examples include Costco, Southwest Airlines, JetBlue, Amazon.com, Tata, Toyota, Trader Joe's, and IKEA. Other conscious companies are positioned at a higher point in the price spectrum but still offer great value to customers, because of the superior quality of their offerings, customer service, and the overall customer experiences that they provide. Examples of such companies include Whole Foods Market, The Container Store, and Starbucks.

Conscious Capitalism works for all kinds of businesses because it achieves a level of *effective efficiency* that traditional businesses just cannot match. Conscious businesses generate higher sales relative to their asset base, have highly productive and effective team members, spend money where it makes a real difference to customers, and do not squander resources on things that do not add value. They run a tight ship.

Wall Street will never see the value of Conscious Capitalism.

As discussed earlier, many individual financial analysts may not appreciate the idea of Conscious Capitalism right now, but financial markets as a whole do reward conscious companies with high valuations because of their superior long-term economic performance. As the legendary investor Ben Graham put it, "In the short run, the market is a voting machine but in the long run it is a weighing machine." The stock market rewards whatever succeeds economically, and it measures financial success over both the short term and the long term. Wall Street is agnostic about the causes of financial success for any business, as long as there is authentic financial success. Over time, mutual funds and stock market indices based on Conscious Capitalism principles will undoubtedly come into existence. As these prove to be financially successful, they will attract more and more imitators, and Wall Street will evolve its values and philosophies accordingly to be able to identify such companies early on.

Unfortunately, too many managers and executives are primarily motivated by short-term considerations, often knowingly short-changing the company's long-term health in the process. For example, in one survey, over 80 percent of executives said they would cut spending in areas such as R&D to make sure they met quarterly earning goals, even if they personally believed this would destroy long-term value.[4]

You have to be born a conscious company. You can't become one if your history has been very different.

As discussed in chapter 17, it is challenging but not impossible for a traditional business to reinvent itself as a conscious business. The transformation of HCL was one example. Another example is Harley-Davidson, which underwent a remarkable transformation after it was sold by AMF Company in 1981. Interface Carpet is another example; after its founder and CEO Ray Anderson had a profound epiphany about the impact his business was having on the planet, he set about reinventing the company as a conscious business.

It is not easy, but it can and must be done if a business wants to be competitive, survive, and flourish over the long term. It takes authentic commitment from the top; you cannot have a conscious business without conscious leadership. It also takes patience; change of this magnitude is a multiyear journey. It usually requires some outside help from consultants too. And it takes the whole stakeholder universe's coming together to collectively envision and commit to a more conscious future.

Even if most existing companies are unable or unwilling to make a successful transition to Conscious Capitalism, it won't matter in the long term because there will be more and more conscious entrepreneurs starting up conscious businesses that will outcompete traditional businesses in the marketplace and eventually replace them. Free-enterprise capitalism is incredibly dynamic and its "creative destruction" processes (whereby more effective and efficient approaches continually supplant older ones) ensure that in the long term, the superior business philosophy triumphs.

Once the founder leaves, companies always revert to the norm.

Reversion after the loss of a strong leader is a real danger, and there are many cautionary tales from recent years to show how easily this can happen. Look at what happened to Hewlett-Packard after the founders retired and the company hired an outsider, Carly Fiorina, as the CEO; Starbucks when Howard Schultz stepped away; and The Home Depot when Bernie Marcus and Arthur Blank handed over the CEO role to GE alum Bob Nardelli. The wrong leader, someone who just doesn't understand the purpose, values, and culture, can quickly undermine and erode the strength of a company that took decades to build. To prevent this from happening, a company must completely imbed a conscious approach into its DNA through its culture. The culture needs to be owned by all the stakeholders, especially team members. Boards of directors must take great care in selecting new CEOs. Ideally, the executive should be promoted from within. Conscious companies that have managed this process well include Tata, UPS, and Southwest Airlines; their cultures and values have endured through many leadership changes.

Becoming a conscious business requires changing everything and is thus impossible.

A conscious business is still a business, first and foremost. Changing a traditional profit-centered business into a purpose-driven conscious business requires a shift in perspective that is challenging but not impossible. The great advantage in such a shift is that the direction feels natural and meaningful to people, once they get past their engrained cynicism about business and about change. The change process soon takes on a momentum of its own. Remember, this is about liberating the heroic spirit of business; the spirit is always present but is largely dormant in most companies. However, it is never dead; the spark of caring and creativity is ever present in all of us and can never be fully extinguished.

What gets measured gets managed. There are too many intangibles here.

Measurement is important, but one of the great fallacies of modern management is that everything that matters must be measured and that if something cannot be objectively measured, it does not matter. This is evidence of our analytical intelligence run amok. We should try to measure what we can in a reasonable way, allowing the people who generate the results to have a strong say in how that is done. But some of the most critical elements of culture, such as love and authenticity, do not lend themselves to hard measures.

It is confusing for managers to be told to optimize stakeholder interests. They need a simple, transparent goal, like maximizing shareholder value.

A principle dubbed Einstein's razor says, "Everything should be made as simple as possible, but no simpler." It can be difficult for some people to understand the larger business system of interdependent stakeholders. As we have discussed, they need a high degree of systems intelligence, and sadly, many people just don't have that yet. However, people who have integrative minds capable of seeing the interdependencies of the larger business system realize that *business is not a math problem to be solved*. Maximizing any one thing necessarily requires that other important things within the larger system are short-changed, possibly even fatally damaged. A business is a complex living organism, and people entrusted with leading and managing such an entity need to have the requisite skill set, mind-set, and heart-set to do so. Their purpose must always be the healthy development of the enterprise, so that it can generate as much value as possible for all stakeholders, including investors. Business leaders must never knowingly allow the overall enterprise to be harmed just to benefit one of its stakeholders in the short term. That path leads to a form of organizational cancer and, left unchecked, the eventual demise of the enterprise.

NOTES

Foreword

1. From *Reason* debate, http://reason.com/archives/2005/10/01/rethinking-the-social-responsi/singlepage.

Chapter One

1. Francois Bourguignon and Christian Morrison, "Inequality Among World Citizens: 1820–1992," *American Economic Review* 92, no. 4 (2002): 731; Shaohua Chen and Martin Ravallion, "The Developing World Is Poorer Than We Thought, but No Less Successful in the Fight Against Poverty," *Quarterly Journal of Economics* 125, no. 4 (2010): 1577–1625.

2. Valued in 1990 international dollars. Angus Maddison, "Statistics on World Population, GDP and Per Capita GDP, 1–2008 AD," Groningen Growth & Development Centre Web page, March 2010, www.ggdc.net/MADDISON/oriindex.htm.

3. These three statistics are from Deirdre N. McCloskey, *Bourgeois Dignity: Why Economics Can't Explain the Modern World* (Chicago: University of Chicago Press, 2010), 48–57.

4. "South Korea GDP," Trading Economics Web page, n.d., www.tradingeconomics.com/south-korea/gdp.

5. Matt Rosenberg, "Current World Population," *About.com*, January 1, 2011, http://geography.about.com/od/obtainpopulationdata/a/worldpopulation.htm.

6. *Wikipedia*, s. v. "life expectancy," last modified June 5, 2012, http://en.wikipedia.org/wiki/Life_expectancy; United Nations, Department of Economic and Social Affairs, Population Division, *World Population Prospects: The 2010 Revision*, CD-ROM ed. (New York: United Nations, 2011).

7. Food and Agriculture Organization of the United Nations, "Hunger," Web portal, 2012, www.fao.org/hunger/en/; Food and Agriculture Organization of the United Nations, *The State of Food Insecurity in the World* (Rome: FAO, 2010); Population Reference Bureau, *2010 World Population Data Sheet* (Washington, D.C.: Population Reference Bureau, 2010).

8. UNESCO Institute for Statistics, "Adult and Youth Literacy," UIS Fact Sheet (Succursale Centre-Ville, Montreal), no. 16, September 2011, www.uis.unesco.org/FactSheets/Documents/FS16-2011-Literacy-EN.pdf.

9. Freedom House, "Democracy's Century: A Survey of Global Political Change in the 20th Century," Freedom House, New York, 1999, www.social-sciences-and-humanities.

NOTES

com/PDF/century_democracy.pdf; Arch Puddington, "Freedom in the World 2011: The Authoritarian Challenge to Democracy," Freedom House, New York, 2011; population statistics from Population Reference Bureau, *2010 World Population Data Sheet.*

10. James D. Gwartney, Joshua C. Hall, and Robert Lawson, 2010 Economic Freedom Dataset, in *Economic Freedom of the World: 2010 Annual Report* (Fraser Institute, Vancouver, Canada, 2010). See also Saamah Abdallah et al., *The (Un)Happy Planet Index 2.0: Why Good Lives Don't Have to Cost the Earth* (New Economics Foundation, London, 2009). Of course, the data does show that above a certain level of material satisfaction, further increases in income are not correlated with increases in happiness.

11. McCloskey, *Bourgeois Dignity.*

12. Candace A. Allen, "The Entrepreneur as Hero," *Economic Insights* (Federal Reserve Bank of Dallas) 2, no. 1 (1997), available at www.dallasfed.org/assets/documents/research/ei/ei9701.pdf.

13. Gallup Consulting, *State of the American Workplace: 2008–2010* (Washington, D.C.: Gallup, 2010); 2010 percentages from Alana K. Farrell (regional marketing consultant for Gallup Consulting), e-mail to authors, November 9, 2011.

14. Sarah Anderson (Institute for Policy Studies), e-mail to author, November 22, 2011.

15. Jeffrey M. Jones, "Americans Most Confident in Military, Least in Congress," *Gallup Politics,* June 23, 2011, www.gallup.com/poll/148163/Americans-Confident-Military-Least-Congress.aspx.

16. Bill Frezza, "Exactly What is Crony Capitalism, Anyway?" *Real Clear Markets,* December 12, 2011.

17. Sandy Cutler, interview with authors, April 10, 2012.

18. Marc Gafni, interview with authors, March 15, 2012.

19. R. Edward Freeman, Jeffrey S. Harrison, and Andrew C. Wicks, *Managing for Stakeholders: Survival, Reputation, and Success* (New Haven: Yale University Press, 2007).

20. Marc Gafni, interview with authors, March 15, 2012.

Chapter Two

1. Jonathan Plucker, ed., "The Flynn Effect," in *Human Intelligence: Historical Influences, Current Controversies, Teaching Resources,* Indiana University, 2002, www.indiana.edu/~intell/flynneffect.shtml.

2. Tim Berners-Lee, "Homepage," n.d., www.w3.org/People/Berners-Lee/.

3. The downside of this, of course, is accuracy. Anyone can publish anything on the Web, and some will believe it without question.

4. Mary Lennighan, "Number of Phones Exceeds Population of World," *Total Telecom,* May 2011, www.totaltele.com/view.aspx?ID=464922.

5. David B. Wolfe, "The Psychological Center of Gravity," *American Demographics,* April 1998.

6. David Wolfe defined the "psychological center of gravity" as the median age of adults plus or minus five years. See ibid.

7. GfK Mediamark Research & Intelligence, "Median Age, Household Income and Individual Employment Income," GfK MRI Spring Technical Guide, www.gfkmri.com/mri/techguide/spr2011/med_age_hhi_iei_sp11.pdf.

8. Women were granted the right to vote in the United States in 1920. Shockingly, women did not have the right to vote in most of Switzerland until 1971; in 2010, a majority of Switzerland's cabinet ministers were women.

NOTES

9. Steven Pinker, *The Better Angels of Our Nature: Why Violence Has Declined* (New York: Viking, 2011). These examples illustrate that as we become more conscious, our ethical standards and practices evolve upward to higher levels. Lawrence Kohlberg and Carol Gilligan's research provides evidence that our ethics tend to evolve over time up several distinct ethical levels or stages from "obedience to avoid punishment" at the first stage up to "universal justice and love" at the highest stage. See Lawrence Kohlberg, *The Philosophy of Moral Development* (New York: Harper & Row, 1981); Lawrence Kohlberg, *The Psychology of Moral Development* (New York: Harper & Row, 1984); Carol Gilligan, *In a Different Voice* (Cambridge, Mass.: Harvard University Press, 1993).

10. Abraham Lincoln, Annual Message to Congress, December 1, 1862.

11. Over the past ten years, Gallup has found that overall employee engagement levels have fluctuated between 26 percent and 30 percent, while 15 to 20 percent of employees have been "actively disengaged." Gallup defines engaged employees as "emotionally attached to their workplace and motivated to be productive," and actively disengaged employees as those who "view their workplaces negatively and are liable to spread that negativity to others." By contrast, we have found that many conscious businesses enjoy the passionate commitment of 95 percent or more of their employees. Gallup Consulting, Gallup Consulting, *State of the American Workplace: 2008–2010* (Washington, D.C.: Gallup, 2010).

12. Kip Tindell, telephone interview with authors, May 2009.

13. Bill George, telephone interview with authors, March 13, 2012.

14. Our inspiration for the comment "Conscious businesses do what is right because it is right" comes from *Letters from Iwo Jima*, directed by Clint Eastwood (Warner Brothers, 2006).

15. David Grayson and Adrian Hodges, *Corporate Social Opportunity! Seven Steps to Make Corporate Social Responsibility Work for Your Business* (Greenleaf Publishing, Sheffield, U.K.: 2004).

16. This metaphor was suggested by Debashis Chatterjee, director of the Indian Institute of Management, Kozhikode.

Part One

1. Jeff Bezos, quoted in John A. Byrne, *World Changers: 25 Entrepreneurs Who Changed Business as We Knew It* (New York: Portfolio/Penguin, 2011).

Chapter Three

1. Bill George, telephone interview with authors, March 15, 2012.

2. Roy Spence and Haley Rushing, *It's Not What You Sell, It's What You Stand For: Why Every Extraordinary Business is Driven by Purpose* (New York: Portfolio, 2009).

3. Richard R. Ellsworth, *Leading with Purpose: The New Corporate Realities* (Stanford: Stanford Business Books, 2002).

4. Jerry Porras, quoted in Lan Liu, *Conversations on Leadership: Wisdom from Global Management Gurus* (New York: Wiley, 2010).

5. John A. Byrne, *World Changers: 25 Entrepreneurs Who Changed Business as We Knew It* (New York: Portfolio/Penguin, 2011).

6. Jennifer Reingold, "Can P&G Make Money in Places Where People Earn $2 a Day?" *Fortune*, January 17, 2011, 86–91.

7. See http://www.guardian.co.uk/sustainable-business/unilever-ceo-paul-polman-interview.

NOTES

8. We are grateful to Doug Levy, CEO of MEplusYOU, for this insight.

9. John Simons, "Pharma, Heal Thyself," *Fortune*, February 28, 2006.

10. Viktor E. Frankl, *Man's Search for Meaning* (Boston: Beacon Press, 1959; first published in Austria in 1946 under the title *Ein Psycholog erlebt das Konzentrationslager*).

11. Ibid.

12. Mat Gelman et al., "Viktor Emil Frankl, 1905–1997," *American Journal of Psychiatry* 157, no. 4 (2000): 625, available at http://ajp.psychiatryonline.org/article.aspx?articleid=174067.

13. "[Viktor E. Frankl] Life and Work," Viktor Frankl Institut, Vienna, last updated June 20, 2012, www.viktorfrankl.org/e/lifeandwork.html.

14. Ibid.

15. Studs Terkel, *Working: People Talk About What They Do All Day and How They Feel About What They Do* (New York: New Press, 1997).

16. George Bernard Shaw, epistle dedicatory to Arthur Bingham Walkley, *Man and Superman: A Comedy and a Philosophy* (originally published in 1923).

17. Gallup Consulting, *State of the American Workplace: 2008–2010* (Washington, D.C.: Gallup, 2010).

18. Paul Hawken, *Blessed Unrest: How the Largest Movement in the World Came into Being and Why No One Saw It Coming* (New York: Viking, 2007).

19. Spence and Rushing, *It's Not What You Sell*.

20. Financial incentives can also backfire because they have been shown to decrease intrinsic motivation by making it "all about the money."

21. Dan Schawbel, "Biz Stone on His Biggest Challenges, Influences and the Future of Social Media," *Forbes*, June 14, 2012; accessed at http://www.forbes.com/sites/danschawbel/2012/06/14/biz-stone-on-his-biggest-challenges-influences-and-the-future-of-social-media/.

Chapter Four

1. Marc Gunther, "Waste Management's New Direction," *Fortune*, December 6, 2010, 103–108. See also the Waste Management Web site, www.wm.com.

2. Associated Press, "Analyst Downgrades Waste Management," September 14, 2009.

3. This section benefited greatly from Nikos Mourkogiannis, *Purpose: The Starting Point of Great Companies* (New York: Palgrave Macmillan, 2006).

4. Muhammad Yunus, *Banker to the Poor: Micro-Lending and the Battle Against World Poverty* (New York: Public Affairs, 1999).

5. For follow-up reading, we recommend the following books: T. Colin Campbell, *The China Study: The Most Comprehensive Study of Nutrition Ever Conducted and the Startling Implications for Diet, Weight Loss and Long-Term Health* (Dallas: BenBella Books, 2005); Caldwell Esselstyn, *Prevent and Reverse Heart Disease: The Revolutionary, Scientifically Proven, Nutrition-Based Cure* (New York: Avery, 2007); Joel Fuhrman, *Eat to Live: The Revolutionary Formula for Fast and Sustained Weight Loss* (Boston: Little, Brown and Co., 2003); Joel Fuhrman, *Super Immunity: The Essential Nutrition Guide for Boosting Our Body's Defenses to Live Longer, Stronger, and Disease Free* (New York: HarperOne, 2011); John McDougall and Mary McDougall, *The Starch Solution: Eat the Foods You Love, Regain Your Health, and Lose the Weight for Good!* (New York: Rodale, 2012); Neal Barnard, *Dr. Neal Barnard's Program for Reversing Diabetes: The Scientifically Proven System for Reversing Diabetes Without Drugs* (New York: Rodale, 2007).

6. Sally Jewell, telephone interview with authors, March 22, 2012.

NOTES

Part Two

1. R. Edward Freeman, Jeffrey S. Harrison, and Andrew C. Wicks, *Managing for Stakeholders: Survival, Reputation, and Success* (New Haven: Yale University Press, 2007).

2. Casey Sheahen, telephone interview with authors, March 22, 2012.

Chapter Five

1. Peter F. Drucker, *Management: Tasks, Responsibilities, Practices* (New York: Harper Collins, 1973).

2. Doug Rauch, telephone interview by Kee Yup Lee for POSCO in-house magazine.

3. John A. Byrne, *World Changers: 25 Entrepreneurs Who Changed Business as We Knew It* (New York: Portfolio/Penguin, 2011).

4. We are grateful to Doug Levy, CEO of MEplusYOU, for this insight.

5. Byrne, *World Changers*.

6. This is an evolutionary principle taken from the Red Queen's race in Lewis Carroll's *Through the Looking-Glass* (chapter 2). It states that continual adaptation is needed for a species to maintain its relative fitness among the systems with which it coevolves; see F. Heylighen, "The Red Queen Principle," Principia Cybernetica Web page, December 2, 1993, http://pespmc1.vub.ac.be/REDQUEEN.html.

7. Doug Rauch, telephone interview, July 12, 2012.

8. Michael P. Zeisser, "A Closing View: Marketing in a Post-TIVO World," *McKinsey Quarterly Special Edition: Technology*, 2002; per-person spending is calculated on the basis of mid-2011 U.S. population data: Population Reference Bureau, *2011 World Population Data Sheet* (Washington, D.C.: Population Reference Bureau, 2011).

9. Melinda Davis, *The New Culture of Desire: The Pleasure Imperative Transforming Your Business and Your Life* (New York: Free Press, 2002).

10. Kip Tindell, telephone interview by Kee Yup Lee for POSCO in-house magazine.

11. Glen Urban, *Don't Just Relate, Advocate! A Blueprint for Profit in the Era of Customer Power* (Upper Saddle River, N.J.: Pearson Prentice Hall, 2005).

12. We are grateful to Doug Levy, CEO of MEplusYOU, for these insights.

Chapter Six

1. Research published in journals such as the *American Journal of Hypertension* and the *British Medical Journal* shows that blood pressure rises and heart attacks spike by 20 percent or more on Monday mornings. See "Monday Morning Bad for Your Health," CNN.com International, February 3, 2005, http://edition.cnn.com/2005/BUSINESS/02/03/monday.pressure/index.html. Research also shows that the stress hormone cortisol peaks early in the day, around the time people head off to work. See "Amazing Facts About Heart Health and Heart Disease," July 2, 2009, www.webmd.com/heart/features/amazing-facts-about-heart-health-and-heart-disease_?page=2.

2. Jim Clifton, *The Coming Jobs War* (New York: Gallup Press, 2011). Italics added.

3. Thomas Petzinger Jr., *Hard Landing: The Epic Contest for Power and Profits That Plunged the Airlines into Chaos* (New York: Three Rivers Press, 1996).

4. Amy Wrzesniewski et al., "Jobs, Careers, and Callings: People's Relations to Their Work," *Journal of Research in Personality* 31, no. 1 (March 1997): 21–33.

5. Walter Robb, e-mail to authors, April 9, 2012.

6. Gary Hamel, *What Matters Now: How to Win in a World of Relentless Change* (San Francisco: Jossey-Bass, 2012).

7. Daniel H. Pink, *Drive: The Surprising Truth About What Motivates Us* (New York: Penguin, 2011).

8. Kip Tindell, telephone interview by Kee Yup Lee for POSCO in-house magazine.

9. Jeffrey A. Krames, *The Jack Welch Lexicon of Leadership* (New York: McGraw Hill, 2002).

10. The 400- or 500-to-1 ratio is based largely on the value of huge stock and stock option grants routinely made to senior executives; some of the grants may amount to nothing if the options expire worthless. While executives sometimes hit the jackpot with very large stock price increases, and the spread increases significantly, cash compensation alone seldom has that big of a spread. We address the issue of stock options in chapter 7.

11. This doesn't mean we believe the government should pass laws restricting executive compensation. Compensation policies need to be voluntary to be meaningful.

12. *Economic Report of the President Transmitted to the Congress February 2011, Together with the Annual Report of the Council of Economic Advisers* (Washington, D.C.: U.S. Government Printing Office, 2011), appendix B, tables B-16 and B-30, available at http://origin.www.gpoaccess.gov/eop/tables11.html.

13. Doug Rauch, telephone interview by Kee Yup Lee for POSCO in-house magazine.

Chapter Seven

1. The best book we know on the causes of the financial meltdown is Gretchen Morgenson and Joshua Rosner, *Reckless Endangerment: How Outsized Ambition, Greed, and Corruption Led to Economic Armageddon* (New York: Times Books, 2011).

2. Warren Buffet, letter to Berkshire shareholders, 2010, available at www.berkshirehathaway.com/letters/2010ltr.pdf.

3. John A. Byrne, *World Changers: 25 Entrepreneurs Who Changed Business as We Knew It* (New York: Portfolio/Penguin, 2011).

4. David Hunkar (pseudonym), "Duration of Stock Holding Periods Continue to Fall," TopForeignStocks.com blog, September 6, 2010, http://topforeignstocks.com/2010/09/06/duration-of-stock-holding-period-continues-to-fall-globally/.

5. An exit strategy does make sense when a particular kind of investor hands off an investment to another kind of investor at the appropriate time, like a well-thought-out succession plan. Venture funding that is targeted at high-risk, early-stage investments appropriately ends when the company reaches a certain stage of development.

6. Tom Gardner and David Gardner, telephone interview with authors, March 23, 2012.

7. Bill George, telephone interview with authors, March 13, 2012.

8. "Customer Centric: Going Beyond the Mission Statement," Karma Blog, February 16, 2011, http://www.karmacrm.com/blog/general/customer-centric-going-beyond-the-mission-statement.html.

9. Academic research bears out our concerns. One study showed that large stock option grants to CEOs result in negative stock performance for shareholders, due to opportunistic behavior by CEOs. See Jean M. Canil and Bruce A. Rosser, "CEO Stock Options: Evidence That Large Grants Are Bad News for Shareholders," paper presented at FMA European Conference, Barcelona, June 1, 2007, available at http://69.175.2.130/-finman/Barcelona/Papers/CEO_barc.pdf. Another paper shows that CEOs with large option grants take excessive risks that can backfire for shareholders. See Gerard Sanders and Donald Hambrick, "Swinging for the Fences: The Effects of CEO Stock Options on Company Risk-Taking and Performance," *Academy of Management Journal* (October–November 2007).

NOTES

10. Ray C. Anderson, *Confessions of a Radical Industrialist* (New York: St. Martin's Press, 2009).

11. Jeffrey M. Jones, "Americans Most Confident in Military, Least in Congress," *Gallup Politics*, June 23, 2011, www.gallup.com/poll/148163/Americans-Confident-Military-Least-Congress.aspx.

12. The B (or Benefit) Corporation movement is largely predicated on this belief. It seeks to create a special mode of incorporation that permits companies to explicitly seek to create societal benefits and consider the interests of all their stakeholders, in addition to creating wealth for shareholders. Companies also are required to report on their social and environmental performance using independent standards. Nine U.S. states have passed Benefit Corporation legislation as of July 13, 2012, and bills have been introduced in six others.

Chapter Eight

1. C. K. Prahalad and Gary Hamel, "The Core Competence of the Corporation," *Harvard Business Review*, May–June 1990. See also C. K. Prahalad and Gary Hamel, *Competing for the Future* (Boston: Harvard Business School Press, 1994).

2. Mohanbir Sawhney, presentation at "Does Marketing Need Reform?" conference, Bentley University, Boston, 2004.

3. CNNMoney, "World's Most Admired Companies: Metals Industry," CNNMoney, March 21, 2011, http://money.cnn.com/magazines/fortune/mostadmired/2011/industries/36.html; Steelads.com, "Top 25 Largest Steel Producers in the World According to the World Steel Organization," 2011, www.steelads.com/info/largeststeel/TOP30_Worlds_Largest_Steel_Companies.html.

4. The discussion of POSCO in this book is based on POSCO Research Institute and Firms of Endearment Institute Korea, research report, Seoul, July 2011.

5. Terri Kelly, telephone interview with authors, March 23, 2012.

6. Sally Jewell, telephone interview with authors, March 23, 2012.

7. John A. Byrne, *World Changers: 25 Entrepreneurs Who Changed Business as We Knew It* (New York: Portfolio/Penguin, 2011).

Chapter Nine

1. Milton Friedman, "The Social Responsibility of Business Is to Increase Its Profits," *New York Times Magazine*, September 13, 1970. For an interesting debate on corporate social responsibility, see Milton Friedman, John Mackey, and T. J. Rodgers, "Rethinking the Social Responsibility of Business," *Reason*, October 2005, http://reason.com/archives/2005/10/01/rethinking-the-social-responsi.

2. We are grateful to Jo Ann Skousen, associate producer of FreedomFest, for this example.

3. For more information, see the Whole Planet Foundation Web page, www.wholeplanetfoundation.org.

4. Marianne McGee, "IBM Launches Corporate 'Peace Corps' Program for Employees," *InformationWeek*, March 26, 2008, http://www.informationweek.com/news/206905657.

5. Chris Edwards, "U.S. Corporate Tax Rate the Highest," *Cato @ Liberty Blog*, December 15, 2010, www.cato-at-liberty.org/u-s-corporate-tax-rate-the-highest/.

NOTES

6. This total includes income taxes, payroll taxes, property, rent, and other taxes; and payroll taxes that are withheld from Whole Foods team members and recognized as compensation expense.

7. Tata, "Values and Purpose," Tata Web page, www.tata.com/aboutus/articles/inside.aspx?artid=CKdRrD5ZDV4=&sectid=SD7sjPUVBkw=, accessed June 22, 2012. Emphasis added.

8. Ibid.

9. Karambir Singh Kang, presentation at Fourth International Conference on Conscious Capitalism, Bentley University, Waltham, MA., May 23, 2012.

10. Ann Graham, "Too Good to Fail," *Strategy & Business* 58 (Spring 2010), accessed at http://m.strategy-business.com/article/10106?gko=74e5d.

Chapter Ten

1. Casey Sheahen, telephone interview with authors, March 22, 2012.

2. Angus Maddison, *The World Economy: A Millennial Perspective* (Paris: Development Centre of the Organization for Economic Co-operation and Development, 2001).

3. Ibid.; Population Reference Bureau, *2011 World Population Data Sheet* (Washington, D.C.: Population Reference Bureau, 2011).

4. United Nations, Department of Economic and Social Affairs, Population Division, Population Estimates and Projections Section, "Population," interactive Web page, http://esa.un.org/wpp/unpp/panel_population.htm, accessed June 22, 2012.

5. Ibid.

6. Henning Steinfeld et al., *Livestock's Long Shadow* (Rome: Food and Agricultural Organization of the United Nations, 2006).

7. Water Footprint, "Introduction: Some Facts and Figures," Water Footprint, Enschede, Netherlands, www.waterfootprint.org, accessed June 22, 2012.

8. U.S. Senate Committee on Agriculture, Nutrition, and Forestry, *Animal Waste Pollution in America: An Emerging National Problem*, 104th Congr., December 1997.

9. Steinfeld et al., *Livestock's Long Shadow*.

10. See T. Colin Campbell, *The China Study: The Most Comprehensive Study of Nutrition Ever Conducted and the Startling Implications for Diet, Weight Loss and Long-Term Health* (Dallas: BenBella Books, 2005); Caldwell Esselstyn, *Prevent and Reverse Heart Disease: The Revolutionary, Scientifically Proven, Nutrition-Based Cure* (New York: Avery, 2007); Joel Fuhrman, *Eat to Live: The Revolutionary Formula for Fast and Sustained Weight Loss* (Boston: Little, Brown and Co., 2003); Neal Barnard, *Dr. Neal Barnard's Program for Reversing Diabetes: The Scientifically Proven System for Reversing Diabetes Without Drugs* (New York: Rodale, 2007); John McDougall and Mary McDougall, *The Starch Solution: Eat the Foods You Love, Regain Your Health, and Lose the Weight for Good!* (New York: Rodale, 2012).

11. See http://animalrights.about.com/od/animalrights101/tp/How-Many-Animals-Are-Killed.htm.

12. Kenneth T. Frank et al., "Trophic Cascades in a Formerly Cod-Dominated Ecosystem," *Science* 308, no. 5728 (2005): 1,621–1,623.

13. Jonathan Everett and Shahid Thaika; "3P: Pollution Prevention Pays," research paper, Bentley University, Waltham, Mass., available at http://solutions.3m.com/wps/portal/3M/en_US/3M-Sustainability/Global/Environment/3P/.

14. Geoff Colvin, "The UPS Green Team," *Fortune*, December 27, 2010, 44–51.

15. Information derived from research report on POSCO produced by The Firms of Endearment Institute Korea and POSCO Research Institute, Seoul, May 31, 2011.

16. Edward Humes, *Force of Nature: The Unlikely Story of Walmart's Green Revolution* (New York: Harper Business, 2011).

17. Michael Strong, *Be the Solution: How Entrepreneurs and Conscious Capitalists Can Solve All the World's Problems* (New York: Wiley, 2009).

18. Richard A. Kerr, "Acid Rain Control: Success on the Cheap," *Science* 282, no. 5391 (November 1998): 1,024.

19. Index of Leading Economic Indicators, 2003, published by the American Enterprise Institute; Steve Raynor, "The International Challenge of Climate Change," November 24, 2004, 12.

20. Jack Hollander, *The Real Environmental Crisis: Why Poverty, Not Affluence, Is the Environment's Number One Enemy* (Berkeley: University of California, 2004).

Chapter Eleven

1. Sam Walton, *Made in America* (New York: Bantam, 1993).

2. *Wikipedia*, s.v. "labor unions in the United States," last modified June 8, 2012, http://en.wikipedia.org/wiki/Labor_unions_in_the_United_States; Morgan Reynolds, "A History of Labor Unions from Colonial Times to 2009," *Mises Daily* (Ludwig von Mises Institute), July 17, 2009, http://mises.org/daily/3553#part12.

3. Ibid.

4. Steven Greenhut, *Plunder: How Public Employee Unions Are Raiding Treasuries, Controlling Our Lives and Bankrupting the Nation* (Santa Ana, Calif.: Forum Press, 2009).

5. Remarks shared at a private dinner in Dallas, October 6, 2011.

6. We are grateful to Ed Freeman for suggesting this point.

7. James Gattuso, "Congress Should Rein in the Regulators," *Washington Times*, December 8, 2010, available at www.washingtontimes.com/news/2010/dec/8/gattuso-congress-should-rein-in-the-regulators; Nicole V. Crain and W. Mark Crain, "The Impact of Regulatory Costs on Small Firms," *Small Business Research Summary* (SBA Office of Advocacy) 371 (September 2010), available at http://archive.sba.gov/advo/research/rs371.pdf.

8. Crain and Crain, "Regulatory Costs."

9. This is known as regulatory capture. *Wikipedia* provides evidence that this has happened in the United States with the following agencies and the industries they regulate: Bureau of Ocean Energy Management, Regulation and Enforcement; Commodity Futures Trading Commission; Environmental Protection Agency; Federal Aviation Administration; Federal Communications Commission; Federal Reserve Bank of New York; Food and Drug Administration; Interstate Commerce Commission; Nuclear Regulatory Commission; Office of the Comptroller of the Currency; and Securities and Exchange Commission. See *Wikipedia*, s.v. "regulatory capture," last modified June 9, 2012, http://en.wikipedia.org/wiki/Regulatory_capture, for details.

Chapter Twelve

1. Bill George, telephone interview with authors, March 13, 2012.

2. See the following books by Ken Wilber and published by Shambhala in Boston: *A Theory of Everything* (2001); *A Brief History of Everything* (2001); *Sex, Ecology, Spirituality* (2001); *Integral Spirituality* (2006); *Integral Psychology* (2000). See also Don Edward Beck and

NOTES

Christopher C. Cowan, *Spiral Dynamics: Mastering Values, Leadership and Change* (Boston: Blackwell, 1996); Jenny Wade, *Changes in Mind: A Holonomic Theory of the Evolution of Consciousness* (New York: SUNY Press, 1996).

3. Experiments conducted in the 1960s demonstrated that people tend to try to confirm the beliefs they already hold. Research has also shown that when people test ideas, they tend to focus on one possibility and ignore alternatives, biasing the outcome. Confirmation bias has been attributed to wishful thinking and the inability to process significant amounts of information. It leads to people's overconfidence in their own beliefs, even when presented with evidence to the contrary. This can lead to poor decisions in business, scientific, military, political, and other spheres. For a nontechnical summary, see Jason Zweig, "How to Ignore the Yes-Man in Your Head," *Wall Street Journal*, November 19, 2009.

4. R. Edward Freeman, Jeffrey S. Harrison, and Andrew C. Wicks, *Managing for Stakeholders: Survival, Reputation, and Success* (New Haven: Yale University Press, 2007).

5. Whole Foods Market, "Declaration of Interdependence," accessed June 20, 2012, www.wholefoodsmarket.com/company/declaration.php.

6. The future-search approach was created by Marvin Weisbord. See Marvin Weisbord and Sandra Janoff, *Future Search: Getting the Whole System in the Room for Vision, Commitment, and Action*, 3rd ed. (San Francisco: Berrett-Koehler Publishers, 2010).

Part Three

1. Pivot Web page, http://pivotleadership.com/.

2. Kamal Sarma, presentation on conscious leadership at the launch of Conscious Capitalism Australia in Sydney, April 30, 2012.

3. Stephanie Holland and She-conomy, "Marketing to Women Quick Facts," *She-conomy*, n.d., accessed June 20, 2012, www.she-conomy.com/report/marketing-to-women-quick-facts.

4. Debashis Chatterjee, quoted in Lan Liu, *Conversations on Leadership: Wisdom from Global Management Gurus* (New York: John Wiley & Sons, 2010).

5. John Kotter, quoted in Lan Liu, *Conversations on Leadership: Wisdom from Global Management Gurus* (New York: Wiley, 2010).

Chapter Thirteen

1. Bill George, quoted in Lan Liu, *Conversations on Leadership: Wisdom from Global Management Gurus* (New York: Wiley, 2010).

2. See Robert Kegan, *The Evolving Self* (Boston: Harvard University Press, 1982); Robert Kegan, *In Over Our Heads* (Boston: Harvard University Press, 1998); *Wikipedia*, s.v. "Howard Gardner," last modified June 12, 2012, http://en.wikipedia.org/wiki/Howard_Gardner; see also Howard Gardner, *Frames of Mind: The Theory of Multiple Intelligences* (New York: Basic Books, 1993).

3. Daniel Goleman, *Emotional Intelligence: Why It Can Matter More Than IQ* (New York: Bantam, 1995). Goleman also wrote another excellent book *Social Intelligence: The New Science of Human Relationships* (New York: Bantam, 2006). We have not separated social intelligence from emotional, spiritual, and systems intelligence into its own category, because we believe it is better seen as a characteristic of the other three categories.

4. Danah Zohar and Ian Marshall, *Spiritual Capital: Wealth We Can Live By* (San Francisco: Berrett-Koehler, 2004), 3.

5. John A. Byrne, *World Changers: 25 Entrepreneurs Who Changed Business as We Knew It* (New York: Portfolio/Penguin, 2011), 52.

6. We first heard this articulated by Debashis Chatterjee.

7. Liu, *Conversations on Leadership*.

8. Zohar and Marshall, *Spiritual Capital*, 55.

9. *Wikipedia*, s.v. "Buckminster Fuller," last modified June 18, 2012, http://en.wikipedia.org/wiki/Buckminister_Fuller.

10. The best book we are aware of on servant leadership is still the one that identified it originally: Robert K. Greenleaf, *Servant Leadership: A Journey into the Nature of Legitimate Power and Greatness* (New York: Paulist Press, 1977).

11. Robert C. Solomon, *A Better Way to Think About Business: How Personal Integrity Leads to Corporate Success* (New York: Oxford University Press, 1999), 40–43.

12. Martin Luther King Jr., "Where Do We Go from Here?" speech delivered at the 11th Annual Southern Christian Leadership Convention, Atlanta, August 16, 1967, available at http://mlk-kpp01.stanford.edu/index.php/encyclopedia/documentsentry/where_do_we_go_from_here_delivered_at_the_11th_annual_sclc_convention/.

13. Howard Gardner, quoted in Liu, *Conversations on Leadership*.

14. Debashis Chatterjee, quoted in Liu, *Conversations on Leadership*.

15. Ibid.

16. Joseph Badaracco, quoted in Liu, *Conversations on Leadership*.

17. See T. Colin Campbell, *The China Study: The Most Comprehensive Study of Nutrition Ever Conducted and the Startling Implications for Diet, Weight Loss and Long-Term Health* (Dallas: BenBella Books, 2005); and Caldwell Esselstyn, *Prevent and Reverse Heart Disease: The Revolutionary, Scientifically Proven, Nutrition-Based Cure* (New York: Avery, 2007).

18. Ibid.

19. Fred Kofman, *Conscious Business: How to Build Value Through Values* (Boulder, Colo.: Sounds True, 2006).

Chapter Fourteen

1. Frank Herbert, *Dune* (Philadelphia: Chilton Books, 1965).

2. There are hundreds of valuable self-help books. Here are some of the ones we have found to be most valuable: Viktor Frankl, *Man's Search for Meaning*; Joseph Campbell with Bill Moyers, *The Power of Myth*; Deepak Chopra, *The Seven Spiritual Laws of Success*; Stephen Covey, *The Seven Habits of Highly Effective People*; Gerald Jampolsky, *Love Is Letting Go of Fear*; Mihaly Csikszentmihalyi, *Flow*; Daniel Goleman, *Emotional Intelligence*; James Hillman, *The Soul's Code*; M. Scott Peck, *The Road Less Traveled*; Anthony Robbins, *Awaken the Giant Within*; Martin Seligman, *Learned Optimism*; Samuel Smiles, *Self-Help*; James Allen, *As a Man Thinketh*; Roberto Assagioli, *Psychosynthesis*; Abraham H. Maslow, *Motivation and Personality*; Carl Rogers, *On Becoming a Person*; George S. Clason, *The Richest Man in Babylon*; Alice Schroeder, *The Snowball: Warren Buffett and the Business of Life*; Benjamin Franklin, *The Autobiography of Benjamin Franklin*; David Gershon and Gail Straub, *Empowerment*; the Foundation for Inner Peace, *A Course in Miracles*; Dan Millman, *Way of the Peaceful Warrior*; Eckhart Tolle, *The Power of Now*. A good Web site with an overview of hundreds of self-help books is found at http://www.entheos.com/philosophersnotes/books.

3. In addition to Daniel Goleman's book, we recommend Robert C. Solomon's numerous books on emotions, particularly *The Passions* (Hackett, 1993) and *True to Our Feelings* (New York: Oxford University Press, 2001).

4. Some recommended books on love include Gerald Jampolsky, *Love Is Letting Go of Fear* (Berkeley: Celestial Arts, 2010); Stephen G. Post, *Unlimited Love: Altruism, Compassion, and Service* (Philadelphia: Templeton Foundation Press, 2003); and Pitirim Sorokin,

NOTES

The Ways and Power of Love: Types, Factors, and Techniques of Moral Transformation (Philadelphia: Templeton Foundation Press, 2002).

5. Jean M. Twenge and W. Keith Campbell, *The Narcissism Epidemic: Living in the Age of Entitlement* (New York: Free Press, 2009).

6. Jean Piaget and Barbel Inhelder, *The Psychology of the Child* (New York: Basic Books, 1972).

7. See the following books by Abraham H. Maslow: *Motivation and Personality* (New York: Harper Collins, 1987); *Toward a Psychology of Being* (New York: Wiley, 1968); *The Farther Reaches of Human Nature* (New York: Penguin/Arkana, 1993).

8. Don Edward Beck and Christopher C. Cowan, *Spiral Dynamics: Mastering Values, Leadership and Change* (Boston: Blackwell, 1996); Ken Wilber, *A Theory of Everything* (Boston, Shambhala, 2001); Steve McIntosh, *Integral Consciousness and the Future of Evolution* (St. Paul, Minn.: Paragon House, 2007).

9. See Lawrence Kohlberg, *The Philosophy of Moral Development* (New York: Harper & Row, 1981); Lawrence Kohlberg, *The Psychology of Moral Development* (New York: Harper & Row, 1984). See also Carol Gilligan, *In a Different Voice* (Boston: Harvard University Press, 1993).

10. Jane Loevinger and Ruth Wessler, *Measuring Ego Development*, vol. 1 (San Francisco: Jossey-Bass, 1970).

11. This is a Buddhist exercise that is described in detail in Roger Walsh, *Essential Spirituality* (New York: Wiley, 2000), 202–203.

12. Holotropic Breathwork is "a practice that uses breathing and other elements to allow access to non-ordinary states for the purpose of self-exploration." *Wikipedia*, s.v. "Holotropic Breathwork," last modified June 2, 2012, http://en.wikipedia.org/wiki/Holotropic_Breathwork. See also Stanislav Grof and Christina Grof, *Holotropic Breathwork: A New Approach to Self-Exploration and Therapy* (Albany: State University of New York Press, 2010).

13. "68 percent of Americans Found to Be Overweight as Obesity Becomes Global Epidemic," *International Business Times*, February 4, 2011.

14. We recommend the following books: T. Colin Campbell, *The China Study: The Most Comprehensive Study of Nutrition Ever Conducted and the Startling Implications for Diet, Weight Loss and Long-Term Health* (Dallas: BenBella Books, 2005); Caldwell Esselstyn, *Prevent and Reverse Heart Disease: The Revolutionary, Scientifically Proven, Nutrition-Based Cure* (New York: Avery, 2007); Joel Fuhrman, *Eat to Live* and *Super Immunity: The Revolutionary Formula for Fast and Sustained Weight Loss* (Boston: Little, Brown and Co., 2003); and by John McDougall, *The Starch Solution: Eat the Foods You Love, Regain Your Health, and Lose the Weight for Good!* (New York: Rodale, 2012).

15. Owen Bond, "Caffeine Withdrawal and Insomnia," Livestrong.com, April 22, 2011, www.livestrong.com/article/426152-caffeine-withdrawal-insomnia/.

16. Stephen S. Cherniske, *Caffeine Blues* (New York: Warner Books, 1998).

17. See John Abramson, *Overdosed America* (New York: Harper, 2004).

18. There are many books on insight meditation. A good introduction is Joseph Goldstein and Jack Kornfield, *Seeking the Heart of Wisdom: The Path of Insight Meditation* (Shambhala, 2001).

19. Peter Koestenbaum, quoted in Polly LaBarre, "Do We Have the Will to Lead?" *Fast Company*, February 2000, 222.

20. McIntosh, *Integral Consciousness*, 146.

Chapter Fifteen

1. James Heskett, presentation at 4th International Conference on Conscious Capitalism, Bentley University, Waltham, Mass., May 22, 2012.

2. Walter Robb, e-mail to authors.

3. Francis Fukuyama, *Trust: The Social Virtues and the Creation of Prosperity* (New York: Free Press, 1996).

4. Doug Levy, CEO of MEplusYOU, e-mail to authors.

5. Jeffrey Pfeffer, *What Were They Thinking? Unconventional Wisdom About Management* (Boston: Harvard Business School Press, 2007).

6. Marc Gafni, interview with authors, Big Sur, Calif., March 13, 2012.

7. Jane Dutton, "Creating a Caring Economics: Theory, Research, and Practice," presentation at the Academy of Management Annual Meeting, Montreal, August 6, 2010.

8. See Mihaly Csikszentmihalyi, *Flow* (New York: Harper Perennial Modern Classics, 2008). A flow state is defined as "the mental state of operation in which a person in an activity is fully immersed in a feeling of energized focus, full involvement, and success in the process of the activity" (*Wikipedia*, s.v. "flow [psychology]," last modified June 14, 2012, http://en.wikipedia.org/wiki/Flow_%28psychology%29).

9. Howard Behar, "Ten Principles of Personal Leadership," in *It's Not About the Coffee: Leadership Principles from a Life at Starbucks* (New York: Portfolio, 2007); list of ten principles available at www.howardbehar.com/principle.shtml.

10. Wayne Dyer, *The Power of Intention: Learning to Co-Create Your World Your Way* (Carlsbad, Calif.: Hay House, 2005).

Chapter Sixteen

1. Brian Robertson, telephone conversation with authors, June 19, 2012.

2. Daniel H. Pink, *Drive: The Surprising Truth About What Motivates Us* (New York: Penguin, 2011).

3. Douglas McGregor, *The Human Side of Enterprise* (New York: McGraw Hill, 1960), 33–57.

4. John Kao, *Jamming: The Art and Discipline of Business Creativity* (New York: Harper Business, 1997), makes this argument very well.

5. F. A. Hayek, "The Use of Knowledge in Society," *American Economic Review* 35, no. 4. (September 1945): 519–530. See also F. A. Hayek, *The Constitution of Liberty* (Chicago: University of Chicago Press, 1978); and F. A. Hayek, *Law, Legislation and Liberty* (Chicago: University of Chicago Press, 1978).

6. Ironically, this well-known phrase is actually a misquotation of Mao Zedong's "Let a hundred flowers blossom," a slogan used for about six weeks in the summer of 1957, when Chinese intellectuals were invited to criticize the country's political system. Mao said, "Letting a hundred flowers blossom and a hundred schools of thought contend is the policy for promoting progress in the arts and the sciences and a flourishing socialist culture in our land." It turned out that this was really a ploy to surface dissidents critical of the regime; many who expressed views contrary to Mao's were executed. See *The Phrase Finder*, s.v. "Let a thousand flowers bloom," accessed June 20, 2012, www.phrases.org.uk/meanings/226950.html.

7. Terri Kelly, telephone interview with authors, March 23, 2012.

8. Howard Behar, *It's Not About the Coffee: Leadership Principles from a Life at Starbucks* (New York: Portfolio, 2007); quote available at www.howardbehar.com/principle.shtml.

9. In recent years, the company has started supplementing this with a more detailed handbook with specific rules and legal regulations, reflecting the increasingly defensive and litigious culture in the United States.

10. Bill George, telephone interview with authors, March 13, 2012.

11. Geoff Manchester, presentation at Conscious Capitalism Australia launch event, Sydney, May 1, 2012; see Intrepid Travel, Home Page, accessed June 20, 2012, www.intrepidtravel.com/.

12. Gary Hamel, *What Matters Now: How to Win in a World of Relentless Change* (San Francisco: Jossey-Bass, 2012).

Chapter Seventeen

1. *Inception* is a popular 2010 science fiction movie directed by Christopher Nolan. In the movie, an original idea is implanted into the subconscious of another.

2. See http://www.bizstone.com/.

3. Dan Schawbel, "Biz Stone on His Biggest Challenges, Influences and the Future of Social Media," *Forbes*, June 14, 2012; accessed at http://www.forbes.com/sites/dan-schawbel/2012/06/14/biz-stone-on-his-biggest-challenges-influences-and-the-future-of-social-media/.

4. This is not to assert that we have arrived at some kind of gospel truth by articulating the tenets in the way that we have done. Our understanding of the key characteristics of conscious businesses will evolve and become richer with experience and further research. But in light of what we have already learned, we are quite confident in being prescriptive with the four tenets.

5. We have developed our own proprietary methodology for this audit, which can be accessed through authorized consulting firms.

6. This process is modeled on one called *Future Search*, which was developed by Marvin Weisbord (see his book, *Future Search: Getting the Whole System in the Room for Vision, Commitment, and Action* [San Francisco: Berrett-Koehler, 2010]) and was successfully used by Whole Foods Market and many other organizations to craft a meaningful agenda for the future that reflects the priorities and passions of all key stakeholders. We describe the process in chapter 12.

Chapter Eighteen

1. Neil Howe, William Strauss, and R. J. Matson, *Millennials Rising: The Next Great Generation* (New York: Vintage, 2000).

2. Jeanne Meister and Karie Willyerd, "Mentoring Millennials," *Harvard Business Review*, May 2010, 68–72.

3. See http://www.ushistory.org/paine/commonsense/sense1.htm.

4. Marc Gafni, telephone interview with authors, March 13, 2012.

5. Lynne Twist is author of *The Soul of Money: Transforming Your Relationship with Money and Life* (New York: Norton, 2003), and founder of the Soul of Money Institute.

Appendix A

1. Rajendra Sisodia, David B. Wolfe, and Jagdish N. Sheth, *Firms of Endearment: How World-Class Companies Profit from Passion and Purpose* (Upper Saddle River, N.J.: Pearson Prentice Hall, 2007).

2. The eighteen companies are Amazon.com, BMW, CarMax, Caterpillar, Commerce Bank, Costco, eBay, Google, Harley-Davidson, Honda, JetBlue, Johnson & Johnson, Southwest Airlines, Starbucks, Timberland, Toyota, UPS, and Whole Foods Market.

3. CNN Money, "100 Best Companies to Work For: 2012," *CNN Money*, February 6, 2012, http://money.cnn.com/magazines/fortune/best-companies/2012/full_list/.

4. Glassdoor, "Best Places to Work: Employees' Choice Awards," *Glassdoor*, 2012, www.glassdoor.com/Best-Places-to-Work-LST_KQ0,19.htm.

5. Gallup Consulting, "Employee Engagement: What's Your Engagement Ratio?" 2010, available at www.gallup.com/consulting/121535/Employee-Engagement-Overview-Brochure.aspx.

6. Jennifer L. Mitchell and Ethisphere, "Ethisphere and the World's Most Ethical Companies Ring NYSE Opening Bell," *Ethisphere*, September 30, 2011, http://ethisphere.com/ethisphere-and-the-worlds-most-ethical-companies-ring-nyse-opening-bell/.

7. John Kotter and James Heskett, *Corporate Culture and Performance* (New York: Free Press, 1992).

8. Mary Sully de Luque et al., "Unrequited Profit: How Stakeholder and Economic Values Relate to Subordinates' Perceptions of Leadership and Firm Performance," *Administrative Science Quarterly* 53 (2008): 626–654.

9. Jim Collins, *Good to Great : Why Some Companies Make the Leap—and Others Don't* (New York: HarperBusiness, 2001).

10. United Nations, "Tobacco Could Kill a Billion People This Century, UN Health Official Warns," *UN News Centre*, April 29, 2011, www.un.org/apps/news/story.asp?NewsID=38240&Cr=tobacco&Cr1; *Wikipedia*, s.v. "health effects of tobacco," last modified July 6, 2012, http://en.wikipedia.org/wiki/Health_effects_of_tobacco.

11. Gregory David Roberts, *Shantaram* (New York: St. Martin's Press, 2004), 610.

12. Jeanne Bliss, "Wegmans Food Markets Excels by Throwing Away the Rule Book," *Think Customers: The 1to1 Blog*, July 14, 2011, www.1to1media.com/weblog/2011/07/customer_bliss_jeanne_bliss_we.html.

13. RetailSails, "Retail Quick Facts: 10 Things About Costco You Probably Don't Know," April 27, 2011, http://retailsails.com/2011/04/27/retail-quick-facts-10-things-about-costco-you-probably-dont-know/.

14. Michael Roberto, "Jordan's Furniture: Shoppertainment," *Professor Michael Roberto's Blog: Musings About Leadership, Decision Making, and Competitive Strategy*, October 27, 2009, http://michael-roberto.blogspot.com/2009/10/jordans-furniture-shoppertainment.html.

15. Doug Rauch, telephone interview with authors, March 22, 2012.

16. For details on marketing spending trends over the past fifty years, see Jagdish N. Sheth and Rajendra S. Sisodia, "Feeling the Heat: Making Marketing More Productive," part I, *Marketing Management* 4, no. 2 (fall 1995): 8–23.

17. We are grateful to Doug Levy, CEO of MEplusYOU, for his suggestions on this subject.

18. We thank Doug Levy for this example.

Appendix B

1. Paul Hawken, Amory B. Lovins, and L. Hunter Lovins, *Natural Capitalism: Creating the Next Industrial Revolution* (New York: Back Bay Books, 2008).

2. John Elkington, *Cannibals with Forks: The Triple Bottom Line of 21st Century Business* (Gabriola Island, B.C., and Stony Creek, Conn.: New Society Publishers, 1998).

3. Andrew W. Savitz, *The Triple Bottom Line: How Today's Best-Run Companies Are Achieving Economic, Social, and Environmental Success—and How You Can Too* (San Francisco: Jossey-Bass, 2006).

NOTES

4. Michael E. Porter and Mark R. Kramer, "Creating Shared Value: How to Reinvent Capitalism—and Unleash a Wave of Innovation and Growth," *Harvard Business Review*, January–February 2011, 2–17.

5. Bill Gates, "Making Capitalism More Creative," *Time*, July 31, 2008, available at www.time.com/time/business/article/0,8599,1828069,00.html.

6. The late C. K. Prahalad popularized this idea through his book *The Fortune at the Bottom of the Pyramid* (Philadelphia: Wharton School Publishing, 2004).

7. B Lab, "B Corps Redefine Success in Business," annual report, 2012, www. bcorporation.net/.

Appendix C

1. Viktor E. Frankl, *Man's Search for Meaning* (Boston: Beacon Press, 1959; first published in Austria in 1946 under the title *Ein Psycholog erlebt das Konzentrationslager*).

2. Kevin Armata, presentation in Raj Sisodia's Conscious Capitalism class, Bentley University, Waltham, Mass., fall 2010.

3. David Whitford, "Can Compassionate Capitalists Really Win? Interview with Raj Sisodia," *Fortune*, March 30, 2011, http://management.fortune.cnn.com/2011/03/30/can-compassionate-capitalists-really-win/.

4. Ian Davis, "How to Escape the Short-Term Trap," *McKinsey Quarterly*, April 2005, www.mckinseyquarterly.com/Corporate_Finance/Performance/How_to_escape_the_short-term_trap_1611.

INDEX

Note: Page numbers followed by *f* refer to figures; page numbers followed by *t* refer to tables.

INDEX

INDEX

INDEX

Robertson, Brian, 236
role models for leaders, 198
Rothbard, Murray, 4
Rowling, J. K., 198
Rushing, Haley, 47

Safer Way, 2, 3–4, 5, 48
Safeway, 112, 245
Sam's Club, 285
Savitz, Andrew, 293
Schein, Edgar, 215
schools, nutritional education in, 133–134
Schultz, Howard, 121, 185–186, 303
Schweitzer, Albert, 187
seafood sustainability, 64, 142, 143, 146
Sears, 167
Securities and Exchange Commission
    (SEC), 207, 208
self-actualization, 204
self-awareness of leaders, 196–197, 201,
    206, 212
self-learning organizations, 248, 260
self-management, 31, 236, 249, 288
self-managing teams, 91–92, 98, 185, 238
senior management
    compensation of, 92, 172
    egalitarianism and, 220
    transformation to conscious business
        and, 257
    trust and, 221–222
    See also CEOs; executives
servant leadership, 187–188
shared fate concept, 242–243
shared-value capitalism (SVC), 293–294
shareholder rights movement, 178
Shaw, George Bernard, 53
Sheahen, Casey, 71, 139
Six Sigma, 262
sleep, 212
Small Business Administration
    (SBA), 163
Smith, Adam, 16–17, 27
smoking, 97, 211, 282
social capital, 137, 221

social democracy, 2, 4
social media, 84
social responsibility, corporate (CSR),
    36–38, 38*t*, 123–124, 137, 293
Socrates, 188
Solzhenitsyn, Alexander, 188
Sony, 42
South Korea, 12, 13, 118, 120, 148
Southwest Airlines, 32, 46, 48, 66–67, 87,
    107, 193, 218, 226, 267, 280, 299, 302,
    304
Sowell, Thomas, 4
speculators, 102–104
Spence, Roy, 47
Spiral Dynamics (Beck and Cowan), 204
Spiritual Capital (Zohar and Marshall), 185
spiritual intelligence (SQ), 184, 185–186
stage absolutism, 205
stakeholders
    activists and critics as, 156–157
    analytical thinking about, 168–169, 170
    communities as, 113–137
    competitors as, 153–155
    conflicts among, 165
    conscious businesses and, 270, 273
    corporate philanthropy and, 125,
        129–130
    customers as, 75–84
    environment as, 130–152
    financial performance and orientation
        toward, 280–281
    government as, 163–165
    hidden synergies among, 170–171
    higher purpose and, 42
    inner circle of, 153–154
    integration of, in Conscious Capitalism,
        33, 33*f*, 34, 69–175
    interdependence of, 167–175
    investors as, 99–109
    labor unions as, 157–161
    lack of cooperation between businesses
        and, 171–172
    legal control of business and, 175
    media as, 161–162
    multiple roles of, 71

ACKNOWLEDGMENTS

Writing this book has been a labor of great love and joy for us, one in which we have had extraordinary inspiration and support from many wonderful people. We thank Bill George for his insightful Foreword to the book. Bill is one of the most conscious leaders we have ever met and has inspired us in many ways through his ideas and his example. Our debt to Ed Freeman and his pioneering work on stakeholder theory is apparent on virtually every page of the book.

We want to thank Stacey Hayes for her research help and Jo Ann Skousen for her editing. We received invaluable feedback on early drafts of the book from Doug Levy, Rand Stagen, Ed Freeman, Alex Green, Jo Ann Skousen, Mark Skousen, Roy Spence, Doug Rauch, Michael Strong, Jay Ogilvy, Philip Sansone, Shubhro Sen, and Glenda Flanagan. We also want to thank our colleagues on the board of Conscious Capitalism, Inc. (www.ConsciousCapitalism.org) for their support and encouragement, including Doug Rauch, Kip Tindell, Jeff Klein, Phyllis Blees, Shubhro Sen, Rick Voirin, Roberta Lang, Susan Niederhoffer, Timothy Henry, Vidar Jorgensen, Raff Viton, Cheryl Rosner, Carrie Freeman-Parsons, Rand Stagen, Doug Levy, and Michael Strong.

We owe an intellectual debt to numerous entrepreneurs, business leaders, and business thinkers, of whom we would like to particularly thank Peter Drucker, Peter Senge, Robert C. Solomon, Gary Hamel, C.K. Prahalad, Howard Schultz, Herb Kelleher, Colleen Barrett, Larry Page, Sergey Brin, Ratan Tata, Jeff Bezos, Steve Jobs, Bill Gates, Chip Conley, Ron Shaich,

ACKNOWLEDGMENTS

Sally Jewell, Terri Kelly, Tim Brown, Abraham Maslow, Ken Wilber, Don Beck, Clare Graves, Steve McIntosh, Jenny Wade, Linda Mason, George Zimmer, Casey Sheahan, Richard Barrett, and Nikos Mourkogiannis.

We are also grateful to Bud Sorenson, Debashish Chatterjee, Deepak Chopra, Michael Gelb, Fred Kofman, Rick Frazier, Scott Minerd, Peter Derby, Jeff Cherry, Judi Neal, Ron Pompei, Sam Yau, Sir Ken Robinson, David and Tom Gardner, Mark Gafni, Howard Behar, Richard Leider, Srinivasan Pillay, Alan Webber, and Youngsul Kwon for their support and help.

We would like to thank our agent Rafe Sagalyn and our wonderful team at HBRP: our editor Melinda Merino, Nina Nocciolino, and Jen Waring. It was a delight to work with them. We also thank Kate Lowery and Mark Fortier for their work in getting the word out about the book.

John Mackey: I want to thank my fellow executives at Whole Foods who have supported this book from its inception, including Walter Robb, Glenda Flanagan, A.C. Gallo, Jim Sud, Ken Meyer, and David Lannon. Evening Galvin and Falesha Thrash provided amazing administrative support for the many iterations of the book. I thank Glenda Flanagan and Jessica Agneessens from Whole Foods for creating the Conscious Leadership Academy to teach many of the Conscious Capitalism concepts (www.academyforconscious-leadership.com).

Raj Sisodia: I would like to acknowledge the great impact that my late friend and co-author David Wolfe had on my life and work. I would also like to thank Jag Sheth for his friendship and guidance over the last twenty years. I thank my wonderful daughters Priya and Maya, who helped greatly with transcribing and editing, and became passionate believers in Conscious Capitalism along the way. I thank my wife Shailini for cheerfully accepting my many absences from home in service of the Conscious Capitalism movement. I also thank Gloria Larson, Mike Page, Tony Buono, David Perry, Chip Wiggins, Alan Hoffman, and Nada Nasr at Bentley University for their support and encouragement. Numerous other individuals have played important roles in helping me and supporting the movement worldwide, including Abilio Diniz, Alan Webber, Amit Chatterjee, Amy Powell, Anand Mahindra, Andre Kaufman, Anil Nayar, Anil Sachdev, Ann Graham, Anton Musgrave,

ACKNOWLEDGMENTS

Anu Agha, Arsenio Rodriguez, Ashley Munday, Ashwini Malhotra, Betsy Sanders, David Cooperrider, Deborah Wallace, Dipak Jain, Bharat Singh, Ernie Cadotte, F.A.L. Caeldries, Gary Hirshberg, George Araneo, Glen Urban, Haley Rushing, Harsh Mariwala, Hildy Teegen, Indrajit Gupta, J.J. Irani, Jeffrey Sonnenfeld, Jim Stengel, John Sterman, Karambir Singh Kang, Kate Walker, Kee Yup Lee, Ketan Mehta, Kevin Armata, Kiran Gulrajani, Mark Albion, Maurizio Zollo, Michael Jensen, Nancy Koehn, Nilima Bhat, Nitin Nohria, Phil Clothier, Phil Kotler, Phil Mirvis, Polly LaBarre, Poonam Ahluwalia, Pradeep Kashyap, Prasad Kaipa, R. Gopalakrishnan, Raghav Bahl, Richard Whiteley, Richi Gil, Rosabeth Moss Kanter, Sandra Waddock, Shereen Bhan, Srikumar Rao, Sudhakar Ram, Ted Malloch, Uday Kotak, Vijay Bhat, Vineet Nayar, Vineeta Salvi, and Vinit Taneja.

ABOUT THE AUTHORS

John Mackey, cofounder and co-CEO of Whole Foods Market, has led the natural and organic grocer as it has grown into an $11 billion *Fortune* 300 company. With more than 340 stores and 70,000 Team Members in North America and the United Kingdom, the company has been named to *Fortune*'s "100 Best Companies to Work For" list for fifteen consecutive years.

While devoting his career to helping shoppers satisfy their lifestyle needs with quality natural and organic foods, Mackey has also focused on building a more conscious way of doing business. He was the visionary for the Whole Planet Foundation to help end poverty in developing nations, the Local Producer Loan Program to help local food producers expand their businesses, the Global Animal Partnership's rating scale for humane farm animal treatment, and the Health Starts Here initiative to promote health and wellness.

Mackey has been recognized as Ernst & Young's "Entrepreneur of the Year," *Institutional Investor*'s "Best CEO in America," one of *Barron's* "World's Best CEOs," *MarketWatch*'s "CEO of the Year," *Fortune*'s "Businessperson of the Year," and one of *Esquire*'s "America's Most Inspiring CEOs."

A strong believer in free market principles, Mackey cofounded the Conscious Capitalism movement (consciouscapitalism.org). He aims to boldly defend and reimagine capitalism, and encourage a way of doing business that is grounded in ethical consciousness.

Mackey cut his pay to $1 in 2006 and continues to work for Whole Foods Market out of a passion to see the business realize its potential for deeper purpose, for the joy of leading a great company, and to answer the call to service he feels in his heart.

ABOUT THE AUTHORS

A founding member of the Conscious Capitalism movement, **Raj Sisodia** is professor of marketing at Bentley University and cofounder of the Conscious Capitalism Institute. He has an MBA from the Bajaj Institute of Management Studies in Bombay and a PhD in marketing from Columbia University. In 2003 he was cited as one of "50 Leading Marketing Thinkers" and named to the "Guru Gallery" by the UK-based Chartered Institute of Marketing. Bentley University honored him with the Award for Excellence in Scholarship in 2007 and the Innovation in Teaching Award in 2008. He was named one of "Ten Outstanding Trailblazers of 2010" by Good Business International, and one of the "Top 100 Thought Leaders in Trustworthy Business Behavior" by Trust Across America for 2010 and 2011.

Raj has published seven books and more than 100 academic articles. His work has been featured in the *Wall Street Journal*, the *New York Times*, *Fortune*, and the *Financial Times*. His book *The Rule of Three: How Competition Shapes Markets* was a finalist for the Best Book in Marketing award from the American Marketing Association. His book *Firms of Endearment: How World-Class Companies Profit from Passion and Purpose* was named one of the best business books of 2007 by Amazon.com. He has consulted with and taught executive programs for numerous companies, including AT&T, Nokia, LG, Deutsche Post DHL, POSCO, Siemens, Sprint, Volvo, IBM, Walmart, Rabobank, McDonald's, and Southern California Edison. He is on the board of directors at Mastek Ltd. and is a trustee of Conscious Capitalism, Inc.